International Series on Sport Sciences, Volume 2

SWIMMING II

Proceedings of the Second International Symposium on Biomechanics in Swimming, Brussels, Belgium

Editors: **Léon Lewillie**
Laboratoire de l'Effort
Université de Bruxelles
and
Jan P. Clarys
Instituut voor Morfologie
Vrije Universiteit Brussel

UNIVERSITY PARK PRESS

Baltimore · London · Tokyo

University Park Press
International Publishers in Science and Medicine
Chamber of Commerce Building
Baltimore, Maryland 21202

Typeset by The Composing Room of Michigan, Inc.
Printed in the United States of America by Universal Lithographers, Inc.

Library of Congress Cataloging in Publication Data

International Symposium on Biomechanics in Swimming,
2d, Brussels, 1974.
Swimming II.

(International series on sport sciences; v. 2)
Includes index.
1. Swimming--Congresses. 2. Human mechanics--
Congresses. 3. Swimming for handicapped persons--
Congresses. I. Lewillie, L. II. Clarys, J. P.
III. Title. IV. Series. [DNLM: 1. Swimming--
Congresses. 2. Motor skills--Congresses. W3
IN916NR 1974s / QT260 I613 1974s]
QP310.S95I57 1974   612'.76   75-16131

ISBN 0-8391-0817-6

Swimming II

International Series on Sport Sciences

Series editors: **Richard C. Nelson and Chauncey A. Morehouse**

This series presents professional reference works derived from congress and symposium proceedings and advanced-level texts of special interest to researchers, clinicians, students, physical educators, and coaches involved in the growing field of sport sciences. The Series Editors are Professors Richard C. Nelson and Chauncey A. Morehouse of The Pennsylvania State University.

The series will cover all aspects of sport sciences, including physiology, biomechanics, medicine, psychology, sociology, history, philosophy, and education. Individual volumes will feature important original contributions, written by leading international authorities, on specific current topics of primary interest to the world-wide community of sport scientists. One of the highlights of this series will be the publication in English of the highly significant research conducted by scientists from many countries. Because many of these authors normally publish their work in languages other than English, the series volumes will be a rich resource for material often difficult if not impossible to obtain elsewhere.

In addition to assisting individuals involved directly with sports-related activities, the *International Series on Sport Sciences* will serve as a valuable source of authoritative, up-to-date information. It will include original scientific studies of interest to those concerned with: (1) the improvement of sports performance, (2) the health and safety of amateur and professional athletes, (3) the role of sport sciences in rehabilitation and public health, (4) the historic, philosophic, and sociologic aspects of sport, (5) the education and training of future sport scientists and professionals, and (6) the free exchange of knowledge about these topics across international boundaries.

Volume 1:
Nelson and Morehouse: **BIOMECHANICS IV** (Fourth International Seminar on Biomechanics)

Volume 2:
Clarys and Lewillie: **SWIMMING II** (Second International Symposium on Biomechanics of Swimming)

Contents

CONTRIBUTORS   ix
SYMPOSIUM ORGANIZATION   xii
PREFACE   xiii

OPENING SESSION

Welcome from the Symposium President   *L. Lewillie*   3
Welcome from UNESCO   *E. Jokl*   5
Welcome from the International Society of Biomechanics   *J. Wartenweiler* 7
Keynote Address   Factors Governing Success in Competitive
   Swimming: A brief review of related studies   *T. K. Cureton*   9

INSTRUMENTATION AND METHODOLOGY

A Device to Measure Forces at the Hands during the Grab Start
   P. R. Cavanagh, J. V. Palmgren, and B. A. Kerr   43
Dual Media Cinematography   *D. R. McIntyre and J. G. Hay*   51
A Device for the On-Line Measurement of Instantaneous
   Swimming Velocity   *M. R. Kent and J. Atha*   58
A Hydrokinetic Apparatus for the Study and Improvement of
   Leg Movements in the Breaststroke   *V. Belokovsky and E. Ivanchenko* 64
Dynamic Measurement Techniques on Swimming Bodies at
   the Netherlands Ship Model Basin   *J. D. van Manen and H. Rijken*   70
Instrumentation and Methods for Complex Investigations of Swimming
   K. Boičev and A. Tzvetkov   80
Response of the Respiratory System to Changes in Pressure
   J. Alexandrov and L. Petrov   90

RESISTANCE, PROPULSION, AND EFFICIENCY

Energetics of Swimming in Man   *D. W. Rennie, D. R. Pendergast,
   and P. E. di Prampero*   97
Body Resistance On and Under the Water Surface
   J. Jiskoot and J. P. Clarys   105

Total Resistance of Selected Body Positions in the Front Crawl
  J. P. Clarys and J. Jiskoot   110
A Biomechanical Model for Swimming Performance
  P. R. Francis and N. Dean   118
Intracycle Kinematics and Body Configuration Changes in
  the Breaststroke   *M. R. Kent and J. Atha*   125
Efficiency of Breaststroke and Freestyle Swimming   *I. Holmér*   130
Maximal Oxygen Uptake Rate during Swimming and Bicycling
  N. H. Secher and I. Oddershede   137

ANALYSIS OF SWIMMING TECHNIQUES

A Model for Upper Extremity Forces during the Underwater Phase
  of the Front Crawl   *R. K. Jensen and B. Blanksby*   145
Three-Dimensional Spatial Hand Patterns of Skilled
  Butterfly Swimmers   *K. M. Barthels and M. J. Adrian*   154
The Division of Swimming Strokes into Phases, Based upon
  Kinematic Parameters   *K. Wiegand, D. Wuensch, and W. Jaehnig*   161
Arm Action in the Crawl Stroke   *M. Miyashita*   167
An Analysis of Arm Propulsion in Swimming   *G. W. Rackham*   174
The Influence of the Leg Kick and the Arm Stroke on the Total
  Speed during the Crawl Stroke   *W. Bucher*   180
Changes in Breaststroke Techniques under Different Speed Conditions
  T. Bober and B. Czabanski   188
Use of Light Trace Photography in Teaching Swimming
  G. Hoecke and G. Gruendler   194
Asymmetry of the Lower Limbs in Breaststroke Swimming
  B. Czabanski   207
Investigation of Hydrodynamic Determinants of Competitive
  Swimming Strokes   *U. Persyn, J. DeMaeyer, and H. Verbaecke*   214

SWIMMING STARTS, WATER POLO, AND LIFESAVING

A Biomechanical Comparison of the Grab and Conventional Sprint
  Starts in Competitive Swimming   *J. E. Bowers and P. R. Cavanagh*   225
A Comparison of Four Styles of Racing Start in Swimming
  A. Ayalon, B. Van Gheluwe, and M. Kanitz   233
Analysis of the Egg Beater and Breaststroke Kicks in Water Polo
  J. P. Clarys   241
An Evaluation of Selected Carrying Methods Used in Lifesaving
  J. G. Hay, D. R. McIntyre, and N. V. Wilson   247

INSTRUCTION FOR NORMAL AND HANDICAPPED SWIMMERS

A Theory-Based Approach to Teaching Swimming   *M. Smith*   257
Special Swimming Instruction for the Multiple Handicapped
  W. P. M. Vis   263
Electromyography for the Evaluation of Handicapped Swimmers
  L. Maes, J. P. Clarys, and P. J. Brouwer   268

Analysis of Techniques used by Swimmers in the Para-Olympic
    Games   *U. Persyn, E. Surmont, L. Wouters, and J. DeMaeyer*   276

ANATOMICAL ASPECTS OF SWIMMING

Body Build and Somatotype of Olympic Swimmers, Divers, and
    Water Polo Players   *M. Hebbelinck, L. Carter, and A. De Garay*   285
Lung Volumes and Swimming   *J. L. Ghesquiere*   306
Residual Reflect Patterns as a Basis for Diagnosing Stroke Faults
    D. Swartz and M. Allen   310
The Shape of the Pectoralis Major Muscle in Swimmers   *G. D. Maas*   314
Spherosomatometric Method for Analysis of Anteroposterior Spine
    Curvatures in Swimmers   *W. Iwanowski*   316

SYMPOSIUM ACTIVITIES

International Coaches Clinic   323
Special Activities   327
Acknowledgments   336

Contributors

In parentheses is the page number for each contribution to this volume.

Adrian, Marlene J. Department of Physical Education for Women, Washington State University, Pullman, Washington 99163 USA (154)

Alexandrov, J. Institut Superieur de Culture Physique, "G. Dimitrov" Rue Tina Kirkova Strasse 1, Sofia, Bulgaria (90)

Allen, Marsha Marin County School District, 201 Chapman Road, Mill Valley, California 94914 USA (310)

Atha, John Department of Ergonomics and Cybernetics, University of Technology, Loughborough, Leicestershire, Great Britain (58, 125)

Ayalon, Alberto Research Department Wingate Institute, Wingate Post, Israel (233)

Barthels, Katharine M. Department of Physical Education, California State University, Fullerton, California 92634 USA (154)

Belokovsky, Viatcheslav V. Department of Swimming, The Central Institute of Physical Culture, Skatertnyi Pereulok 4, Moscow 69, USSR (64)

Blanksby, Brian Department of Physical Education, University of Western Australia, Nedlands, Western Australia (145)

Bober, Tadeusz Biomechanics Laboratory, Higher School of Physical Education, ul. Wiejska, 80-336 Gdansk, Poland (188)

Boičev, Kliment Scientific Sport Center, CNIFK, bul. Tolbuhin 18, Sofia, Bulgaria (80)

Bowers, Judith Department of Physical Education, Moorhead State College, Moorhead, Minnesota 56550 USA (225)

Brouwer, Piet J. Instituut voor Morfologie, Vrije Universiteit Brussel, Eversstraat 2, 1000 Brussel, Belgium (268)

Bucher, Walter Eidg. Technische Hochschule, Kurse für Turnen und Sport, Plattenstrasse 26, 8032 Zurich, Switzerland (180)

Carter, L. Department of Physical Education, San Diego State University, San Diego, California 92115 USA (285)

Cavanagh, Peter R. Biomechanics Laboratory, the Pennsylvania State University, University Park, Pennsylvania 16802 USA (43, 225)

Clarys, Jan P. Laboratorium voor Morfologie, Everstraat-Gebouw D, B-1000 Brussel, Belgium (105, 110, 241, 268)

Cureton, Thomas K. Physical Fitness Institute, 141 Armory Building, University of Illinois, Champaign, Illinois 61820 USA (9)

Czabanski, Bogdan Wyzsza Szkola Wychowania Fizycznego, Banacha 11, 51-617 Wroclaw, Poland (207)

Dean, Nathan Department of Physical Education for Men, Iowa State University, Iowa City, Iowa 52240 USA (118)

De Garay, A. Instituto Nacional de Energia Nuclear, Mexico City, Mexico (285)

De Maeyer, J. Instituut voor Lichamelijke Opvoeding, Katholieke Universiteit Leuven, Tervuurse vest 101, 3030 Heverlee, Belgium (214, 276)

di Prampero, Pietero E. Department of Physiology, School of Medicine, via Mangiagalli 32, 20133 Milan, Italy (97)

Francis, Peter R. Department of Physical Education for Men, Iowa State University, Ames, Iowa 50010 USA (118)

Ghesquiere, Joseph L. Faculty of Medicine and Pharmacy, National University of Zaire, Kinshasa Campus, Kinshasa, XI Zaire, South Africa (306)

Gruendler, Gudrun Department of Sport Science, Friedrich Schiller Universität, Seidelstrasse 20, 69 Jena, German Democratic Republic (DDR) (194)

Hay, James G. Department for Physical Education for Men, Fieldhouse, University of Iowa, Iowa City, Iowa 52240 USA (51, 247)

Hebbelinck, Marcel Navorsingslaboratorium-HILO, Vrije Universiteit Brussel, A. Buyllaan 105, 1050 Brussel, Belgium (285)

Hoecke, Gerhard Department of Sport Science, Friedrich Schiller Universität, Seidelstrasse 20, 69 Jena, German Democratic Republic (DDR) (194)

Holmér, Ingvar Gymnastik och Idrottshogskolan, Department of Physiology, Lidingövägen 1, 114 33 Stockholm, Sweden (130)

Ivanchenko, E. Department of Swimming, The Central Institute of Physical Culture, Skatertnyi Pereulok 4, Moscow 69 USSR (64)

Iwanowski, Wiktor Department of Aquatic Sports, Skoczylasa 22, 54-071 Wroclaw, Poland (316)

Jaehnig, G. Martin Luther Universität Halle, Sektion Sportwissenschaft, Friedemann Bach Platz 5, 402 Halle, German Democratic Republic (DDR) (161)

Jensen, Robert K. Department of Physical Education, Laurentian University, Sudbury, Ontario, Canada (145)

Jiskoot, Jan Academie voor Lichamelijke Opvoeding, Willinklaan 5, Amsterdam-Geuzenveld, The Netherlands (105, 110)

Jokl, Ernst Department of Physical Education, University of Kentucky, Lexington, Kentucky 40500 USA (5)

Kanitz, M. Research Department Wingate Institute, Wingate Post, Israel (233)

Kent, Malcolm R. Wardroom, HMS Collingwood, Fareham, Hants, Great Britain (58, 125)

Kerr, Barry A. School of Physical Education, University of Calgary, Calgary, Alberta T2N 1N4, Canada (43)

Lewillie, Leon Laboratoire de L'Effort, Université Libre de Bruxelles, Av. Paul Héger 28, 1050 Bruxelles, Belgium (3)

Maas, Geerlof D. Jacob van Campenlaan 48, Leiden, The Netherlands (314)

Maes, Luk Instituut voor Morfologie, Vrije Universiteit Brussel, Eversstraat 2, 1000 Brussel, Belgium (268)

McIntyre, Donald R. Department of Physical Education for Men, University of Iowa, Iowa City, Iowa 52242 USA (58, 247)

Miyashita, Mitsumasa Department of Physical Education, Faculty of Education, University of Tokyo, Bunko-Ku, Tokyo, Japan (167)

Oddershede, I. Laboratory for the Theory of Gymnastics, August Krogh Institute, University of Copenhagen, Denmark (137)

Palmgren, John Biomechanics Laboratory, The Pennsylvania State University, University Park, Pennsylvania 16802 USA (43)

Pendergast, David   Department of Physiology, State University of New York at Buffalo, 120 Sherman Hall, Buffalo, New York 14214 USA (97)

Persyn, Ulrik   Instituut voor Lichamelijke Opvoeding, Katholieke Universiteit Leuven, Tervuurse vest 101, 3030 Heverlee, Belgium (214, 276)

Petrov, L.   Institut Superieur de Culture Physique, "G. Dimitrov" Rue Tina Kirkova Strasse 1, Sofia, Bulgaria (90)

Rackham, George W.   Swimming Teacher Association, 8 Copperfields, Kemsing, Sevenoaks, Kent, Great Britain (174)

Rennie, Donald W.   Department of Physiology, State University of New York at Buffalo, 120 Sherman Hall, Buffalo, New York 14214 USA (97)

Rijken, H.   N. S. P. Nederlands Scheepsbouwkundig, Proefstation, Haagsteeg 2, Postbus 28, Wageningen, The Netherlands (70)

Secher, Niels H.   Laboratory for the Theory of Gymnastics, August Krogh Institute, University of Copenhagen, Denmark (137)

Smith, Murray   Faculty of Physical Education, University of Alberta, Edmonton 7, Alberta T6G OX6, Canada (257)

Surmont, E.   Instituut voor Lichamelijke Opvoeding, Katholieke Universiteit Leuven, Tervuurse vest 101, 3030 Heverlee, Belgium (276)

Swartz, Don   Marin Aquatic Club, San Rafael, California 94901 USA (310)

Tzvetkov, A.   Scientific Sport Center, CNIFK, bul. Tolbuhin 18, Sofia, Bulgaria (80)

Van Gheluwe, Bart   Research Department, Wingate Institute, Wingate Post, Israel (233)

Van Manen, J. D.   N. S. P. Nederlands Scheepsbouwkundig, Proefstation, Haagsteeg 2, Postbus 28, Wageningen, The Netherlands (70)

Vervaecke, H.   Instituut voor Lichamelijke Opvoeding, Katholieke Universiteit Leuven, Tervuurse vest 101, 3030 Heverlee, Belgium (214)

Vis, W. P. M.   Fédération des Instructeurs de Natation des Pays-Bas, Rambrandt Van Rijn laan 26, Berkel/Enschot (Ntr Brabant), The Netherlands (263)

Wartenweiler, Jurg   Eidg. Technische Hochschule, Plattenstrasse 26, 8032 Zurich, Switzerland (7)

Wiegand, Klaus   Martin Luther Universität Halle, Sektion Sportwissenschaft, Friedemann Bach Platz 5, 402 Halle, German Democratic Republic (DDR) (161)

Wilson, Neela V.   Department of Physical Education for Men, University of Iowa, Iowa City, Iowa 52242 USA (247)

Wouters, L.   Instituut voor Lichamelijke Opvoeding, Katholieke Universiteit Leuven, Tervuurse vest 101, 3030 Heverlee, Belgium (276)

Wuensch, Diethard   Martin Luther Universität Halle, Sektion Sportwissenschaft, Friedemann Bach Platz 5, 402 Halle, German Democratic Republic (DDR) (161)

Symposium Organization

SITE

University of Brussels
Sociology Building
44, Avenue Jeanne
1050 Brussels, Belgium

MAIN THEME

Biomechanical studies on human motion and their applications to competitive and recreational swimming, water polo, motor learning, therapy, and re-education.

ORGANIZING COMMITTEE

Chairman: *Léon Lewillie*
Secretary General: *Jan P. Clarys*
Treasurer: *Jean Claude De Potter*
Adm. Secretary   *Mrs. M. Plasch*
Ass. Adm. Secretary: *Miss B. Pion*
Member: *Jean Pierre Coenraets*

SCIENTIFIC COMMITTEE

P.O. Astrand, Sweden
D. Barr, Great Britain
H.N. Bleasdale, F.I.N.A.
P.J. Brouwer, Belgium
J. Counsilman, U.S.A.
T.K. Cureton, U.S.A.
G. Hoecke, D.D.R.
J. Jiskoot, The Netherlands
R. Leek, New Zealand
R.C. Nelson, U.S.A.

Preface

It was four years ago that the First International Symposium on Biomechanics in Swimming was held in Brussels, and because of its success a second meeting was organized. This book contains the papers presented at that second meeting, which also took place in Brussels.

Interest in the scientific approaches to swimming is increasing, as demonstrated by the number and quality of papers presented at the second symposium. There is a noticeable trend toward a more exact scientific approach to competitive swimming. The knowledge which is being gained of the factors that underlie all aspects of swimming may be of the greatest importance in the development of methods of teaching swimming to the handicapped. Several symposium papers dealing with this subject have been included here.

It is hoped that the contact between researchers from the world of competitive swimming and those concerned with therapeutic swimming will contribute to the future development of scientifically based swimming programs for handicapped individuals.

P. J. BROUWER
Head of the Instituut Voor Morfologie
Vrije Universiteit
Brussels, Belgium

Opening
session

Welcome from the Symposium President

L. Lewillie

It is indeed a pleasure to see all of you here at this Opening Session of the 2nd International Symposium on Biomechanics in Swimming. As Symposium President and Chairman of the Organizing Committee, I wish to extend to you a most sincere welcome. Four years ago many of us met here for the first symposium. Our purpose then was to bring together persons interested in the biomechanical aspects of swimming so that better communication and exchange of ideas among scientists and practitioners would be possible. In so doing, we would complement the work undertaken through the International Seminars on Biomechanics. Your presence today indicates that interest generated during the first symposium continues to grow and develop.

A part of human knowledge becomes scientific when it is effectively quantified. Over the door of the auditorium of physiology of our Faculty of Medicine stands a quotation from the Belgian poet, Emile Verhaeren:

"What lengths of time
poured down the abyss of years

The anguish and hope
of destinies to come

and the minds steeped in
noble lassitude

That were needed to grasp
a small bit of truth"

This short poem clearly describes our problem. Man must continue regardless of the lack of scientific knowledge available to him. The man who stands beside a swimming pool, teaching swimming for leisure and safety, the one who trains for competitive swimming, or the one who uses swimming as a tool for therapeutics and rehabilitation—that man must act, today, whatever the limits of our knowledge. It may be said in referring to the present meeting that it brings together men and women who attempt to master scientific precision without losing touch with daily human reality.

Application of instrumentation to swimming is not easy, but difficulties seem to have stimulating effects: the Symposium communications cover the entire field, from film analysis to myoelectric signals, force-time, speed, and resistance measurements. But instrumentation has meaning only to the extent that it leads us to a better understanding of man.

Applied anatomy, applied human motion, specific problems of energy cost and efficiency in movement through water, and mathematical models are some of the areas which we look to for progress. Two new subjects which show promise for future development are therapeutic and reeducational swimming, both rich in practical experience but lacking scientific bases for progress.

Motor learning may be the key of knowledge because, when the elaboration of the basic motor vocabulary, the means of transfer and the ways of learning are known, all our behavior will be shown in a new light.

I cannot end this address without rendering homage to those who are pioneers in biomechanics and who are once more with us today: Professor Ernst Jokl, President of the Research Committee of the International Council for Physical Education and Sport, UNESCO, who covers all the problems of research in sport, but who, among all the branches with which he has been associated, has a special regard for biomechanics; Professor Jurg Wartenweiler, organizer of the 1st International Seminar in Zurich and President of the young International Society of Biomechanics who, from among all branches of biomechanics, has always shown a special regard for swimming.

It is my hope that we will all benefit from this meeting and that the conclusions of the communications will establish the foundation for the research and practice of tomorrow.

Welcome from UNESCO

E. Jokl

Once again it is my privilege to convey to this meeting the good wishes of the UNESCO International Council of Sport and Physical Education. The Council, which sponsored the first symposium on "Biomechanics of Swimming," was glad to do so again. It is very appreciative of the fine work done by the organizers of today's event, especially by Dr. Lewillie, Dr. Clarys, Dr. Nelson, Dr. Morehouse, and Dr. Hebbelinck. It is with pleasure that the Council complies with the wish for a Working Group on "Biomechanics of Swimming" henceforth to be directly associated with its Research Committee. The Group can rest assured that every support it may need from the Committee will be forthcoming.

This is, I think, an appropriate occasion to acquaint you with the design, structure, and over-all organization of the Council's scientific activities to which the Biomechanics of Swimming Group now belongs. I shall enumerate its various investigative teams as well as the names of the chief experts who have contributed and continue to contribute to their work.

First, I refer to the two secretaries the Research Committee has had since its inception, Dr. Simon and Dr. Hebbelinck, and to point to the Committee's numerous publications, including its comprehensive report entitled "International Research in Sport and Physical Education" issued at the occasion of the 1964 Olympic Games in Tokyo. Günter Erbach, Günter Luschen, Kalevi Heinila, Peter McIntosh, Gerald Kenyon, and Andrzey Wohl founded the Sociology of Sport Committee, which publishes the "International Review of Sport Sociology." The first President of the History of Sport Committee was Frantisek Kratky, who has recently been succeeded by Günter Wonneberger, ably assisted by Maurice Verhaegen and Jujiro Narita, under whose guidance the Committee's first "Yearbook on History of Physical Education and Sport" has appeared. The International Society of Sport Psychology has lately indicated its desire to coordinate its work with that of the Research Committee of the I.C.S.P.E.; among its leading members are Miroslav Vanek, Vladimir Rudichenko, Hermann Rieder, John Kane, and Ferrucio Antonelli, editor of the "International Journal of Sport Psychology." Other important contributions to sport research have been made by the Council's Working Groups on Biomechanics and on Biochemistry of Exercise, the former directed by Jurg Wartenweiler, the latter by J. R. Poortmans and Josef Keul. The recently created Committee on Art and Sport owes its formation to the efforts of Don Masterson, Christoph Wagner, and M. Nemessuri. The last wrote a book entitled, "The Physiology of Violin Playing," with O. Szende. A Working Group on Physical Activity and Aging is led by M. Karvonen, Kenneth Cooper, D. Brunner, and A. Carlsten; one on Ergometry by H. Mellerowicz, A. Venerando, and H. Buhlmann; one on Clinical Pathology of Exercise by J. T. McClellan, who coauthored the monograph "Exercise and Cardiac Death." A group studying special Physiological and Medical Problems of Swimming, including skin and scuba diving, operates under the leadership of M. Milani Comparetti, L. Lewillie, and J. P. Clarys. The Research Committee is at present holding discussions on the establishment of a Working Group on Philosophy of Sport with Paul Weiss, Ommo Grupe, Hans Lenk, and J. M. Cagigal.

The committees and groups to which I have referred have organized over 50 conventions, symposia, and round-table conferences, and issued about the same number of books and monographs.

The various research units operate at different degrees of autonomy, some of them in virtual independence. By accepting such a policy of flexibility as well as by realizing the fact that many of the teams' activities overlap, the Research Committee has been able to obtain an overview of the sports sciences in their entirety. The Research Committee has cultivated relations with virtually all other international bodies that concern themselves with research in the sports sciences, chief among them F.I.M.S., I.C.H.P.E.R., F.I.E.P., the International Sports Federations, the International Congress of Internal Medicine, the International Congress of Physiology, and the Epidemiology Section of the World Health Organization.

The International Council of Sport and Physical Education is confident that the Biomechanics of Swimming Working Group will fit nicely into the Research Committee's program, and I reiterate the good wishes which have accompanied the early efforts of the Working Group and which will always be with it in future.

Welcome from the International Society of Biomechanics

J. Wartenweiler

I bring you the greetings of the International Society of Biomechanics, and I sincerely wish you a successful meeting. You have assembled here to present your papers, report on your research findings, and discuss practical problems in biomechanics of swimming. It will be possible for those who participated in the first symposium 4 years ago to compare it with this meeting. Formerly the main topic was the analysis of various movements in swimming; measurements of the resistance of the water with different positions of the body; and measurements of force when swimming, taking off, and diving. Furthermore, experiments were shown, theories discussed, and models demonstrated as an explanation of the pushing power by arms and legs. Many of these studies were somewhat unsophisticated. The developments that have occurred in the interim will be readily apparent. The fact that so many of you are present today is proof that more scientific information is needed on swimming, diving, and water polo. The necessity of sharing information justifies the efforts the president of this symposium, Leon Lewillie, and his general secretary, Jan P. Clarys, have put forth in organizing this second symposium.

An international symposium such as this requires a great deal of effort on the part of the organizing committee. Our hosts have included both professional and social activities on the program, assuring us of a very worthwhile experience. Certainly the opportunity to renew old friendships and make new ones while exchanging ideas and discussing problems adds greatly to our scientific endeavors. The program provides for ample personal and professional interaction, highlighted by the cocktail party at the Castle of Ham and the Symposium Banquet both at the invitation of Professor and Mrs. Lewillie.

Water has always fascinated man, and for thousands of years he has been able to move through water by his own physical effort. Quite on his own, with little help from biomechanics, he has developed many strokes such as the breaststroke, crawl, and butterfly. Swimming is used for fitness development, therapy, sport, and recreation. It is, therefore, not surprising that those interested in biomechanics have chosen it as a topic for scientific investigation. Biomechanics includes studies of human and nonhuman movements from their mechanical and biological points of view. Swimming represents only one area within the total scope of the science known as biomechanics.

Up to now four international congresses on biomechanics have taken place (Zurich, 1967; Eindhoven, 1969; Rome, 1971; and Penn State University, 1973) during which most fields of pure and applied biomechanics were discussed. The proceedings of these congresses are available for individuals who are interested. Following the biennial cycle the Vth International Congress on Biomechanics will be held in Jyväskylä in 1975; you will hear more about it from Paavo Komi during this Symposium. An International Symposium of Biomechanics in Track and Field was held in Budapest in 1973. After having organized two colloquiums which took place in Lille, 1972, and Paris, 1973, the Societe d'Ergonomie de Langue Francaise has now organized the third colloquium on Biomechanics of Movements, which will also be arranged by Mr. Lewillie here in Brussels next month.

The international contacts made possible by biomechanics have resulted in two international organizations: the Working Group on Biomechanics ICSPE-UNESCO and the International Society of Biomechanics (ISB), who work closely together. You will find among the material handed out to you for this congress, a pamphlet on and the constitution of the ISB. You are welcome to join the society and may do so by presenting your subscription at the registration desk or you may send it to me.

Biomechanics has made rapid progress these past 10 years, thanks to the cooperative spirit of many of you present. Those of you who are with us for the first time will be able to contribute to its future development. With this prospect in mind, I welcome all of you to this Second International Symposium on Biomechanics in Swimming.

Keynote
Address

Factors governing success in competitive swimming: A brief review of related studies

T. K. Cureton

HISTORICAL PERSPECTIVE

In the time of Duke Kahanamoku's swimming (1905–1928) the training procedures for competitive swimming were rather indefinite and hardly deserved the connotation of "scientific training." There was little specialization up to 880 yards, as most good swimmers competed over the entire range, and usually in several events. Johnny Weismuller held almost all of the freestyle records, with Jamison Handy and Perry McGillivray holding the middle distance titles, and Bob Skelton holding the breaststroke titles. Girls were not yet accepted in hard training camps, and physiological analysis of swimming and training methods for competition were vague, in fact almost nonexistent.

During this period, 1905–1928, Weismuller's body build was considered the ideal: wide shoulders, 6 ft 2 in in height, slim hips, and large feet with very flexible ankles. Still the most important thing was "the stroke" whether it was the "Australian crawl," the new "American six-beat crawl," or the "legless crawl," as practiced and utilized by Jamison Handy. Very little attention was paid to how much work was done, or how it was done; or to systematic alternation of work and rest; or to diet, temperature of the water, warm-up (sauna or exercise), or use of supplements like vitamins C, B-complex, E, minerals, or wheat germ oil. Such terms as interval training, circuit training, repetitious bursts, or "total work load" had hardly appeared and were generally unknown. Medley swimming as an individual event was seldom practiced; and the "dolphin-butterfly" was just appearing as a novelty-fun stroke. It had not yet been incorporated into regular competitive meets—nor had flutter boards (better kick boards), drag-tubes, hip floats, hair shaves, silk racing trunks, high take-off blocks, turning lines, or overhead

9

wires with warning flags appeared. There were no particular rules or known advantages of various styles of breathing, premeet relaxation, or agonistic training and other sophisticated training aids, such as "pleasure pills" (Van Rossen, 1968). There was almost no consideration of "distribution of power" as conceived now. Since 1928 all of these previously mentioned training aids have come into generalized use, as well as some improvements in stroke mechanics, such as: the "whip-kick," the "fish-tail kick," "finning," "the flip-turn," and timed "energy packing." Also, a series of testing techniques have emerged to be used as part of the training work, day by day, or at least from month to month, just to provide coaching intelligence. In addition to Weismuller, Arne Borg of Sweden, Eric Rademacher of Germany, Warren Keoloha, the Spence (Marten and Leonard) brothers, and also Mike McDermott and Bob Skelton were the great stars. Meanwhile girls such as Ann Curtis, Sybil Bauer, Martha Norelius, Helen Meeny and Sue Zimmerman began to set records.

THE FACTORS GOVERNING SUCCESS IN COMPETITION

I can now extend the summary that I made previously (Cureton, 1934) based upon studies made of the Olympic and collegiate swimmers of the 1930–1932 period. I concluded then that Japan won the 1932 Olympics because of better fitness, and at that time I published research on these factors (Cureton, 1933, 1934, 1936). My prediction that the Japanese men swimmers would win surprised Bob Kiphuth, who collaborated with me in this research at Los Angeles and at Berlin. Kiphuth permitted his Yale swimmers to be tested with our "diagnostic fitness tests" as did Sid Hazelton at Dartmouth and others. This testing continued at the University of Illinois under Coach Ed Manley and Al Klingle, and was done by myself or my students. We added a collection of long distance swimmers and many women swimmers, after testing several hundred college and high school varsity swimmers. It was also adopted as a method by the Japanese and Australians, under Yanagita and Ikai in Japan and Carlile and Carlile in Australia (1961, 1963).

At the outset of this period we postulated that there were four principal sets of factors which were operative, but we did not know the relative value of these factors. These factors are listed as follows:
1. Stroke mechanics and coordination
2. Structural aptitude, body build (somatotype), strength, and flexibility
3. Organic condition (fitness)
4. Mental attitude (to train hard enough), personality, and confidence

The ideas that we have had about these major groups of factors are very much the same, but more detailed information has become available. It is the major function of this article to spell out briefly these additional developments.

In 1950, Forbes Carlile and Ursula Carlile visited with us and were very interested in the heartometer work (stroke volume test) that we were using, and also the electrocardiogram test, both of which were being used to indicate the range of cardiovascular adjustment possible in a given swimmer to various levels of work. That led to the use of these tests by the Carliles and the publication of their very successful results (1961). The idea of stress tolerance was a leading topic with Carlile (1963). More and more work, yes, but up to a limit—and beyond that, when the tests changed from getting better and better to worse, then a taper-off was ordered. This "taper" has now become a major concept and is widely applied by coaches. The materials that I published in my books—*Physical Fitness Appraisal and Guidance* (1947), *Endurance of Young Men* (1945), and *Physical Fitness of Champion Athletes* (1951)—stimulated Carlile's interest (Cureton, 1947, 1951).

Major experimentation was projected on a) value of land drills (Kiphuth, 1942, 1950), b) value of varying the pattern of work (Haskell, 1965), c) value of wheat germ oil and wheat germ (Cureton, 1972), and d) psychological motivators (Van Rossen, 1968). However, when we asked Johnny Weismuller why the records were better now, he said, "The pools are better now, not the men." The basic stock of men or women is probably not better, but I must say that the training is now relatively more scientific, with many diligent, shrewd, and scientifically trained coaches working at getting results, and working harder and harder. There is better selection of manpower, and that selection now begins much earlier than formerly, owing mainly to the age-group swimming plan. The much larger number of competitors, including girls, now working out and entering meets is many times greater. There is a larger pool of talent from which to draw, and greater motivations are applied by more meets, better individualized coaching, more writings, and clinics. There are more pools, and the work under the better coaches is longer and harder. Biomechanics is being applied to analyze swimming and diving.

THE NEW ERA, SCIENTIFIC APPLICATIONS

I shall summarize some of the studies which apply scientific methods to improving competitive swimmers. The idea of streamlining swimming to reduce resistance of the body at speeds over 1.5 yards per sec is most dominant because all formulas indicate a great disproportionately high resistance at higher speeds: Karpovich (1933, 1937) reported resistance (R) is proportional to $3.17 \, V^2$ in the crawl stroke, $3.66 \, V^2$ in the orthodox breaststroke, and $3.17 \, V^2$ in the backstroke. These indicate that it takes higher and higher energy to swim faster, above 1.5 yards per sec, with the energy increasing according to the square, rather than as a straight proportionality. In top swimmers, the oxygen used $(\dot{V}O_2)$ in swimming goes almost as high as in a) runners on the treadmill, b) cycling on a bicycle ergometer, and c) skiing cross-country style (Magel and Faulkner, 1967). Below 1.5 yards per sec a straight-line equation may be employed, but a logarithmic form curve is needed at higher speeds. A faster turn-over stroke, as exemplified by the Australian, Wenden, has indicated its better possibilities for fastest speed up to 200 m. In the longer swims the total working capacity appears dominant, influenced a great deal by nutritional reserves. The high relationship of muscular endurance, at moderate effort, is demonstrated by the high relative correlation of a 10-Item Muscular Endurance Test (Cureton, 1960). Correlations as high as 0.83 with performance at 100 and 400 yards suggest that great muscular stamina should be sought in swimming, and in imitative swimming exercises such as: a) flutter kicks (front and back); b) side leg-raises; c) leg whipping with trunk held firm (front and back); d) pulley weights, resistance pulling, or medicine ball throwing; e) continuous endurance in running with crawl strokes, or the breaststroke coordination exercise (Counsilman, no date). Power of the shoulder girdle, while imitating the pull-through movement, as in medicine ball throw for distance, seems to be very important. Although studies have not proven this point conclusively (Schleicher, 1965), there is a great deal of practical coaching support for it (Cureton, 1960; Kiphuth, 1950). Ankle flexibility is of moderate importance and is worth something in all strokes (Yanagita, 1936). While the correlations are rather low with kicking times, the real value of the ankles has not been tested during swimming itself (Alley, 1952). Most swimmers have to kick in order to keep their legs afloat, and perhaps in longer swims they kick only moderately because of the great oxygen cost of kicking. The tank swimmers do drive their legs as they come away from the turns. At a time when Japanese swimmers were generally superior to those in the U.S.A., they were shown to be stronger in both arm and leg strength, and they practiced very much on their kick. They were also shown to be much more flexible (Cureton, 1933). Some coaches have said, "Just swim enough in your event and strength and flexibility will take care of themselves." Studies, including underwater observations during swimming itself, seemingly confirm the important role of flexibility—for example, Yorzyk and Spitz had great ankle flexibility, approximating $100°$ for combination of extension and flexion (total range). I noted also the improvement of Spangaro, the Italian, at the Olympic Games of 1960, after we stretched his ankles in hot towels (for 3 weeks), leading to a 6-sec improvement in the 200-m breaststroke. Tight shoulder muscles or leg muscles and tight suits which restrict shoulder muscle function will tire a swimmer prematurely; and overly slack and poorly conditioned leg extensor and back muscles will weaken a kick that is normally needed to stabilize the body and keep it on keel.

It has been noted that in a given swimming season, strength will diminish unless there are some maintenance exercises. Up to a certain point strength is important, but above that limit it is not, as witnessed by two 13- and 14-year old girls, both doing 16:49.9 for the 1500 m. Jenny Terrell weighed only 46

Table 1. Contribution* of biomechanics tests to swimming performance (crawl)

Test	Time, 20-yard swim β^2 or r^2	%	Time, 100-yard swim β^2 or r^2	%	Time, 440-yard swim β^2 or r^2	%
Coordination			(0.102)	10.2	(0.106)	10.6
test (table			0.043*	4.3		
for Wilson-	0.355	35.5	0.090	4.0	0.045	4.5
Cureton Eq.)	(0.058)	5.5	0.013	1.3	0.025	2.5
Gliding 20 ft,			(0.334)	33.4	0.44	44.0
push-off in	0.089	8.9	0.033	3.3	0.135	13.5
water, prone	0.103	10.3	0.101	10.1	0.385	38.5
Leg kicking			(0.317)	31.7	0.573	57.3
test, 60 ft	0.045	4.5	0.011	1.1	0.102	10.2
	(0.463)	46.3				
Arm stroke			(0.351)	35.1	0.269	26.9
(alone) test,	0.032	3.2	0.124	12.4	0.124	12.4
legs floated			(0.532)	53.2		
			0.180	18.0	0.314	31.4
			0.096	9.6	0.102	10.2
			0.144	14.4		
Whole stroke			(0.317)	31.7		
test, 20 ft in			(0.53)	53.0	0.364	36.4
100 yards,			(0.144)	14.4	0.281	28.1
in 440 yards						
Endurance			(0.477)	47.7	(0.207)	20.7
drop-off test	(0.116)	11.6	0.091	9.1	0.36	36.0
(top speed 1st			0.228	22.8	0.448	44.8
lap—then			(0.148)		0.035	3.5
swim 100 yards						
with 1st lap fast)						

*The figures given in the table are net betas squared for the most part, coming from several available regression equations, or if they are in parentheses, they are correlations squared. Such figures as betas and correlations are not exactly comparable but if squared the betas represent the relative percentage of the *net* variance; and if the rs or Rs are squared, the result is the percentage of *gross* variance. The difference is not great enough to make much difference in the present usage. An r^2 represents the *direct* and *indirect* contributions to a criterion (time) but the β^2 represents only the *direct* net contribution.

kg (101 lbs) and was credited with a world's record. Strength is worth somewhat more at sprint distances, as the research shows (Table 2).

More attention is paid now to streamlining the swimmer to reduce resistance, as extreme effort is required to hold the body high, to hydroplane, or to lift the head. This effort will quickly fatigue the swimmer. Breathing, too, can cause body instability, hip sway, and widening of the legs. Fewer

Table 2. Structural factors of physique related to swimming times

Test	Time in 20-yard swim		Time in 100-yard swim		Time in 440-yard swim		Olympians differentiated from college swimmers (using biserial r^2 to differentiated groups)	
	β^2 or r^2	%	β^2 or r^2	%	β^2 or r^2	%	β^2 or r^2	%
Trunk extension backward flexibility	0.012	1.2	0.02	2.0	0.147	14.7	(0.635)	63.5
Trunk forward flexibility	(−0.025)	−2.5					(−0.41)	−41.0
Ankle flexion plus extension	(0.025)	−2.5					(0.33)	−33.0
Vertical buoyancy test (7 ft water)	(0.10)	1.0					(0.049)	4.9
Shoulders flexibility							(0.19)	19.0

Vital capacity (spirometer)					(0.24)	24.0
Cureton plinth leg-kick strength	0.145	14.5	(0.312)* 0.029	31.25* 2.95	0.083	8.3
Roger's strength index	0.033	3.3	(-0.006)	-0.61	(-0.002)	-0.25
Cureton, 4-dyn. strengths	(0.0025)	0.25			(-0.0035)	-0.35
Cureton plinth arm-pull strength	0.120	10.12	0.440	4.42	0.034	3.39
Age of young men	0.53	5.3			(0.0367)	6.7
Height of young men	0.104	10.4			(0.005)	0.5
Fat on gluteals with calipers					(0.433)	43.3
Fat on face with calipers	(0.105)	10.5				
Size of hands	(0.159)	15.4				
Length of legs	(0.172)	17.0				

*Women.

breaths may be taken up to 100 m, but for longer distances this is probably not recommended. Progressive training of the breath-holding ability, which is well correlated with oxygen debt capacity, is needed, as swimmers adopt "tumble-turns" and hold their breath on the turns and push-off glides (Collis, 1970; Van Huss and Cureton, 1955).

Prediction of crawl swimming times from various tests

It is necessary to point out that statistical prediction of swimming times is dependent on the type of sample at hand. Very precise generalizations should not be made because of the sampling variation in the coefficients presented.

No precise formulas for prediction exist at the very highest speeds, for prediction requires a generalized equation demanding a wide distribution of cases. The data can be fitted with a straight line below 1.5 yards per sec, but above this speed a parabolic fit needs to be made; the V^2 law fits quite well. The weighted coefficients as taken from regression equations are valuable to indicate the relative importance of various test elements for prediction of swimming times. There are no recent "engineering" equations which fit all human bodies in motion. The beta weights are better than raw correlation coefficients and represent the best evidence available; otherwise "r^2" is used in Tables 1, 2, and 3. The "path coefficient" defining an influence over a direct path from item to criterion (the time) is indicated proportionately by the beta squared (β^2), or by the multiple R^2. The latter indicates the percentage of relative relationship of a test item to the total gross variance in the criterion. The *net* relationship of the beta squared is better, as the influence of the intercorrelation effects are eliminated, and only the direct relationship from item to criterion is given in the net, β^2 (Wright, 1922).

All correlational procedures are but approximations; but gross differences can be observed in the results shown in Tables 1, 2, and 3 in which tests of various types have been related to swimming performances at 20, 100, and 440 yards. The data are from 10 studies (Cureton, 1930, 1933, 1934, 1935; Homan, 1947; Krizan, 1948; Tilley, 1951; Geistweit, 1952; Houston, 1952; Luther, 1952). All studies listed are theses sponsored by the author and conducted at the University of Illinois.

Parallelism between fitness state and performance

The data taken on a girl swimmer, Sara Barber (Figure 1) show that 4 years of progressive training (progressive overload) were paralleled by improved swimming backstroke times and also paralleled by improved amplitudes and areas of the brachial pulse wave. The waves were progressively taller, sharper, and higher in velocity at the peak of training and decreased when she was out of training. The capability of the heart for ejecting blood also steadily improved during training, as indicated by the brachial pulse waves.

In an interesting experiment it was shown that at four levels of work (gradually increased step by step) the amplitudes of the brachial pulse waves which were taken during work increased progressively with the work and paralleled the stroke volume. John Shepherd at the University of Minnesota and John Faulkner at the University of Michigan have shown that it is typical of the stroke volume to increase, even after the pulse rate and the maximal oxygen intake have leveled off, and also after the arteriovenous oxygen difference has leveled off. Therefore, the most critical adjustment of the swimmer would seem to be in the ability of the heart to produce a larger and larger stroke as stress is built up in the work and to develop "stress tolerance." It is interesting that the postexercise brachial pulse wave is the one most affected by training, and presumably it is the most important one for indicating the effects of training. Notice this in Figure 1.

Carlile (1961) adopted this method after he visited our laboratory and worked with us. He followed through with this type of testing with the Australian swimmers in the last 8 weeks of training before the Rome Olympic Games. He demonstrated that those who did not adapt to the training and had some deterioration in their brachial pulse waves in the last 8 weeks either went stale and had poorer relative times or did not make the team (Carlile, 1958; Carlile and Carlile, 1961). Counsilman (1968) supported the same concepts of fatigue and staleness.

BIOMECHANICS: THE TEST ITEMS

Six principal types of tests are shown in Table 1 which have to do with actual swimming. It is also this group of tests which gives the best relationships to swimming times. Prediction equations were generated by Wilson (1933) and Cureton (1940) working together at Springfield College:

$$\text{Time in 20-yard crawl sprint (sec)} = 0.343 \text{ (time of arms alone*)} + 0.106 \text{ (time of legs alone)} + 5.16 \tag{1}$$

$$\text{Time in 20-yard backstroke (sec)} = 0.52 \text{ (time of arms alone*)} + 0.18 \text{ (time of legs alone)} + 1.35 \tag{2}$$

$$\text{Time in 20-yard breaststroke (sec)} = 0.265 \text{ (time of arms alone*)} + 0.131 \text{ (time of legs alone)} + 8.68 \tag{3}$$

*Feet floated, tied to polo ball.

Table 3. Circulatory-respiratory factors related to swimming times

Test	Time in 20-yard swim		Time in 100-yard swim		Time in 440-yard swim		Olympians differentiated from college swimmers (using biserial r^2 to differentiate)	
	β^2 or r^2	%	β^2 or r^2	%	β^2 or r^2	%	β^2 or r^2	%
Terminal pulse rate after 2-min step test 30 steps/min	(0.062)*	6.2			0.324 0.75†	32.3 75.0†	(0.35)	35.0
Terminal pulse rate after swim					0.459	45.9		
Heartograph, sys. amplitude					(0.025)	2.5	0.007	0.7
HGF fatigue ratio							0.384† 0.466	38.4 46.6
HGF diastolic amplitude					(0.050)	5.0	0.023 (0.254)†	2.3 25.4
HGF diastolic surge					(0.084)	8.4	0.307 0.157	30.7 15.7

HGF area	(.001) 0.10		(0.045) 4.5	(0.352)† 35.2
HGF obliquity angle				(0.000) 00.0
HGF rest-to-work ratio			(0.096) 9.6	0.025 12.5
Barach index	(0.16) 16.0			(0.130) 13.0
Oxygen intake (liters/min)	(0.185) 18.5	0.000 0	0.113 12.7	
Oxygen debt (liters)		(0.047) 4.7	(0.295) 29.5	0.013 1.3
5-min step test	(0.020) 2.0	0.000 0	(0.141) 14.1	(0.05) 0
Breath-holding time	(0.071) 7.10	0.135 13.5	(0.330) 33.0	0.40 40.0
Underwater swim distance	(0.000) 0	0.034 3.4	(0.016) 1.6	0.000 0
Diastolic blood pressure	(0.018) 1.8	0.146 14.6		(0.080) 8.0
Systolic blood pressure		0.072 7.2	0.248 24.8	(0.463) 46.3
T-wave, highest		0.156 15.6		
ST-segment		0.130 13.0		

*Figures in parentheses r^2; others β^2.
†Women.

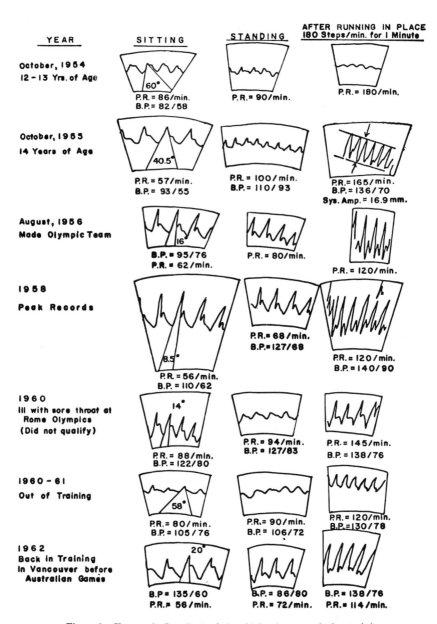

Figure 1. Changes in Sara Barber's brachial pulse wave during training.

If a swimmer beats his predicted mark, this *residual* (unpredicted part) may indicate that he has coordination better than average and can be rated on a scale of such differences (Table 4). But if the swimmer is poorer than the predicted time, then his coordination is poorer than average. It was found by testing many swimmers that there was a wide distribution of such scores, plus (poorer) and minus (better), and so a scale was prepared. The same thing may be done by using Karpovich's equation, V^2 (arms and legs) = V^2 (arms) + V^2 (legs).

In a similar way, Cureton (1935) developed an endurance test based on the principle that speed could be separated statistically from endurance. Time is taken at top speed, starting in the water with a push-off, and multiplying the 20- or 25-yard time by the number of laps in the 100 yards. This product yields the total time for the 100 yards. In this case there is no loss or "drop-off." Then the swimmer is told to swim the 100 yards, but to swim the first lap as fast as possible, and then do the best he can on the remaining laps. This gives his actual time in the 100-yard swim. The difference between the calculated time and the actual time is the "drop-off index." This has been found to be as low as 1.0 sec in the top swimmers, who are fit enough to hold a fast pace without much drop-off; and it has been found to be as great as 20 or more sec in very poorly fit swimmers. This technique eliminates the speed and gives a rating which is mainly *endurance.* It was found to correlate as high as 0.74 with the McCurdy-Larson Cardiovascular-Respiratory Test. The equation for the 20-yard pool is:

$$\text{Time in 100 yards (sec)} =$$
$$5.98 \text{ (time in 20-yard sprint)}$$
$$+2.88 \text{ (drop-off index)} +2.63 \tag{4}$$

$$r = 0.912 \pm 3.28 \text{ sec}$$

The net contribution to the 100-yard time was 54.6 percent for speed and 45.4 percent for endurance. The coefficients are 4 (for sprint time) and 2.6 (for drop-off) in a 25-yard pool. The constant is then 5.5 Table 5 gives the scale.

A comparison shows that items in Table 1 (biomechanics) are better related to performance than those in Tables 2 and 3 and that Table 3 has items with greater importance than Table 2. Thus we can say generally and inclusively that *swimming itself* and its separate elements (arms alone, gliding, legs alone, and coordination) are better related to swimming times than any other type of tests. It is also apparent, however, that body build, size, flexibility, horizontal floating capacity, and buoyancy are worth something but static strength is very low in importance. It has been shown that maximal static strength is not as highly related as muscular endurance to 100-yard

Table 4. Cureton's coordination scale* for comparing the difference between the predicted time and actual time in short sprint swimming.

Percentile rating	Difference between computing and actual times for 60 ft	Coordination Scale	
100	−5.47	50	0.00
98	−5.24	48	0.23
96	−5.01	46	0.46
94	−4.77	44	0.69
92	−4.55	42	0.93
90	−4.33	40	1.15
88	−4.10	38	1.38
86	−3.82	36	1.61
84	−3.64	34	1.85
82	−3.38	32	2.06
80	−3.13	30	2.28
78	−2.92	28	2.43
76	−2.72	26	2.57
74	−2.49	24	2.71
72	−2.26	22	2.85
70	−2.03	20	3.19
68	−1.81	18	3.42
66	−1.58	16	3.68
64	−1.36	14	3.90
62	−1.27	12	4.13
60	−1.09	10	4.56
58	−0.91	8	4.59
56	−0.68	6	4.82
54	−0.46	4	5.05
52	−0.23	2	5.28
		0	5.51

*Equations 1–3 indicate how well an average swimmer will combine arms with legs. The better swimmers will "beat" these equations by making faster time. Poorer swimmers will be poorer in coordination. Coordination is defined as proper movements, made with proper regulation of force and intertimed so as to achieve the most perfect action as willed by the performer with a minimum of waste. Swimmers who better the average prediction have better coordination than those who do not equal the expected average. This idea permits the construction of a *coordination scale*. This test is designed to see how well a swimmer can combine arms with legs for a short distance. A short distance is chosen because it is desirable to exclude endurance. Deduct the computed time from the actual. Look up the difference in the table for the percentile rating on coordination.

swim time. Swimming uses moderate strength in an endurance way. It must be directed specifically to the right point of application.

Table 3 is perhaps the most interesting because the circulatory-respiratory factors are hard to see or appreciate. Terminal pulse rate and the Heartograph tests relate quite well to swimming the crawl stroke; and, while the data are not given, the results are not very different either for the back- or breast-strokes. Oxygen intake is not very well related, nor is oxygen debt or breath holding, except at the highest level of swimming competition. The faster and faster a person goes, the more oxygen debt he will develop (if his anaerobic metabolism is well trained). The 5-min step test is disappointingly poor, much poorer than the terminal pulse rate test. The lower the swimmer can keep the pulse rate during the work, the better is his endurance; and the stronger the pulse pressure (or heart stroke) he can develop, the better is the endurance. These results support the validity of the McCurdy-Larson equation to predict 440-yard swimming (Cureton, 1947).

$$\text{Time in 440 yards} = \frac{623.5 - [\text{standing normal diastolic pressure}]}{3.81}$$
$$- \frac{[\text{breath holding after 2-min bench stepping (17 in, 30/min)}]}{3.45}$$
$$+ \frac{[\text{pulse rate at end of 440 swim}]}{1.46}$$
$$- \frac{[\text{increase of the diastolic pressure after exercise}]}{1.68}$$

For young competitors, the multiple R for four measures of the heartograph is 0.61 for men and is 0.70 for women subjects. With nonchampions and a well distributed group, the multiple R for the McCurdy-Larson equation is 0.81. The latter test is based upon 2 min of step test exercise and also an actual 440-yard swim for best time. The test begins by taking the diastolic pressure standing; then the 2-min step test is conducted, and 20 sec after it a breath-holding test is given. The diastolic blood pressure is taken right after the breath holding. The subject then swims the 440 yards, the time is taken, and immediately after the swim the pulse rate is taken. From these data the test can be scored. If a subject fails to equal his actual 440-yard time as a result of the prediction calculation, then he is assumed to be in relatively poor condition, whereas if he makes a cardiovascular-respiratory (CV-R) fitness score better than his swim time, he is in a very good state of fitness. Fitness may help swimming, but in no way does it provide a substitute for good mechanics and a streamlined body position.

Good swimming also depends upon muscular endurance, strong shoulders and leg-kicking muscles, and good flexibility—in addition to CV-R fitness. In Ohnmacht's (1958) experiment with young men, a multiple R was obtained of 0.83 (S = ±17.8 sec) for predicting the 440-yard swim time. This was based

Table 5. A test for endurance in speed swimming

Percentile rating	Rungs to climb	Time of short sprint (start in water)		Endurance index (1st lap from last) (sec)	Time in 100 yards (sec)
		60 ft (sec)	75 ft (sec)		
100	0	8.8	10.8	.5	49.7
99	1	9.0	11.0	1.0	51.9
98	2	9.4	11.4	1.1	54.1
97	3	9.6	11.6	1.2	55.7
96	4	9.8	11.8	1.3	57.4
95	5	10.0	12.0	1.6	59.0
94	6	10.1	12.1	2.0	60.7
93	7	10.3	12.3	2.3	62.3
92	8	10.5	12.5	2.6	63.9
91	9	10.7	12.7	3.0	65.6
90	10	10.9	12.9	3.3	67.3
88	12	11.0	13.0	3.5	68.5
86	14	11.1	13.1	3.8	69.6
84	16	11.2	13.2	4.1	70.2
82	18	11.3	13.3	4.4	71.3
80	20	11.4	13.4	4.7	72.5
78	22	11.5	13.5	4.8	73.4
76	24	11.6	13.6	5.0	74.0
74	26	11.65	13.65	5.2	74.8
72	28	11.7	13.7	5.4	75.7
70	30	11.75	13.75	5.6	76.5
68	32	11.8	13.8	5.8	77.4
66	34	11.9	13.9	6.0	78.3
64	36	12.0	14.0	6.2	79.2

62	38	12.1	14.1	6.3	80.2
60	40	12.2	14.2	6.5	81.1
58	42	12.3	14.3	6.7	81.9
56	44	12.35	14.35	6.9	82.5
54	46	12.4	14.4	7.1	83.4
52	48	12.5	14.5	7.2	84.2
50	50	12.6	14.6	7.4	84.9
48	52	12.7	14.7	7.6	85.9
46	54	12.8	14.8	7.7	86.7
44	56	12.9	14.9	7.9	87.8
42	58	13.1	15.1	8.0	88.7
40	60	13.2	15.2	8.1	89.7
38	62	13.3	15.3	8.3	90.4
36	64	13.35	15.35	8.4	91.1
34	66	13.4	15.4	8.5	91.7
32	68	13.5	15.5	8.7	92.4
30	70	13.6	15.6	8.8	93.1
28	72	13.8	15.8	9.0	94.7
26	74	14.0	16.0	9.2	96.2
24	76	14.2	16.2	9.4	97.6
22	78	14.3	16.3	9.7	98.9
20	80	14.4	16.4	10.0	100.2
18	82	14.7	16.7	10.4	102.2
16	84	15.0	17.0	10.7	104.3
14	86	15.2	17.2	11.0	106.4
12	88	15.5	17.5	11.4	108.4
10	90	15.7	17.7	11.7	110.5
5	95	17.3	19.3	15.1	126.3
0	100	19.3	21.3	18.6	143.9

*From Cureton (1935).

upon the ten-item test devised by Cureton (1960). The items were*: a) medicine ball throw for distance from a lying position (12-lb ball); b) trunk extension flexibility, backward; c) extension press-ups (boys), forearm press-ups (girls); d) flutter-kicks on the front; e) flutter-kicks on the back; f) 2-min step test (17-in bench or chair) plus terminal pulse rate; g) breath holding immediately after the 2-min step test and terminal pulse rate; h) side-support leg raisings, right and left; i) breaststroke imitation exercise; j) ankle flexibility, right and left. Each item is scored on the basis of 100 points, with a possible maximum of 1000. It is a good test for young swimmers and has developmental value. It illustrates that speed swimming requires considerable muscular and structural fitness, as well as CV-R fitness.

Related land tests of physical aptitude for swimming, tests of physical performance for evaluating swimmers, and analytical tests for swimming are presented in Tables 6–8, respectively.

TRAINING PROGRAMS AND TOTAL AMOUNT OF WORK DONE IN TRAINING

No one pattern of work has proven to be very superior to others. It has long been the practice to work at repetitious sprints, as well as longer, slower work. Haskell (1965) tested three programs comparing the following work-outs: a) moderate pace, many repetitions, interval style; b) fast pace, repetitious sprints; c) rather long, continuous work. The improvements were 51 sec for an all-out endurance trial on a treadmill, 59 sec for intensive repetitions, and 101 sec for continuous pattern, respectively. Counsilman, in a report to the AAAS Meeting at Dallas, 1968, advocated the principle of mixed types of workouts, alternating the locomotive build-up pattern with fast sprints and also considerable long distance swimming. But what has stood out over the years has been more and more work. This has steadily gone up over the years for men and women, boys and girls. From 1 hr per day, it has advanced to as much as 4 or 5 hr per day, and to as many as three workouts per day, totaling 9,000–12,000 yards/day.

In trying to identify the most critical factors for 30 top girl swimmers in Sweden, Astrand et al. (1963) could only conclude that the most successful ones had done more total work than the others. But, in addition, they were taller and heavier and had larger vital capacities and oxygen intakes. Correcting the latter for weight eliminated any significant net contributions of these tests and also eliminated the effects of total hemoglobin, even though it was 19 percent above average, and likewise heart volume (22 percent above) and

*In the original test the 5-min step test was used, but this was dropped in favor of the terminal pulse rate, and the medicine ball throw was inserted in place of the extension press-up.

blood volume (14 percent above). Inuring the muscles to fatigue does not seem to be a matter of size but of specific conditioning of muscle groups. The final conclusion indicates that the total amount of fast swimming is the critical factor.

Carlile and Carlile (1961) made a dramatic reversal of overtraining (staleness) with the Australian Olympic swimmers of 1960. When they saw this staleness developing from observing the results of weekly heartometer and electrocardiogram tests, they instituted changes in the training. They reduced the workouts, ordered more sleep, and added vitamins and wheat germ oil daily. These measures seemed to work, and the team gave a wonderful account of itself at Rome in 1960. Kiphuth was also of the opinion that definite rest periods should be provided for his best swimmers. Most coaches want to use "taper-off" before their top meets.

Homan (1947) obtained a multiple R of 0.75 by combining arms alone (20 yards), less face fat with calipers and lying systolic blood pressure (the higher the pressure the better). The relative contribution of these items was, respectively, 66.5, 20.8, and 12.7 percent. The prediction of the 440-yard time gave a multiple R of 0.65 for three events: 100-yard swim (76.8 percent), pulse rate 3 min after a 5-min step test (14.0 percent), and trunk extension backward (9.2 percent).

In the study by Houston (1952) on the electrocardiogram measurements, only two showed significant helpful relationships: a) the T-wave, highest and b) the ST-segment. The former gave a net beta square coefficient of 0.156 (15.6 percent) and the latter 0.130 (13.0 percent), with the interpretation in the usual direction. The S-wave was negatively related, larger S with poorer time, −0.253 for r^2 (25.3 percent).

It is shown in Tables 1, 2, and 3 that there are many factors affecting swimming performance but they operate differently at different distances, and somewhat differently between the sexes. There are very definite limitations to respiration in swimming, and the problem seems to be more related to being economical and getting more work done on relatively less oxygen, the oxygen debt (anaerobic factor) being fully as important as the oxygen intake (aerobic) factor (Van Huss and Cureton, 1955; Collis, 1970).

A comment should be made about body type. The tall, slim type has been shown to glide better through the water if the legs are supported. This refers to the body type of Mark Spitz, or Ronald Matthes of East Germany, or of a type like Ann Curtis or Sybil Bauer. These types are generally more flexible than other types and have less resistance passing through the water. Most swimmers are medial mesomorphs, except for this tall, wiry, and flexible type. If the thinner type is given enough strength work (medicine balls) and enough endurance training, they may be the best of all. Great strength, such as would go with an extreme mesomorph, is not needed. The strength cannot be exerted fully on the water because it gives. The slip is about 75 percent.

Table 6. Land test of physical aptitude for swimming*

Test items	Specifications	Poor 0 to 25	Fair 26–35	Average 50	Good 65–75	Excellent 76–100	Points earned
1. Medicine ball throw, 12 lbs (ft)	Lie on back ball overhead, throw for distance	10	15	20	25	30+	
2. Average of right and left ankle flexion plus extension (degrees)	Trace ankle against paper pad with pencil	40	60	75	85	90+	
3. Trunk extension backward, warm-up is permitted (in)	Lying on front, legs held, hands behind neck—raise chin upward	8	14	18	20	22+	
4. Shoulder girdle flexibility (in)	Lying on front, chin to floor throughout, rod in hands	8	12	18	21	24+	
5. Sum of side leg-raisings Right side down Left side down	Lift top leg to horizontal as many times as can	20	30	44	60	100+	
6. Flutter-kicks on front (number)	Arched back, hands under thighs, legs straight	100	300	600	750	1000+	

		50	100	200	300	400
7. Flutter-kicks on back	Hands behind neck, legs low and straight					
8. Run in place with crawl or butterfly arm movements 180/min	Finish run, sit down and after 2 breaths hold the third for time (sec)	10	20	30	45	60
9. Breaststroke imitation, arms pull, then squat jump—out and back	At 30/min rate, legs spread 24 in wide and back together	20	35	50	75	100
10. Pulse rate taken immediately after squat-jumps above (beats/min.)	Take pulse rate on carotid, neck, or wrist for 30 sec × 2	200	180	150	130	110

TOTAL SCORE

*Instructions: Take the test in a bathing suit in the order given as there is a built in warm-up in the test. Score your result, then encircle the score opposite the test by ringing the nearest resulting score; then estimate points on basis of 100 given in the top line. Total all points and put score at bottom to the right in space given.

Table 7. University of Illinois norm tables—varsity swimming squad, 1947–1948, Cureton's physical fitness for aquatic leadership

Classifica-tion	S.P.W. amplitude (cm)	D.P.W. amplitude (cm)	Diastolic surge (cm)	Angle of obliquity (degrees)	Schneider test scores	5-min step test (pulse)	B.H. after 2-min stepping 30/min (sec)
	2.83	1.93	1.10	27.72	22	79	81.0
Superior	2.71	1.84	1.07	27.08	21	86	78.0
	2.59	1.75	1.04	26.44	21	93	75.0
	2.47	1.66	1.01	25.80	20	100	72.0
Very good	2.35	1.57	0.98	25.16	20	107	69.0
	2.23	1.48	0.95	24.52	19	114	65.5
	2.11	1.39	0.91	23.88	18	121	60.5
Above average	1.99	1.30	0.82	23.14	17	128	55.5
	1.87	1.21	0.73	22.50	16	135	50.5
	1.75	1.12	0.64	21.86	15	142	45.5
Average	1.63	0.93	0.55	21.22	14	149	40.5
	1.51	0.84	0.46	20.58	13	156	35.5
	1.39	0.75	0.37	19.92	12	163	30.5
Below average	1.27	0.66	0.28	19.28	11	170	25.5
	1.15	0.57	0.19	18.64	10	177	20.5
	1.03	0.48	0.15	18.00	9	184	15.5
Poor	0.91	0.39	0.12	17.36	8	191	12.0
	0.79	0.30	0.09	16.72	8	198	9.0
	0.67	0.21	0.06	16.08	7	205	6.0
Very poor	0.55	0.12	0.03	15.44	7	212	3.0
	0.43	0.03	0.00	14.80	6	219	0.0
M	1.63	0.93	0.55	21.22	13.99	148.85	40.51
σ	0.40	0.30	0.29	2.15	3.38	23.43	16.87
N	79	79	79	79	79	78	79
Range	0.93–2.50	0.27–1.58	0.06–1.28	16.8–26.3	6–22	91–204	5–110

QUESTIONNAIRE STUDIES OF TRAINING METHODS

Several questionnaire studies have been made of coaches and swimmers, at the top competitive level. These have been made by Cureton (1933, 1936, 1947, 1960), Essick (1956), and Chivers (1952). A condensed summary is as follows:

1. Total amount of work done—3 to 7 miles per day by top swimmers
2. Pace—worked upon at shorter distances, then more and more distance

Table 7. Continued

Surface area (m²)	V.C. corrected (in)	V.C. residuals (in)	Trunk flexion (in)	Trunk extension (in)	Extension press up (times)	Side leg raisings (right)	Side leg raisings (left)	Flutter kicks on back (times)
2.31	466	+126	0.00	31.50	12.0	78.0	70.0	270
2.27	453	+115	0.55	30.20	11.0	75.0	68.0	260
2.23	440	+104	1.10	28.90	11.0	71.0	66.0	250
2.19	427	+ 93	1.65	27.60	10.0	67.0	64.0	240
2.15	414	+ 82	2.20	26.30	10.0	63.0	61.0	230
2.11	401	+ 71	2.76	25.00	9.0	59.0	58.0	220
2.07	388	+ 60	3.66	23.70	9.0	55.0	55.0	210
2.03	375	+ 49	4.56	22.40	8.0	51.0	50 0	200
1.99	362	+ 38	5.46	21.10	8.0	47.0	45.0	190
1.95	349	+ 27	6.36	19.80	7.0	43.0	40 0	180
1.91	336	+ 16	7.26	18.50	6.0	39.0	35.0	170
1.87	323	+ 4	8.16	17.20	5.0	35.0	30.0	160
1.83	310	− 7	9.06	15.90	4.0	31.0	25.0	150
1.79	297	− 18	9.96	14.60	4.0	27.0	20.0	140
1.75	284	− 29	10.86	13.30	3.0	23.0	15.0	130
1.71	271	− 40	11.76	12.00	3.0	19.0	12 0	120
1.67	258	− 51	12.32	10.70	2.0	15.0	9 0	110
1.63	245	− 62	12.87	9.40	2.0	11.0	6.0	100
1.59	232	− 73	13.42	8 10	1.0	7.0	4.0	90
1.55	219	− 84	13.97	6.80	1.0	3.0	2.0	80
1.51	206	− 95	14.52	5.50	0.0	0.0	0.0	70
1.91	336.46	+ 16.22	7.26	18.51	6.05	39.00	35.34	170.12
0.12	42.40	36.00	3.11	4.35	5.75	13.20	16.74	35.0
55	79	79	79	79	78	77	77	77
1.60–	257–	− 67–	0–	3.6–	0–	10–	6–	60–
2.20	428	+ 98	15.8	25.5	47	63	68	414

Continued

3. Year-round developmental work (land training and longer endurance work), competitive period 4–5 months, possibly with two peaks and tapers-off between

4. Regular use of pulleys, medicine balls, pull-over weights, iso-cords, and elastic rubber strips—continuously, throughout the entire year

5. Use of diagnostic (coaching intelligence) tests in early season, or preseason, which also may have some possible motivational effect

6. Attention to balanced and adequate nutrition, with supplements of vitamins and wheat germ oil

Table 7. Continued

Flutter kicks–front (times)	2-min run B.H. (sec)	Breaststroke squat jump (times)	Total points	Letter grade	Numerical grade	Standard score	T-score by formula	Percentage by tables
1433	58	118	1000		100	100	80	99.8
1396	57	116	989	A+		95	77	99.6
1313	55	114	949			90	74	99.1
1275	53	112	909			85	71	98.2
1192	51	109	869	A		80	68	96.4
1109	49	106	829		90	75	65	93.3
1026	45	103	789		89	70	62	88.4
943	41	92	749	B		65	59	81.6
860	37	81	709		80	60	56	72.6
777	33	70	669		79	55	53	61.8
694	29	59	629	C+		50	50	50.0
611	25	48	589		75	45	47	38.2
528	21	37	549		74	40	44	27.4
445	17	26	509	C		35	41	18.4
362	13	15	469		70	30	38	11.5
279	9	12	429		69	25	35	6.7
196	7	9	389	D		20	32	3.6
113	5	6	349	Pass	60	15	29	1.8
75	3	4	309	Fail		10	26	0.8
37	1	2	269			5	23	0.3
0	00	258			0	20	0.1	
694	29.15	58.82	629.20					
276	15.33	36.60	135.00					
77	78	77	77					
140–	10–	33–	340–					
1360	75	201	901					

7. Motivational devices used during the season, rewards, recognition, publicity

8. A good deal of competition, two seasons per year, to keep swimmers working

9. More full length, competitive size pools

10. Tests to check fitness levels, throughout the year

The use of preliminary developmental training exercises is strongly indicated, as used by most top coaches (Kiphuth, Haines, Chàvoor, Counsilman, Silvia). After the Australians did rather poorly in the 1948 Olympic Games,

Table 8. Careton's analytical advanced tests: crawl swimming analysis percentile scoring chart (college men)*

	Endurance	Racing start time at 20 ft and 60 ft	Push and swim turns fast (widths)	Push and glide (widths)	Coordination (using Wilson's equations)	Whole stroke 20-yard sprint (with push)	Ball between knees 20 yard arm stroke (with push)	Ball in front 20-yard flutter-kick (with push) 234 cases	Percentile score
36	0.5	1.0	18	22	−5.0	8.0	10.9	10.5	100
	2.6	1.25	20	24	−4.55	9.6	11.4	12.0	92
26	4.3	1.5	22	26	−3.51	11.0	11.9	14.1	83
	5.1	1.75	25	29	−2.60	11.5	12.8	16.1	75
6	5.9	2.0	29	33	1.69	11.9	13.8	18.3	67
	6.7	2.25	32	36	−0.91	12.2	14.2	20.4	58
0 (median)	7.4	2.5	36	40.0	0	12.6	14.7	22.5	50
	8.0	2.75	39	43	0.93	13.1	15.6	25.7	42
6	8.6	3.0	43	43	1.95	13.5	16.6	28.9	33
	9.3	3.26	46	50	2.64	15.1	12.8	32.1	25
26	10.5	3.5	50	54	3.55	14.8	19.0	35.4	17
	13.1	3.75	54	58	4.59	16.0	20.2	38.6	8
36	18.6	4.0	58	62	5.51	17.2	21.4	41.9	0

*Developed in research at Springfield College. (Pool, 24 feet wide.)

compared to the Japanese and the Americans, they adopted the land-training system. It has seemingly improved their team. These are well covered in Kiphuth's book (1942, 1950).

Counsilman has detailed the training for many top swimmers in his book, *Science of Swimming* (1968). Such material has been available just in recent years. Kiphuth (1942, 1950) has the best exercises in his book, *Swimming*.

NUTRITIVE NEEDS FOR SWIMMERS

Youth may have definite nutritional deficiencies today, due to: a) economic conditions; b) processing and adulteration for preservation; c) cooking and reheating and storing in freezer, thawing and reheating; d) poor choices: eating for taste rather than for good balance in the 60 percent carbohydrates, 20 percent fat, and 20 percent protein proportion; e) eating old food, packaged and shelved too long; f) erroneous dieting fad; g) poor food (empty calories); h) induced deficiencies due to sickness, overstress, alcoholism, confinement, drugs, or hospitalization; i) indoor swimming only, lack of vitamin D; j) biological individuality (Cureton, 1968A, 1972).

Hard work in swimming training requires a good oatmeal or whole wheat cereal with milk and honey, one egg per day and some lean meat, a good mixed green-yellow-red salad, citrus fruit and apples, potatoes, assorted vegetables and green or dried beans (lima), and added vitamins: C, B-complex and wheat germ and wheat germ oil. Regularity is important in eating. Fish and milk or cottage cheese are good sources of protein, along with beans. The problem is to avoid overeating or undereating. Lemon, lime, apple, orange, and grapefruit juices are to be taken freely. Contraindicated are smoking, excessive use of "pop" drinks, greasy meals, excessive use of poor meats, lack of vegetables and fruits. A few days before a time trial or race it is well to reduce fat and protein food and eat mainly carbohydrates. In this case additional B-complex vitamins and C vitamins may be taken.

It has been shown that wheat germ oil is a potent supplement for athletes in hard training (Cureton, 1957, 1968A). In very hot weather, the salt may be increased somewhat and overeating should be strictly avoided. Water may be freely drunk, along with milk. There should be some restriction of pastries, hot breads, pies, doughnuts, and any food which produces "excessive fullness" or gas or indigestion. On a day-to-day basis the peak point of efficiency is about 3–4 hr after the last meal. The precontest meal should be rather light and easily digestible.

Bill Yorzyk reported that he took 35 × 6 minim capsules of viobin wheat germ oil throughout the season and 10 per day in the off season, along with multivitamins. His stamina in the 200-yard dolphin race at Melbourne and his Olympic record at that time are noted (Cureton, 1968A). Essick (1956) did another study, *The Training Habits of the 1956 U.S.A. Men's Olympic*

Table 9. Progressive changes in the physical fitness of an adult male during a season of training for competitive swimming

Progression by months	Gale (% BMR)	Resting state								Hard work (in, or immediately after)			
		Basal TPR (mm Hg/cc X time/beat)	Area/SA (cm²)	Systolic amplitude (cm)	Stroke volume (cc/beat)	Sitting pulse rate (beats/min)	Rest/work (Heartograph)	O₂ intake (liters/min)	Net O₂ intake (liters/min/kg)	PP (1 min after) (mm Hg)	Net total O₂ (liters)	Stroke volume (cc/beat)	Time of run (min & sec)
1. Detrained	6	1.352	0.178	1.21	60.3	72	1.53	1.78	0.024	88	8.15	104.7	1:11
2. Land drills	4	1.180	0.199	1.35	82.8	64	2.28	2.57	0.030	106	8.34	127.2	1:13
3.	1	1.233	0.191	1.43	80.3	64	2.40	2.77	0.032	113	10.98	126.9	1:30
4. Pool drills	8	1.093*	0.195	1.26	84.9*	72	2.81	3.21	0.037	110	9.93	153.1	1:34
5.	6	1.262	0.171	1.25	78.5	68	3.00*	3.10	0.036	156	12.38	147.5	1:50
6. Competition	14	1.234	0.213*	1.57*	69.1	64	2.28	3.90*	0.041*	162*	14.47	176.2*	1:53
7.	15*	1.204	0.200	1.40	82.3	72	2.23	3.70	0.039	121	15.12*	163.5	2:00*
8. Detraining	13	1.189	0.185	1.45	72.9	68	2.13	3.78	0.040	80	11.59	160.1	1:37
9.	7	1.226	0.179	1.30	74.8	72	1.86	3.15	0.032	104	10.42	130.7	1:25

*Peak score or performance.

Swimming Team. Shelley Mann and Nancy Ramey, the only two girls on wheat germ oil at that time, won 1st and 2nd in the 100-m butterfly race (Cureton, 1968A). Support for the assumption that the wheat germ oil helped is now published in Cureton's full report on 42 experiments (1972). Ludwig Prokop demonstrated faster recovery after exertion tests attributable to wheat germ oil (including vitamin E) and Gier and Farrell, of Kansas State University, showed support with experiments on animals. These animals had less oxygen debt after swims to exhaustion and recuperated faster. Wheat germ oil improved endurance and also reaction time. The results were relatively greater and more significant statistically at 20 weeks of feeding the wheat germ oil supplement, than at 10 weeks.

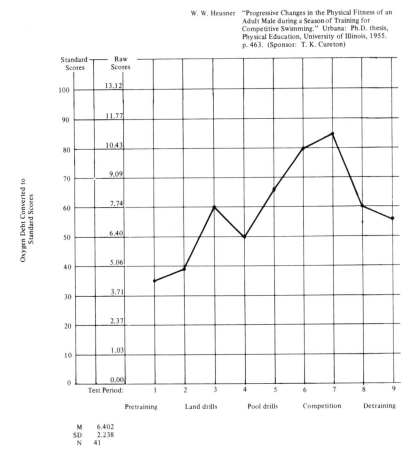

W. W. Heusner   "Progressive Changes in the Physical Fitness of an Adult Male during a Season of Training for Competitive Swimming." Urbana: Ph.D. thesis, Physical Education, University of Illinois, 1955. p. 463. (Sponsor: T. K. Cureton)

Figure 2. The progressive development of oxygen debt in Heusner's full season training experiment.

A table has been published by Cureton (1968A) of the habitual practices of the Russian athletes, which shows that more B_1 and C vitamins are fed as work gets harder, and also the proportionate increase in vitamin E obtained from wheat germ oil. It is not certain that vitamin E causes improvements in the fitness tests, as it has been shown to be due to another substance called octacosanol (Cureton, 1972).

In the data obtained on Heusner at the Physical Fitness Research Laboratory, University of Illinois at Urbana (Table 9), there is impressive evidence that the preliminary land drill period caused significant improvements, the water drills then added more, and the competitive period pushed the subject to his peak for the season. His training curve is shown for the development of oxygen debt, most needed by a swimmer when he is in the terminal throes of pushing for the finish (Figure 2).

REFERENCES

Adams, R. and F. Murphy. 1973. The Good Seeds, the Rich Grains, the Hardy Nuts for a Healthier, Happier Life. Larchmont Books, New York.

Alley, L. 1952. Analysis of water resistance and propulsion in swimming the crawl stroke. Res. Quart. 23: 253—270.

Astrand, P.O., et al. 1963, Girl swimmers. Acta Pediat. Suppl. 147.

Bockman, T., Jr. 1951. The correlation of 37 tests with the 100 yd. drop-off test in swimming. M.S. thesis in Physical Education. University of Illinois, Urbana.

Carlile, F. 1963. Forbes Carlile on Swimming. Pelham Books, London.

_____ 1958. Scientific trends in training the sportsman, Sydney, Australia, Swim Forum (unpublished).

_____ and U. Carlile. 1961. Physiological studies of the Australian olympic swimmers in hard training. Aust. J. Phys. Training. 23: 5—34; and Chapter 9, pp. 99—122 in Ref. 9 therein.

Chivers, W.C. 1952. An inquiry into present day practices in conditioning competitive swimmers. M.S. thesis in Physical Education. Springfield College, Springfield, Mass.

Collis, M.I. 1970. The effects of a sustained training program of breath-hold swimming on selected physiological parameters and swimming performance. Res. Abstr. A.A.H.P.E. and R., Seattle, Washington, April 3.

Counsilman, J.E. 1955. Fatigue and staleness. Athletic J. 15: 164.

_____ 1968. Science of Swimming. Prentice-Hall, Englewood Cliffs, N.J.

_____ Isometric, isotonic and intermediary muscle contraction drills for swimmers. Bloomington, Ind. (privately mimeographed).

Cureton, T.K., Jr. 1930. Relationship of respiration to speed in swimming. Res. Quart. 1: 54—70.

_____ 1933. Observations and tests of swimming at the 1932 Olympic Games. J. Phys. Educ. (Y.M.C.A.). pp. 1—6.

_____ 1934. Factors governing success in competitive swimming. In: Educational Section, N.C.A.A. Official Rules, Spalding's Series, No. 91R, pp. 48—62. American Sports Publishing Co., New York.

_____ 1935. A test for endurance in speed swimming. Res. Quart. Supp., 6:106—112.

_____ 1936. Analysis of vital capacity as a test of condition for high school boys. Res. Quart. 7: 80—92.

_____ 1940. Review of a decade of swimming research at Springfield College. Res. Quart. 11: 68—79.

_____ 1947. Physical Fitness Appraisal and Guidance, pp. 292—295. C.V. Mosby, St. Louis.

_____ 1951. Physical Fitness of Champion Athletes. University of Illinois Press, Urbana.

_____ 1956. The relationship of physical fitness to athletic performance and sports. J.A.M.A. 162: 1139—1151.

_____ 1957. Science aids Australian swimmers. Athletic J. 37: 40—44.

_____ 1960. Ten-item fitness aptitude test for swimmers. In: National Y.M.C.A. Life Saving Manual and Tests Syllabus, p. 47. National Council of the Y.M.C.A., Association Press, New York.

_____ 1968A. Diet related to athletics and performance. J. Phys. Educ. 57: 2—5.

_____ 1968B. Nutritive aspects of fitness. J. Phys. Educ. (Y.M.C.A.). 66: 41—47.

_____ 1969. The relative value of stress indicators. In: J.R. Poortmans (ed.), Biochemistry of Exercise, Medicine and Sport, vol. 3, pp. 73—80. Karger, New York, Basel.

_____ 1971. Biomechanics of swimming with interrelationships to fitness and performance. In: L. Lewillie and J.P. Clarys (eds.), First International Symposium on Biomechanics in Swimming, pp. 31—52. Université Libre de Bruxelles, Brussels.

_____ 1972. The Physiological Effects of Wheat Germ Oil on Humans in Exercise. Charles C Thomas, Springfield, Ill.

Ebbetts, J. 1966. Diet in training and competitions. In: XVI Weltkongress für Sportmedicin, Hannover, West Germany: Fed. Int. de Medico Sportive, pp. 724—734.

Essick, R. 1956. The training habits of the 1956 U.S.A. men's Olympic swimming teams. Research Project, University of Illinois (unpublished).

Fowler, D. 1954. Split-vision photography, above and below water level, simultaneously. Research Project at Fort Lauderdale, Fla. (unpublished).

Geistweit, W.B. 1952. Relationship between the brachial pulse wave and metabolic measures and swimming times. M.S. thesis in Physical Education. University of Illinois, Champaign-Urbana.

Haskell, W.B. 1965. The effects of three endurance training programs on energy metabolism. Ph.D. thesis in Physical Education. University of Illinois, Champaign-Urbana.

Homan, M.L. 1947. A study of basic elements, prediction equations and rating scales for advanced swimming of high school girls. M.S. thesis in Physical Education. University of Illinois, Champaign-Urbana.

Honma, S. 1966. Mental training is necessary for the athlete. Res. J. Phys. Fitness (Tokyo). No. 4, 1—14.

Houston, R.K. 1952. The relationship of the electrocardiogram to various metabolic measures and to crawl swim times. M.S. thesis in Physical Education. University of Illinois, Champaign-Urbana.

Karpovich, P.V. 1933. Water resistance in swimming. Res. Quart. 4: 21—28.

_____ 1937. A mathematical analysis of the crawl. Scholastic Coach. 6: 22+.

Kiphuth, R.J.H. 1942. Swimming. A.S. Barnes and Co., New York.

_____ 1950. Swimming. Nicholas Kaye, London.

Krizan, T.F. 1948. Comparison of Olympic and varsity swimmers on physical fitness characteristics. M.S. thesis in Physical Education. University of Illinois, Champaign-Urbana.

Luther, C.C. 1952. The relationship of selected tests to swimming times and metabolic measures. M.S. thesis in Physical Education. University of Illinois, Champaign-Urbana.

Magel, J.R. and J.A. Faulkner. 1967. Maximal oxygen intake of college swimmers. J. Appl. Physiol. 22: 929–931.

Ohnmacht, F.W. 1958. Causal analysis of the physical fitness test for aquatic leadership (Cureton's). M.S. thesis in Physical Education. University of Illinois, Champaign-Urbana.

Schleicher, R. 1965. The validity of cord-stretching strength exercises in competitive swimming. M.S. in Physical Education. University of Illinois, Champaign-Urbana.

Tilley, J.L. 1951. The relationship of land drills and other tests to speed in swimming. M.S. thesis in Physical Education. University of Illinois, Champaign-Urbana.

Van Huss, W. and T.K. Cureton. 1955. Relationship of selected tests with energy metabolism and swimming performance. Res. Quart. 26: 205–221.

Van Rossen, D. 1968. A study of psychological motivations in experiments with competitive swimmers. Ph.D. thesis in Physical Education. University of Illinois, Champaign-Urbana.

Wilson, C.T. 1934. Coordination tests of swimming. Res. Quart. 5: 81.

Wright, S. 1922. Correlation and causation. J. Ag. Res. 20: 562 (cf. Ref. 12 for an illustrative application of the method).

Yanagita, T. 1936. Why Japan won the men's swimming. F.I.M.5. Meeting, Berlin (unpublished).

Instrumentation
and
methodology

A device to measure forces at the hands during the grab start

P. R. Cavanagh, J. V. Palmgren, and B. A. Kerr

Recent studies of the grab start have used such techniques as quantitative cinematography to obtain the now generally accepted opinion that the grab start is faster than the conventional circular armswing start (Winters, 1969; Roffer and Nelson, 1972; Bowers and Cavanagh, 1975) when used by both male and female competitive swimmers.

Force dynamography has been successfully used in the evaluation of the forces applied by the feet in the conventional swim start (Elliott and Sinclair, 1971). To gain further insight into the mechanics of the grab start, it seemed desirable to obtain information concerning the forces that are applied by the hands throughout the performance of this movement. Such data might also prove useful for the training of individual swimmers using the grab start by providing visual feedback of the force-time patterns obtained. Howell (1956) found that such feedback facilitated the learning of the sprint start in running.

PURPOSE

It was the purpose of this study to design, construct, and make a preliminary evaluation of a device to measure the forces exerted by the hands during the performance of the grab start in competitive swimming.

DESIGN AND CONSTRUCTION

The block

A board was constructed from ¾-inch plywood which completely replaced the standard 10° inclined starting block utilized at the Penn State Univer-

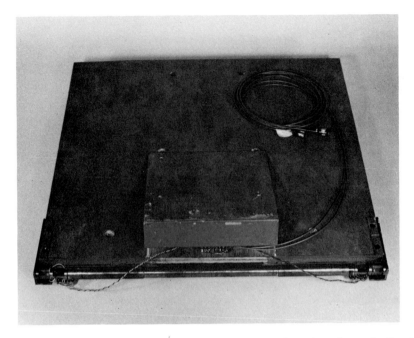

Figure 1. A view of the device with the foot plate removed, to show the continuity of the cross bar.

sity Natatorium. Along the front edge of the board a milled steel bar, 1 inch in diameter, was suspended from angle iron supports at the sides of the board. This arrangement is shown in Figure 1. An abrasive coating was applied to the surface of the block to give the swimmer a normal sensation of friction.

The sensing elements

The horizontal bar was sectioned 3 inches from each end to allow for mechanical linkage to the sensing elements shown in Figure 2. Two orthogonal flats, 1 inch long and 0.25 inch thick, were machined from the small portions of the bar which had been removed. One end of each element was firmly fixed to the angle iron supports at the edge of the board, with a degree of freedom left available for fine adjustment so that one of the flats could be aligned in a vertical position when the block was mounted at the $10°$ inclination.

The linkage between the sensing elements and the horizontal bar was provided by two 0.125-inch spring pins protruding from the sensing elements and mated into holes 0.135 inch in diameter in the bar. This arrangement has the advantage over a continuous bar in that only shear forces can be

Figure 2. Close-up of one of the sensing elements showing the gauges and waterproofing applied.

transmitted to the sensing elements. Moments that are created due to the bending of the solid bar cannot create strain in the sensing elements.

Strain gauging

Foil strain gauges (part CEA-06-375UW-120, Micromeasurements, Romulus, Mich.) were applied to both surfaces of each flat of the sensing elements, making a total of eight gauges in all. This arrangement can be seen in Figure 2, where the subsequent waterproofing with Micromeasurements M-Coat C silicone rubber compound is also visible. A four active arm Wheatstone bridge was formed for both vertical and horizontal measurements by the combination of the two relevant gauges on each side of the block. D.C. excitation of 10 volts was provided for the bridges. The bridge connections are shown schematically in Figure 3, where other details of the construction are also visible.

Foot plate

Since only forces exerted by the hands were required, a piece of galvanized sheet steel, 0.0625 inch thick, was formed to cover the bar over a 12-inch

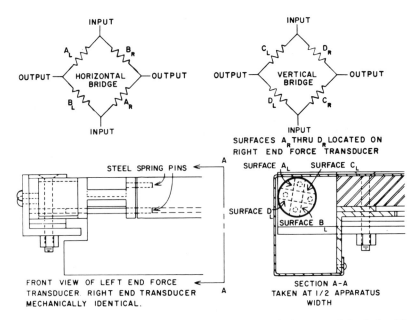

Figure 3. A detailed drawing of the mechanical and electrical aspects of the device. The steel spring pins which transmit forces from the cross bar to the sensing elements can be seen in the front view of the left-hand force transducer. The Wheatstone bridge configurations are indicated with reference to the labeled surfaces of the sensing elements and the subscripts L and R for left and right sides, respectively.

region of foot contact. This plate, shown in the drawing of the instrument in Figure 3, had no physical contact with the bar at any time during the start.

Other instrumentation

The outputs from both bridges were amplified and then recorded on a Sanborn strip chart recorder. In the field trials of the device, a Lo-Cam camera operating at 50 frames per sec was used to obtain data on the movement of the performer. By matching gun flash on the film with a simultaneous electrical contact closure in the gun, which was recorded on the strip chart, synchronization of the force records and film data was achieved.

CALIBRATION, LINEARITY, AND CROSS SENSITIVITY

From the free body diagram of the device, shown in Figure 4A, it is clear that the bridge output $(R_1 + R_2)$ in either vertical or horizontal directions will be proportional to the sum of the applied components of force regardless of the

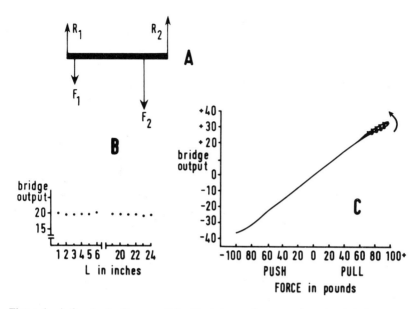

Figure 4. *A*, free body diagram of the block in use (one component only.) R_1 and R_2 represent the reactions at each end measured by the sensing elements. The forces F_1 and F_2 are the components of force applied by the hands. Resolving vertically indicates that the bridge output (proportional to $R_1 + R_2$) is independent of the point of force application. *B*, bridge output (*y*-axis) during the suspension of a 50-lb weight at various distances from the end of the bar, *A*. These results also indicate independence of output from position of force application. Units for bridge output are the same arbitrary units as in part *C*. *C*, bridge output (arbitrary units) (*y*-axis) plotted against applied force (*x*-axis) in the vertical direction. Slight hysteresis is apparent at higher loads with output for the same force being lower in the ascending sequence than for the descending sequence, as indicated by the arrow.

positions in which these components are applied along the bar. Thus the recorded output signals represent the total force applied to the bar by both hands in a given direction. It is not possible with this device to partition the contributions of right and left hands.

Figure 4*B* represents the bridge output in the vertical direction for the same weight of 50 lbs suspended at various distances from one end. It is clear that the signal obtained is independent of position of force application.

The linearity of the device (again in the vertical direction) over the region from −100 lbs to + 100 lbs is shown in Figure 4*C*. Some hysteresis was apparent in these results with sequential loading and unloading at higher force values, but this was always less than 3 percent of full scale.

The cross sensitivity of the device was dependent in part upon correct vertical alignment of the sensing elements. Values measured showed less than 6 percent error in both directions.

PRELIMINARY FIELD TRIALS

Following calibration and testing in the laboratory the device was mounted at the pool side. A male swimmer (5 feet 11 inches, 210 lbs) who was an experienced and accomplished 100-yard breaststroke performer was recruited for a series of pilot trials. Following a warm-up period and several practice attempts, both cine and force recordings were made of starts using the normal cues: "take your mark" and gun.

An annotated chart record from one trial is shown in Figure 5. It is important to notice that both the scales and direction conventions are different for the two force components. An upward deflection represents a "push" on the horizontal trace and an equal upward deflection on the vertical trace represents a "pull" of five times greater magnitude. The conventions for applied vertical force, shown beneath the record, are self-explanatory since the swimmer is always above the board before take-off. The designation of "push" or "pull" for a horizontally applied force is made assuming the swimmer to be behind the front of the block.

In the record shown, the subject exerts a relatively steady force in the set position with components of 90 lbs and 15 lbs in the vertical and horizontal

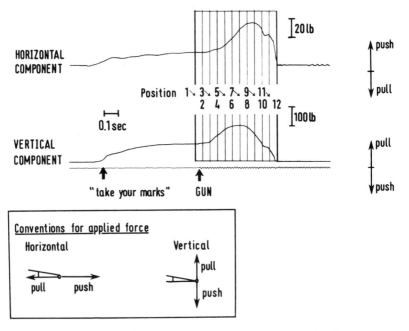

Figure 5. Annotated chart record from one trial of the grab start. The three traces are horizontal component, vertical component, and starter's gun. Scales and conventions are indicated on each force record.

directions, respectively. The vertical component increases rapidly approximately 80 msec after gun flash; since this is less than reaction time, the subject presumably anticipated the starting command. The force rises to a peak of 195 lbs (pull) at 280 msec in the vertical direction and 45 lbs (push) at 320 msec after gun flash in the horizontal component.

From the information contained in Figure 5 it is possible to calculate the magnitude and direction of the resultant force vector at each stage of the start. This has been done for the 12 discrete intervals shown in Figure 5, and the resultant vector is plotted in Figure 6 superimposed upon an outline of the posture at the same instant obtained from film. The vector has been drawn equal and opposite to the reaction on the board and thus represents the force acting on the body due to the action of the hands.

It is clear that the general pattern of force application in this subject was not directed toward the production of forces which will accelerate the body horizontally forward. The force vector stayed within 30 degrees of the vertical for most of the start and actually tended to retard the forward progress of the body. The principle use of the arms in this subject appeared to be simply the provision of a "brace" against which the lower limbs were able to pretense before release of the hands.

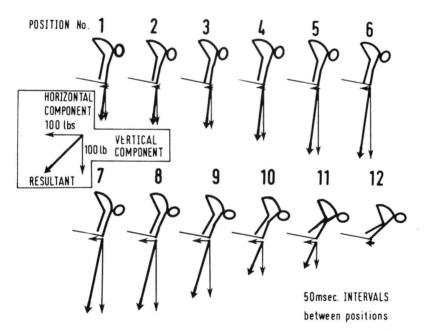

Figure 6. Resultant force vector calculated for each of the instants shown in Figure 5. The vector is drawn to represent the force acting on the body due to the action of the arms. The posture of the body at these instants has been obtained from cine film and superimposed upon the force vector.

CONCLUSIONS

This device appears to present a valid and objective technique for determining the action of the hands during the grab start in competitive swimming. In the near future, we hope to obtain experimental results from a group of world class swimmers. This will aid in the identification of the major determinants of the grab start and should provide a sound base for teaching and coaching the start.

REFERENCES

Bowers, J. E. and P. R. Cavanagh. 1975. A biomechanical comparison of the grab and conventional sprint starts in competitive swimming. *In:* J. P. Clarys and L. Lewillie (eds.), Swimming II, International Series on Sport Sciences, Vol. 2, pp. 225–232. University Park Press, Baltimore.
Elliott, G. M. and H. Sinclair. 1971. The influence of the block angle on swimming sprint starts. *In:* L. Lewillie and J. P. Clarys (eds.), First International Symposium on Biomechanics in Swimming, pp. 183–189. Université Libre de Bruxelles, Brussels.
Howell, M. L. 1956. Use of force-time graphs for performance analysis in facilitating motor learning. Res. Quart. 27: 12–22.
Roffer, B. J. and R. C. Nelson. 1972. The grab start is faster. Swimming Techn., J. Swimming, Diving, Water Polo 8: 101–102.
Winters, C. N. 1969. A comparison of the grip start and the conventional start in competitive swimming. Compl. Res. Health, Phys. Educ. Recr. 11: 196.

Dual media
cinematography

D. R. McIntyre and J. G. Hay

Swimming is an activity in which the performer spends some time with his body completely immersed in the air and some time with it completely immersed in water. However, the vast majority of the time is spent with his body moving simultaneously in both the air and water near the interface between these two media. It follows that anyone concerned with completely observing and evaluating a swimming performance must of necessity obtain an impression of the total performance. There is an obvious need, therefore, for some means of simultaneously recording the actions which take place above and below the water. It is conceivable that two high speed motion picture cameras could be used for this purpose—with one camera above and one below the water level. However, because of the problems associated with accurately synchronizing the two film records, there would appear to be some advantage in using a technique which simultaneously records the above-and-below-water level action on the same film frame. It is the purpose of this paper to describe such a technique.

EQUIPMENT

The inverse periscope shown in Figure 1 consists of two back-silvered mirrors supported in a steel framework. Each of the mirrors is inclined at 45° and their reflective surfaces face each other. With the lower mirror partially submerged in the water the light reflected to the lower mirror from those parts of the swimmer's body both above and below the water level is reflected to the upper mirror. The upper mirror in turn reflects the light through the lens of the motion picture camera.

It should be obvious that the apparatus must provide for as much flexibility of use as possible and allowances should be made to ensure the correct orientation of the mirrors and camera. In the illustrated design it is

Figure 1. The inverse periscope.

possible to alter the distance between the two mirrors, the location of the lower mirror relative to the water level, and the orientation of the upper mirror. Four platform screws permit leveling of the motion picture camera and adjustment of its position relative to the midpoint of the upper mirror. A slot in the platform allows for movement of the motion picture camera either away from or toward the upper mirror.

Whenever quantitative data are to be extracted from motion picture films, it is necessary to establish a linear scale which can be used to convert displacements measured on a film frame to real displacements. A suitable linear scale can be established by lowering an appropriately marked rod, weighted at its lower end, until it comes to rest in a vertical position (and in the anticipated plane of motion of the subject) with part of its length above and part below the water line. If due care is taken to ensure that the rod is indeed vertical, it can also serve as a vertical reference line—a necessary prerequisite to establishing horizontal and vertical displacements.

For the computation of time-based parameters it is necessary to establish a temporal scale which can be used to compute the time interval between selected instances of the performance. In a study by Hay, McIntyre, and Wilson (1975) a temporal scale was established by using a motion picture camera which incorporated built-in timing lights and a timing light generator. Another alternative for the establishment of a temporal scale is to include a large chronometer in the optical field of the camera.

PROBLEMS AND SOME SOLUTIONS

There are several problems associated with the use of the inverse periscope. One of these involves the taking of light readings and the subsequent determination of camera settings. If underwater lighting, sufficient to make the light intensity below the water equal to that above, is not available, it would seem logical to use camera settings based on the light coming from below the water level—especially when it is realized that in most swimming activities the majority of the swimmer's body is below the water level.

Another problem involves the image distortion caused by wave action in the water covering the submerged part of the lower mirror. This distortion can be almost completely eliminated by attaching rigid glass and metal baffles around the submerged part of the mirror. Another way of solving this problem would be to seal the volume in front of the lower mirror completely so that no water covered the reflective surface.

A further problem involves the difficulty encountered in positioning the optical axis of the motion picture camera at the same horizontal level as the water line reflected by the upper mirror. If the optical axis of the motion picture camera is above the horizontal level of the reflected water line, a portion of the performer below the water level near the air-water interface is obscured from the camera. However, if sufficient care is taken to ensure correct camera alignment, the obscured portion of the performer can be made to approximate a line.

The problem discussed in the preceding paragraph is compounded by wave action against the glass baffle. The wave action can be minimized by ensuring that the water in the pool is as nearly motionless as possible prior to the required movement of the performer.

DATA REDUCTION

As with most cinematographic analysis, the investigator will ultimately be concerned with extracting data from the films—both temporal characteristics and the location of selected landmarks. Obviously, the nature of the extracted data and the resulting usage of that data for subsequent computations will depend on the purpose of the study.

If the investigator wishes to locate the coordinates of a selected landmark, there is one phenomenon which must be recognized and accounted for if the location of the landmark is to be accurately determined. It has long been recognized that when light moves from one medium to another of lesser density it bends away from the normal. The angle at which the light from the water strikes the interface between the air and water (the angle of refraction) and the angle at which it moves away from the interface (the angle of incidence in air) are related by the index of refraction. The refraction of light is observed in dual media cinematography. When a body immersed in both the air and the water moves from the center of the optical field to the periphery, it appears as if those parts of the body under the water dissociate themselves from and precede those parts of the body above the water (Figure 2).

For an accurate description of the configuration of a body immersed in both air and water, it is necessary to account for the refractive effects in determining the coordinates of the landmarks of interest. This is accomplished by using a transformation equation based on Snell's law of refraction. The transformation equation permits the determination of the actual displacement of a water-immersed landmark from an established origin.

The derivation of the transformation equation makes use of the refractive index between air and water and geometrical relationships between the landmarks and dimensions as illustrated in Figure 3.

The transformation equation:

$$g = \sqrt{\dfrac{e^2\left(\dfrac{c}{1.33\sqrt{c^2+d^2}}\right)^2}{1-\left(\dfrac{c}{1.33\sqrt{c^2+d^2}}\right)^2}} + \dfrac{cf}{d}$$

(Note: By Snell's law: $\dfrac{\text{sine } i}{\text{sine } r} = 1.33$ [air/water refractive index])

Figure 2. Differences in media density produce scaling differences and distortion.

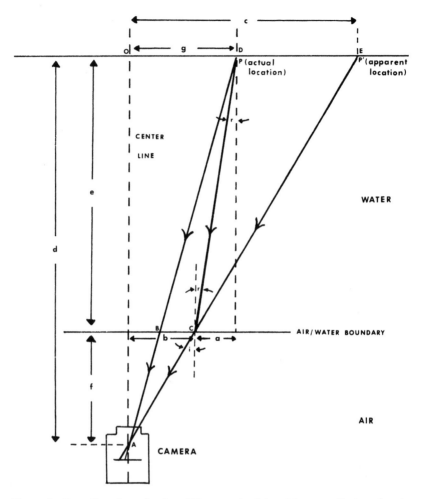

Figure 3. Correction for refractive differences in determining coordinates of water-immersed landmarks.

By using the transformation equation and the following procedural steps, the coordinates of both the air- and water-immersed landmarks can be determined with reference to an origin in a fixed Cartesian coordinate system:

1. The real coordinates of the air-immersed landmarks and the apparent coordinates of the water-immersed landmarks (both measured in units of the film analyzer) are located with reference to a fixed origin in the bottom left-hand corner of the film frame.

2. The scale factor is used to convert the coordinates of both the air- and water-immersed landmarks into real-life distances from the fixed origin.

3. The apparent coordinates of the water-immersed landmarks are determined with reference to a Cartesian coordinate system with the origin at the intersection between the water line and the vertical center line.
4. The apparent coordinates of the water-immersed landmarks are converted to real coordinates by using the transformation equation.
5. The real coordinates of the water-immersed landmarks are again determined with reference to the fixed origin in the bottom left-hand corner of the film frame.

SUMMARY AND CONCLUSION

A one-camera technique utilizing an inverse periscope for filming an activity in which the performer moves simultaneously in two media has been described. Consideration was given to the image distortion caused by wave action and by the difference in the densities of the two media. By using the technique described, it is possible to obtain a simultaneous visual impression and a film record of the above and below the water action—an obvious benefit to both swimming coach and researcher.

REFERENCES

Hay, J. G., D. R. McIntyre, and N. C. Wilson. 1975. An evaluation of selected carrying techniques used in life saving. *In:* L. Lewillie and J. P. Clarys (eds.), Swimming II, International Series on Sport Sciences, Vol. 2, pp. 247–253. University Park Press, Baltimore.

A device for the on-line measurement of instantaneous swimming velocity

M. R. Kent and J. Atha

In the study of the biomechanical characteristics of swimmers the measurement of intracyclic velocity fluctuations is of vital importance. To achieve full value, these measurements must meet certain requirements which may be summarized as follows: a) they should provide an accurate and continuous record of swimming velocity, b) the procedures involved should not impede the swimmer, and c) all records obtained should be synchronized to permit sensible interpretation.

Over the past half-century only a limited number of procedures have been reported for measuring swimming velocity. They have involved both mechanical and optical methods of transduction and a variety of methods of recording.

Karpovich (1930) developed a Natograph which operated on the principle that a line towed away from a drum around which it is coiled will cause the drum to rotate at a speed that is linearly related to the speed of tow. By measuring the times required for the drum to rotate through given distances, a series of discrete average velocities could be calculated and plotted as velocity-time graphs showing stroke-cycle velocity fluctuations. The Natograph may be criticized on several grounds. Harnessing a swimmer to a tow line may or may not violate the second criterion already presented, but the other two criteria are certainly not met. The sampling frequency is variable; it is distance-, not time-dependent; and it provides only a series of discrete average speeds, not continuous records. The swimmer imposes intermittent jerks on the tow line, unless he progresses at a constant speed, which coupled with the inevitable inertia of the system must introduce overrun inaccuracies in the recordings. In addition, the procedure for calculating velocities from recorded signals is laborious.

58

Improvements were introduced subsequently (Karpovich and Karpovich, 1970; Miyashita, 1971), but the inherent disadvantages of the technique still prevent the Natograph from being entirely satisfactory.

Alternative methods for measuring motion have included cinephotography (De Vries, 1959; Dal Monte, 1970) and multiple exposure photography, *e.g.*, chronocyclography (Councilman, 1971). Although the advantages of cinephotography are widely recognized (for instance, it meets without question the second and third criteria stated above), it must be acknowledged that measuring small displacements accurately from motion films is difficult at best, while underwater films introduce additional difficulties. Frame speed must be restricted, and grainy films must be used because of the low light levels; the negatives produced are tiny and magnification errors can occur; water distorts, and therefore parallax corrections must be carefully carried out; and water vortices and bubbles dragged in from the surface tend to obscure recorded images. Taking these factors into account, one must conclude that cinephotography fails to meet the requirements of a good swimming velocity measurement technique.

Little interest has been shown in self-contained velocity measuring instruments mounted on swimmers, although one such device was successfully designed and constructed in England in 1949 (Popham, British Patent Number 623,439). This instrument, called the Autocritic, consisted of a small metal cylinder approximately 220 mm in length which was strapped to the waist of the swimmer. In operation it presented an impeller to the water, which rotated as the swimmer moved. This provided the drive for the recording paper. It also retreated into its housing under the pressure of the water causing an ink writing pen to trace a graph on recording paper.

Although the records that resulted were continuous and immediately available for inspection, the interpretation of the traces was not easy. The paper speed and the trace amplitude both altered as a function of the swimmer's speed. Although theoretically it is possible to separate these two factors, it is not in practice a simple matter and no attempts to do so have been reported. In addition, Popham provided no marker synchronization signal so that it was quite impossible to relate fluctuations of velocity with specific aspects of the swimmer's performance.

THE DEVICE

In view of the foregoing it was concluded that no suitable instrument for measuring the velocity of the swimmer was available, and so a new device was constructed that had among its specifications the requirement that it satisfy the three criteria mentioned earlier. This instrument, which is designed to be strapped to the waist of the swimmer, was found to enjoy distinct advantages over previously available methods (Figure 1).

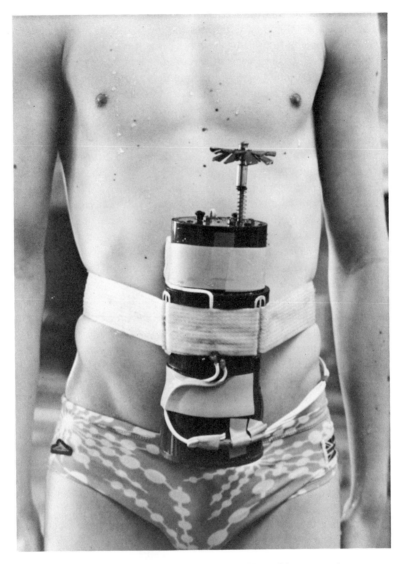

Figure 1. The swim speed recorder mounted in position on a swimmer.

Its design was based on the principle employed by Popham, *viz.* that when a constant frontal area moves through an incompressible fluid at varying speeds it experiences forces that are a simple function of those speeds. The device, called a swim speed recorder (SSR), was constructed around a 60 mm diameter pressure response rotor which consisted of dual-pitched plastic-coated steel blades mounted at the end of a 4.0-mm steel piston. The piston could be displaced axially through a 25 mm long brass bushing. A plated steel compression spring which was symmetrically coiled around the piston provided the only force that resisted this displacement. Attached to the inner end of the piston was a finely pointed fiber tip pen which was positioned so that, when the SSR was in the operational horizontal position, it rested decisively against the internal surface of a cylindrical drum on which the graph paper was fastened (Figure 2).

The graph drum was driven by a 6-volt D.C. Ripmax Orbit 405 motor with a rotational frequency of 180 Hz which was reduced by a gear box constructed to provide a 2700:1 reduction ratio. This resulted in the drum completing one full revolution in 15 sec, while drawing 233 mm of graph paper past the recorder pen.

An event marker consisting of a 6-volt electromagnet, with a fine fiber tip pen rigidly attached to the solenoid, was securely bolted inside the case. A single throw double pole switch operated the event marker and simultaneously activated a marker signal lamp which could be situated in the field of view of the camera during filming.

The SSR as a whole was contained within a stout polyethylene cylinder with a maximum diameter of 97 mm and an over-all length of 213 mm. It was built in two sections. The rotor and response piston projected from the forward section, which also contained the recording pen and electronic event marker. The aft section contained the recording paper drive drum, the electric drive motor, and the speed reduction gear box and batteries.

The reliability of the recorder and in particular the extent to which eddy currents generated by the swimmer influenced the velocity readings were evaluated by comparing a) 30 trials in which the recorder was towed through

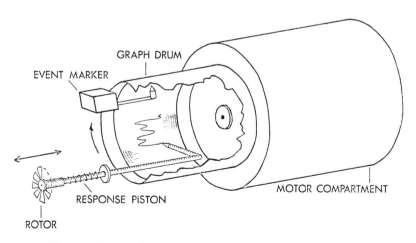

Figure 2. Simplified structural principles of the swim speed recorder.

the water while attached to a streamlined wooden float with b) 60 trials in which the recorder was attached to swimmers who were towed at similar speeds. The wooden float used was 1 m long and had a weighted steel keel. The swimmers generally remained in the glide position while being towed but during each tow which was at a constant speed, they completed one full swimming stroke. When the results were analyzed, none of the variations between traces recorded at the same speed exceeded the resolution of the trace line.

Variations in the alignment of the rotor relative to the direction of travel were examined for their effect on the sensitivity of the rotor response. A series of 120 static flume tests were carried out in the hydraulics laboratory at Loughborough University. The SSR was bolted in the flume at set angles ranging from $0°$ to $50°$ in steps of $10°$. The tests were carried out using a

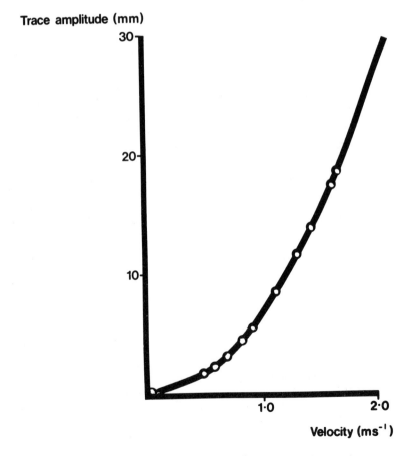

Figure 3. Calibration curve for swim speed recorder response rotor.

variety of water speeds. It was found that altering the angle of the rotor by 10° resulted in less than a 5 percent reduction in the amplitude of response. Subsequently, in a series of 36 dynamic tests when the SSR was towed at four velocities (1.0, 1.2, 1.4, and 1.8 m sec⁻¹) while positioned in each of three angles (−10°, 0°, and +10°) no significant differences in amplitude of trace between the three angles could be detected.

The uniformity of the graph paper speed was checked by recording a series of cam-triggered signals set at 10 and 15 Hz for given periods of 11 sec. The resultant intersignal distances were then measured using a traveling vernier microscope. After not more than 1 sec from the moment of switching on, the paper drive mechanism had attained a constant speed, with the intersignal distances remaining at a constant interval (correct to two decimal places) of 1.55 or 1.04 mm, respectively.

Calibration of the response trace was carried out using the previously mentioned constant speed towing device and a calibration curve drawn from the results (Figure 3). This curve was found to be parabolic and to satisfy the relationship:

$$y = 0.39x^{1/2}$$

where y = velocity in m sec⁻¹ and x = trace amplitude in mm. This self-contained instrument has been successfully employed to measure continuously the speed of swimmers.

REFERENCES

Counsilman, J.E. 1971. The application of Bernoulli's principle to human propulsion in water. *In:* L. Lewillie and J.P. Clarys (eds.), International Symposium on Biomechanics in Swimming, pp. 59–71. Université Libre de Bruxelles, Brussels.

Dal Monte, A. 1971. Presenting an apparatus for motion picture, television and scan shots of the movement of swimming. *In:* L. Lewille and J.P. Clarys (eds.), First International Seminar on Biomechanics in Swimming, pp. 127–128. Université Libre de Bruxelles, Brussels.

De Vries, H.A. 1959. A cinematographical analysis of the dolphin swimming stroke. Res. Quart. 30: 413–422.

Karpovich, P.V. 1930. Swimming speed analyzed. Sci. Amer. 142: 224–225.

Karpovich, P.V. and G.P. Karpovich. 1970. Magnetic tape Natograph. Res. Quart. 41: 119–122.

Kent, M.R. and J. Atha. 1971. A device for the measurement of water resistance. Res. Paper Phys. Educ. 2: 1–6.

Miyashita, M. 1971. An analysis of fluctuations of swimming speed. *In:* L. Lewillie and J.P. Clarys (eds.), First International Symposium on Biomechanics in Swimming, pp. 53-58. Université Libre de Bruxelles, Brussels.

A hydrokinetic apparatus for the study and improvement of leg movements in the breaststroke

V. Belokovsky and E. Ivanchenko

It is well known that powerful movements of the legs counteracted by the least hydrodynamic resistance during the preparatory phases play a decisive role in the creation of the propulsive force of a breaststroke swimmer.

In practice coaches advise swimmers to master various leg movement patterns which differ in the degree of flexion in both hip and knee joints. Most of the recommendations in this respect are based on the analysis of motion pictures of top level swimmers and results of electronic recordings of the selected parameters. These analyses only reflect amplitudes of the movements within the breaststroke cycle. But the main question as to how the power potential of muscles utilized in the leg kick can be used most efficiently remains unanswered.

METHODS

The purposes of this study with regard to the technique of breaststroke swimmers' leg movements were a) to measure the working amplitudes and investigate the variabilities of spatial and temporal characteristics of the hip and knee joint movements performed by top level swimmers; b) to study, by means of a special technique, the level of the dynamic force of muscle groups in the lower extremities for different joint angles; and c) to determine criteria for the most effective joint movements during execution of the breaststroke kick.

The following research methods were used to fulfill the prescribed purposes of this study: a) electrogoniography and goniometry, b) hydrodynamography and dynamometry, and c) direct observations and timing.

The level of the force of swimming movements is usually measured by means of mechanical or electrical measuring dynamometers of different types. However, these techniques did not meet completely the requirements of this investigation since it was necessary to measure the change in resultant efforts during the leg stroke. The environment (water) in swimming has a significant effect upon the specific conditions and requirements of the movements involved. Since the whole leg of the swimmer interacts with the aquatic medium, it is essential that the dynamics of the resultant application of forces be determined.

In view of these requirements, an apparatus was designed and constructed to investigate the force of specific leg movements and at the same time to control the position of the principal body parts involved. The essence of the method is that the platform for the subject is placed on land, while the resistance mechanism operates in the water. The water then provides resistance to the body movements through a cable arrangement. The design was based on the principle proposed by the famous Russian physiologist, Sechenov (1906), "the force of motion in many aspects is determined by the nature of the resistance force."

In swimming the effect of muscle forces is counteracted by the corresponding resistance of the water. The performance of the movements remains specific, because both the body's position and the amplitude of leg movement are the same as in the water. In order to study thoroughly the movements that a swimmer performs in the water, it was necessary to place him on land. The hydrodynamographic apparatus consisted of a movable and an immovable table connected by a hinge. The leading edge of the immovable table was fastened to a rigid metallic frame. A guiding pulley was placed on the shaft of the vertical part of the frame while a working axis with a rope drum and a paddle were attached on the horizontal part. The paddle, the drum, and the resistance transducer and recorder were interconnected by a cord. The hydrodynamograph registered the changes in dynamic force with an accuracy of ± 100 g and the duration of the main competitive movement to an accuracy of 0.05 sec (see Figure 1). To date 72 highly skilled breaststroke swimmers have been investigated by this method.

RESULTS

Comparative analysis of the working amplitudes of hip and knee joints

This part of the study was performed by means of telemetric electrogoniography during competitive swimming. For purposes of analysis a complete cycle of leg movement was divided into the following phases: pulling up of legs into the initial position for performing the preparatory movement (flexion in the joints), the working movement (extension), and the glide

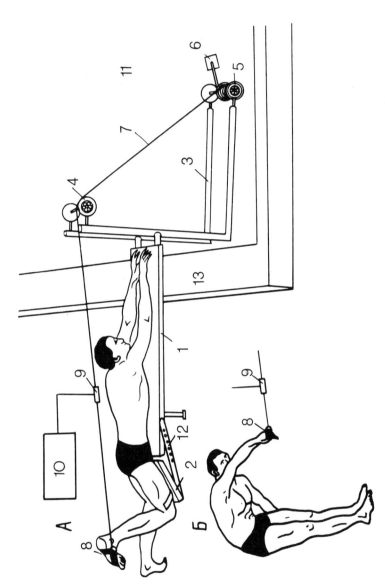

Figure 1. Diagram of hydrodynamic apparatus. 1, immovable table; 2, movable table; 3, metallic frame; 4, guiding pulley; 5, rope drum; 6, paddle; 7, connecting cord; 8, harness attachment; 9, resistance transducer; 10, recorder; 11, pool; 12, hinge; 13, pool edge.

(pause). The second phase of the cycle was considered as the working amplitude. Thus, the working amplitude results from angular changes in joints during execution of the main propulsive movement.

Based on previous research the average angle of flexion in the hip joint was 137.4 ± 8.5°. The angle of the preparatory phase for male swimmers ranged from 130 to 148° and that of female swimmers from 124 to 131°. These can be compared to the swimming technique of 1950's–1960's in which this angle was only 107.0 ± 15.6°. While the angle of flexion for the knee joint of male swimmers reached a right angle, that of female swimmers was 100–124°. In the last 5 years angular changes in the hip joints have tended to decrease by one-half and at present these angles are 34.0 ± 8.5°. Working amplitudes of female swimmers are 44–48° and those of male swimmers are less, 24–32°. At present, the mean knee joint angle in the preparatory phase is 40.1 ± 5.1° compared to 30.2 ± 2.8° in 1950–1960.

Analysis of dynamic forces

By means of a special technique (hydrodynamography) a study was performed to investigate the level of dynamic forces for the hip joint at the following angles: 180, 160, 140, 120, 105, and 90°. Also investigated were the dynamic forces in the initial positions formed by the shank and the thigh (knee angle) for angles of 40, 50, 60, 70, 80, and 90°.

The dynamic force values obtained reflect the pattern of the main leg movement and correspond to a certain degree of flexion in the joints. The highest levels of dynamic force of the extensors were recorded when the knee angle was increased as the hip joint changed from 105 to 160°. Most interesting are the data about the force developed from the initial position of 140° in the hip joint. In this case the maximal value (20.2 ± 1.0 kg) is more than that recorded when extending the legs from the initial position of 160° in the hip joint. It is interesting that in this case the maximal level is achieved faster and is maintained until the angle of the extending knee joints is 110.1 ± 11.1°.

The working phase of the movements beginning from the position where the angle of flexion is 120 and 105° in knee joints also shows a high level of force (20.0 ± 1.4 and 20.3 ± 1.2 kg). But those amplitudes involve sharp decreases of the force level during the first 0.1 sec following the maximal level.

The lowest level of dynamic force (18 ± 2.9 kg) was recorded when the legs moved from the position of 90° at the hip joint. For measurement of the dynamic force of the knee extensors at various amplitudes of movement it was necessary to select a constant position at the hip joint (140°). The results are presented in Figure 2 by a three-dimensional graph in which: y = axis for force in kilograms, x = axis for angles in degrees, and z = axis for time of movements. In the upper part of Figure 2 is located a two-dimensional graph

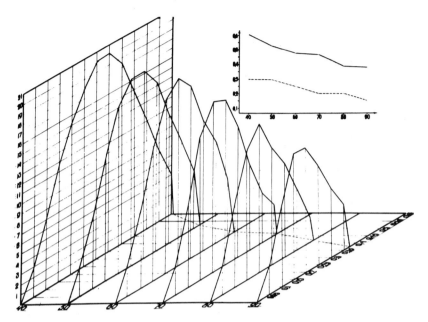

Figure 2. Three-dimensional graph of knee joint angle. x, angle in degrees; y, force in kg; and z, time of movement.

in which the horizontal axis represents the angles in degrees and the vertical axis the time in seconds. The upper curve shows total time of movement and lower curve shows time of achievement of maximal force. As noted in the main graph the maximal level of force was registered during leg movements from the initial knee joint position of 40°. A decrease in the working amplitude in the knee joints by 10–20° is accompanied by some force decrease ($p < 0.03$).

With respect to temporal characteristics, the total duration of the effort is diminished by 0.08 sec. When the knee angle for the initial position is changed from 60 to 40°, the observed decrease is more pronounced— −0.13 sec. In these cases some loss in force is compensated for by the saving in total movement time. When the legs move from the initial position of 70, 80, and 90° in the knee joints, the force drops off markedly.

Improvement of stroke efficiency with the changes of leg movement pattern

In an attempt to improve stroke efficiency an investigation was conducted of the changes in dynamic force and swimming speed resulting from different preset angles of the hip and knee joints. The swimmers who were studied changed the pattern of their preparatory leg movements in the water by means of a special device, that limited the angle of leg flexion to 140° in the hip joint and to 50–60° in the knee joint.

The measurement of the parameters under study over a 1½-month experimental period showed that the changes in the leg movement pattern in the preparatory phase prescribed for the main group of swimmers resulted in improved performance. For example, the maximal level of dynamic force increased by 1.2 kg (t=2.72; p<0.05) and the moment of its complete achievement came 0.03 sec later (t=3.33; p<0.02). The time required for the complete effort was shortened by 0.03 sec (t=3.00; p<0.02) while swimming time over competitive distances decreased significantly.

The obtained data from all these experiments showed that significant improvements in the parameters under study were due to the most efficient execution of the preparatory movements of the lower extremities. This permitted a more effective use of the forces of extension in the hip and knee joints. The proposed hydrodynamographic method may be recommended both for solution of research problems and for practical application to improve performance of breaststroke swimmers.

Determination of the movements' amplitude efficiency with respect to various rates of swimming

It is known that the pattern of movements in each style of swimming is directly related to the rate and speed of the stroke. Various working amplitudes cannot be considered apart from their functional application.

For sportsmen under study, the range of the stroke rates was determined by the achievements of leading Russian and foreign breaststroke swimmers at a distance of 100 m. From our observations this range was from 56.2 to 68.1 cycles per min. In our study the range of the stroke rate included five equal increments: 55, 60, 65, 70, and 75 cycles per min. The rate of movement was set by lighting the signal lamp of an electronic pacemaker installed on a swimming board in front of the subject. The swimming speed was determined by the time required to swim 50-m laps using only leg strokes.

Angular changes in the hip joints at a preparatory stage of movement were 100, 120, 140, and 160° in our study and flexion in the knee joints did not exceed 50–60°. The experiment was performed with 9 high grade breaststroke swimmers with the rate of 58 to 67 cycles per min when swimming 100 m.

In order to utilize the recommended pattern of leg movements in the preparatory phase, the optimal rate is about 65 cycles per min. Exceeding the optimal rate by 10 cycles per min results in substantial changes in swimming technique and a decrease in the swimming speed.

Dynamic measurement techniques on swimming bodies at the Netherlands Ship Model Basin

J.D. van Manen and H. Rijken

Human swimming can be studied by observations or measurements. A swimming pool is a poor facility for making adequate observations since the time needed by a swimmer to pass an underwater window is too short. Making measurements is even more difficult since this can be done only by a wireless transmitting system (telemetry).

The Netherlands Ship Model Basin (NSMB) is equipped with several large concrete basins for experimental studies on ship models. The basins are provided with carriages running over their full lengths at controllable speeds. The carriages comprise extensive instrumentation and recording facilities, including underwater television.

Since 1968 one of these basins, the so-called high speed basin, has been used for a number of experimental studies on swimming. The basin has a length of 220 m, a width of 4 m, and a water depth of 4 m. The towing carriage can attain speeds up to 12 m per sec. The swimming studies are based on measurements and observations, which are continued for as long as necessary for an adequate observation of the swimmer.

The measurements and recordings of forces and other mechanical quantities are analyzed by NSMB and the results discussed with the swimming coaches. The observations, made by underwater television, provide additional information to the coaches. This article presents the test techniques used and gives some of the results and conclusions.

RESISTANCE AND PROPULSION TESTS

The investigations started in 1968 with a study sponsored by the Dutch Sporting Federation in cooperation with the Royal Dutch Swimming Association. The purpose of the initial study was to determine the contribution delivered by the arm or leg stroke separately, for different swimming strokes. A schematic diagram of the equipment used for these measurements is shown in Figure 1. During measurement of the arm stroke, the swimmer who is fixed to the vertical rod by means of a girdle stretches the legs and swims with the arms only. The carriage speed is gradually increased until it exceeds the free swimming speed. At lower speeds, a resulting forward force (thrust) is measured. When the speed is increased the thrust decreases below zero and becomes a resistance.

A similar relation is found when the swimmer stretches the arms forward and swims with the legs only. The output of the strain gauge force transducer is recorded on UV-paper together with the speed of the towing carriage. In Figure 2 some typical recordings are presented for the leg stroke only. It is shown that the thrust during one stroke varies considerably. The average values are plotted in Figure 3. In this diagram additional resistance curves are given for the stretched body (A) and for the swimmer swimming with arms and legs (D). The free swimming speed is still somewhat larger than the speed found at the intersection of curve D with the zero-thrust line. This is caused by an additional resistance of the girdle. The resistance curve (A) is measured by towing the stretched swimmer holding a hand grip.

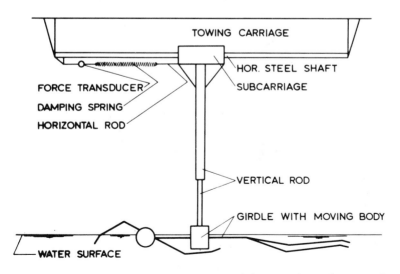

Figure 1. Test equipment to measure the thrust of the arm or leg stroke separately.

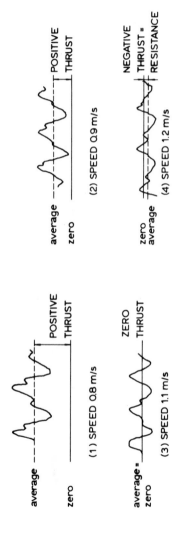

Figure 2. Typical recordings for the leg stroke only (the numbers *1–4* refer to those points indicated in Figure 3).

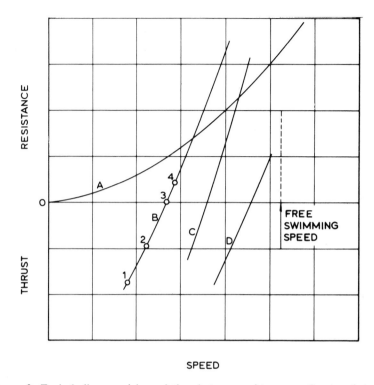

Figure 3. Typical diagram giving relation between resistance or thrust and towing carriage speed. *A*, resistance of stretched body; *B*, resistance for leg stroke only; *C*, resistance for arm stroke only; *D*, resistance when swimming with arms and legs.

In order to demonstrate the significance of these measurements, an example is given for the breaststroke. Two of the best Russian breaststroke swimmers were tested, and it was found that both swimmers showed a positive contribution of the leg stroke at the free swimming speed. This result was different from the results of the majority of a group of Dutch swimmers. In Figure 4, results are given for the world champion Galina Stepanova, a Dutch champion, and an average Dutch breaststroke swimmer. Apparently, a well performed leg stroke is capable of delivering 100 percent of the total propulsion.

Another study (Clarys, Jiskoot, and Lewillie, 1973), sponsored by the "Instituut Voor Morfologie" of the Vrije Universiteit Brussel, was conducted in order to investigate the differences between competition crawl and water polo crawl strokes. Typical recordings are given in Figure 5. The main conclusion of the study was that the total energy output during the water polo crawl is higher than for the competition crawl, in spite of the fact that the free swimming speed for the water polo crawl is lower. The complete

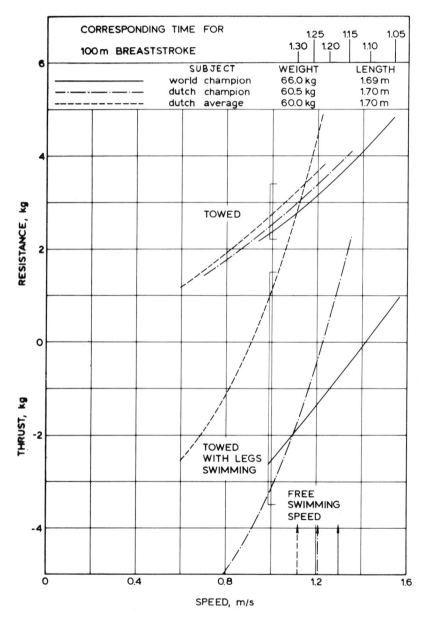

Figure 4. Diagram showing significant differences in the thrust delivered by the leg stroke only for three breaststroke swimmers.

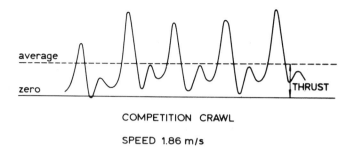

COMPETITION CRAWL

SPEED 1.86 m/s

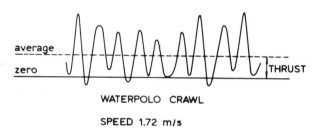

WATERPOLO CRAWL

SPEED 1.72 m/s

Figure 5. Typical thrust recordings for competition and water polo crawl.

results of this study were presented by Clarys, Jiskoot, and Lewillie at an earlier seminar (1973).

The effect of body shape on resistance

The initial investigation was followed by a study of the effect of body shape on resistance (Clarys *et al.,* 1974). For this study a large number of test persons were towed, and the resistance was measured. The body shapes were described by several parameters and it was expected that some indications might be obtained concerning the relationship of body shapes to minimal resistance. An example is presented, in which the dimensionless resistance of six test persons with entirely different body shapes, varying from long and thin to short and fat, has been plotted against the Froude number (Figure 6). In this figure subjects 1, 2, and 3 are heavily built persons, while subjects 4, 5, and 6 are lightly built.

A small project was conducted to determine whether a swimmer has less resistance with or without a swimming suit. The diagram presented in Figure 7 indicates that an increase in resistance of about 9 percent was found for a

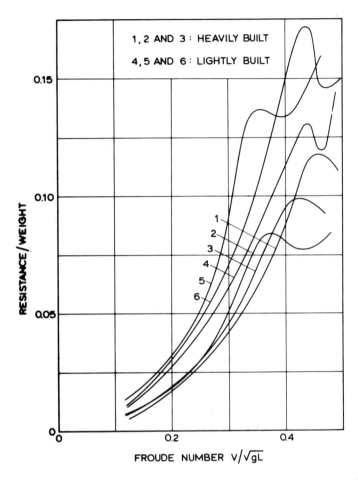

Figure 6. Relation between dimensionless resistance and Froude number for six test subjects having different body shapes.

naked female swimmer compared to the resistance when she wore a slim fitting and high close-necked swimming suit.

Pressure measurements

The latest development in test techniques has been accomplished in response to the demands of the Royal Dutch Swimming Association. In the training and development of young swimmers, new ways had to be found to test their techniques and performance. For this purpose, a pressure pick-up was developed that can be adjusted on the palm of the hands. This device makes it possible to record continuously the pressure during the whole cycle of the

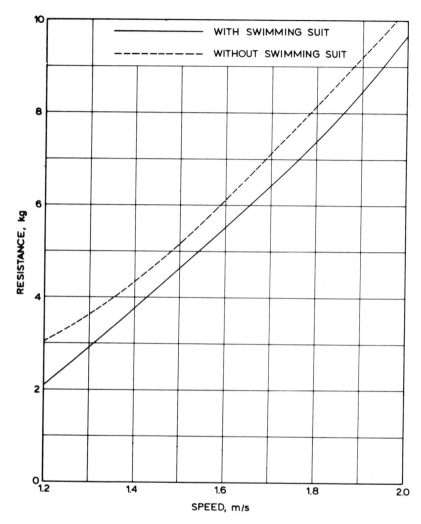

Figure 7. The effect of wearing a swimming suit on the resistance of a female swimmer.

arm stroke for all types of swimming strokes. The significance of this
parameter has already been pointed out by Counsilman (1971). The instrument is shown in Figure 8. Typical recordings for the left and right hand of a
competition crawl swimmer, who breathed on the right side, are given in
Figure 9. The arrow pointing downward indicates the instant the hand
entered the water. The first phase of the stroke was characterized by a pull of
the hand; the second phase by a push of the hand. Finally, the hand left the
water at the moment indicated by the arrow pointing upward.

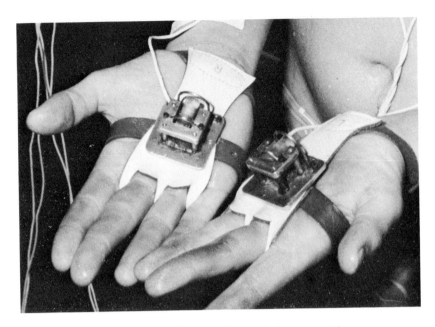

Figure 8. Photograph showing adjustment of pressure pick-ups.

This study started at the end of 1973 and needs more testing before a final evaluation of the method can be made. In any case, an important advantage of this method is the possibility of testing a swimmer almost undisturbed by the test equipment. By means of underwater TV recordings, wrong hand positions which create unusual hand pressure recordings can be explained.

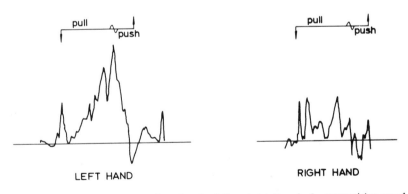

Figure 9. Typical pressure recordings for the left and right hand of a competition crawl swimmer, breathing on the right side.

REFERENCES

Clarys, J.P., J. Jiskoot, and L. Lewillie. 1973. A kinematographical, electromyographical and resistance study of water polo and competition front crawl. *In:* S. Cerquiglini, A. Venerando, and J. Wartenweiler (eds.), Biomechanics III, Medicine and Sport, Vol. 8, pp. 446–452. S. Karger, Basel.

Clarys, J.P., J. Jiskoot, H. Rijken, and P.J. Brouwer. 1974. Frictional resistance in water and its relation to body form. *In:* R.C. Nelson and C.A. Morehouse (eds.), Biomechanics IV, International Series on Sport Sciences, Vol. 1, pp. 187–196. University Park Press, Baltimore.

Counsilman, J.E. 1971. The application of Bernoulli's principle to human propulsion in water. *In:* L. Lewillie and J.P. Clarys (eds.), First International Symposium on Biomechanics in Swimming, pp. 59–71. Université Libre de Bruxelles, Brussels.

Instrumentation and methods for the complex investigations of swimming

K. Boičev and A. Tzvetkov

Methodology of scientific research in the field of physical culture and especially in sports is relatively underdeveloped. This is understandable since it is a very young area. Consequently, it is necessary to improve it, particularly regarding the study of specific movements and training programs of competitors. It is also important to study the competitors' physical characteristics so they can be classified and graded relative to their performance. The practice of conducting pure laboratory experiments has to be gradually directed to investigations of sportsmen in the practical setting. In testing the athlete's condition before and after training, it is necessary to determine the reaction and the effectiveness of the applied work during his performance. To evaluate his condition, the single method of analysis commonly used must be replaced by more complex techniques. All this is in connection with the urgent need for gaining greater knowledge about the requirements of different disciplines, developing greater perfection in the specific utilization of the methods, and ensuring higher effectiveness and rationale for training. In short, this leads to a more complete understanding of the entire sport activity and makes possible greater efficiency.

It is almost impossible to observe and quantify the biomechanical aspects of human motion by visual means. Consequently, it is essential that objective techniques be developed to improve the level of scientific work.

A number of test apparatuses have been used successfully to measure various aspects of the movements involved in swimming. Examples of such work include that of Aručev (1962), Zapnutdinov et al. (1968), Stučinskii (1966), Gavriiski (1962), Bassan (1967), Glaser et al. (1970), and Magel et al. (1969). Related work on the specific techniques of swimming strokes has been reported by Apsaliamov (1964), Belokovskii (1962), Gevlič (1962), Guminskii and Makarenko (1962), Molinskii (1961), Sosin (1965), Ceburaev

(1967), Boičev *et al.* (1969), Boičev and Burzakov (1969), Ringer and Adrian (1969), Mosterd and Jongbloed (1964), Kupper (1960), Koniar (1967), and Kipke (1966).

The problems of respirations were treated by Klećov (1964), Makarenko (1965), Volkov (1965), and Boičev *et al.* (1969), while gas analysis problems were treated by Volkov *et al.* (1968) and Volkov and Cermisinov (1970). Successful electromyograms during swimming have been reported by Ikai *et al.* (1964), Kipke (1966), and Filcak (1971). Some researchers who attempted to register the speed of the swimmer include Klećov (1964), Molinskii (1961), Boičev *et al.* (1969), Karpovich and Karpovich (1970), and Wanke (1960). Interesting investigations of a complex nature have been conducted by Astrand (1970) and Cureton (1933). Some details regarding other investigations in the field of swimming can be found in the works of Botnarenko (1966), Zaćiorskii (1962), Milštein and Slavoliubova (1972), Swegan and Thompson (1970), and Waltker (1969). The researches of Zlatarev and Gruev (1965), Platonov (1969), Pugačev (1966), and Kovrigin (1970) also have practical value. From a theoretical standpoint, quite a number of achievements may be pointed out, but from the viewpoint of current scientific requirements directed toward determining practical solutions to problems, only a few researches can be considered as very useful.

PURPOSE

Our purposes have been to improve scientific instrumentation and methodology so that it is possible to obtain both quantitative and qualitative information concerning parameters that cannot be readily observed and analyzed. Such improvements in research methodologies will ultimately lead to more comprehensive investigations and thus greater knowledge concerning the competitive aspects of swimming.

The first piece of apparatus we perfected was an ideal primary circuit for an electrotensiometer transducer used to record accurately the forces of human movements while swimming. In order to eliminate the disadvantages (shortcomings) of previous transducers, we utilized strain gauges. Therefore, we were able to obtain accurate information concerning the instantaneous pressure of the water during the arm stroke and the leg kick. In order to eliminate the interference due to turbulence of the water, we equalized the static pressure on the inside of the transducer by installing a 5-cm tube which connected the inside of the transducer with the water medium on the outside (see Figure 1).

Our experiments with this tensiocapsule revealed that it was possible to obtain signals for the accurate determination of the water pressure. Figure 2 shows an original recording from this device. By analyzing the curves, we are able to determine the force of the water pressure on the capsule. The

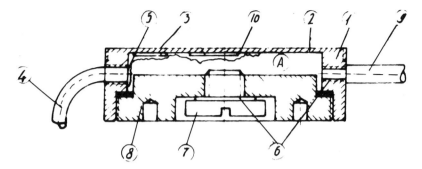

Figure 1. Tensiocapsule consisting of: *1*, the frame; *2*, membrane; *3*, wired tensiotrans-formers; *4*, lead cable; *5*, cable head; *6*, gaskets; *7*, deactivation bolt; *8*, rear cap; *9*, tube for the equalization of the dynamic and static pressures; *10*, water and moisture protection coating.

comparison of the values of the different curves provide a quantification of the effectiveness of each movement. The temporal aspects of the curves reveal the synchronization and coordination of the arms and legs in the execution of the complete stroke. We are also able to determine the times required to complete each phase of the stroke cycle while swimming.

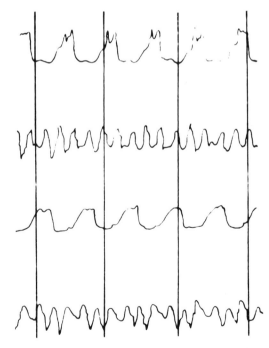

Figure 2. Synchronous recordings of movements while swimming the crawl stroke. Beginning at the top. 1, curve of the strokes of the right hand; 2, curve showing the movements of the right leg; 3, a curve of the strokes of the left hand; 4, a curve of the movements of the left leg.

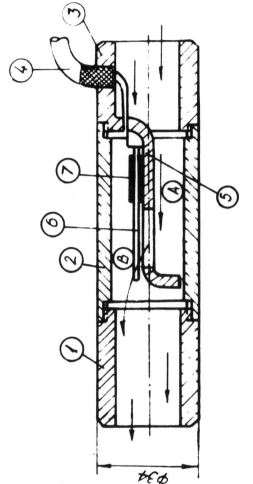

Figure 3. Tensiometric air tube consisting of: 1–3, pipe connection; 2, hose; 4, tensiometric cable; A and B, tow chambers; 6 and 7, tensiometric transformer elements; 5, a base of the tensioelement.

Another instrument we have developed is a transmitter for continuous recording of the three phases of respiration: inhalation, exhalation, and resting phases. Previous transmitters utilized for this purpose have been based on an entirely different principle. Our tensiometric air tube is shown in Figure 3.

In this device, strain gauges are mounted on a base consisting of a movable plate which provides a continuous recording of the characteristics of the air flow (*i.e.*, its force and volume). Gas analysis of the composition of the expired air is also obtained. This tensiometric tube has been registered as an invention by IIR (No. 11691-1969). Figure 4 shows a curve depicting the phases of respiration. This instrument was developed so that its record could by synchronized with the recordings of the movements obtained from the tensiocapsule device previously described. This provides us with a complete analysis of both the movements and respiration during the act of swimming.

Recordings containing synchronized information of movements are not sufficient to provide a complete dynamic analysis of swimming. These data must be interpreted in conjunction with records of swimming speed. In order to obtain records of swimming speeds, the device shown in Figure 5 was developed. This is a plastic speed capsule with built-in semiconductor tensio-transformers utilizing strain gauges. The fluctuations in water pressure result-ing from the minor changes in speed while swimming are received by the tensiotransformers, amplified, and registered on a recorder. An example of a set of curves from this apparatus is shown in Figure 6. This speed capsule is an original invention protected under a registration certificate (No. 17623-1971).

The transducers described enable us to quantify movement techniques, and, to a certain extent, the gas analysis data provide an estimate of the swimmer's endurance. The next problem is one of quantifying the amount of force exerted. In order to provide accurate data concerning force, we have developed an electroforce meter. This device has the capability of registering the force produced by separate muscle groups while an individual performs movements on land which imitate those utilized in swimming. An imitation swimming stroke is performed dynamically on a sliding sled in order to produce force-time curves which can be synchronized with motion picture films.

Figure 7 illustrates a typical force-time curve obtained during the pull phase of the right arm, left arm, and both arms in a middle position. Figure 8

Figure 4. A curve of the circulation and the speed of the air through the tensiometric tube.

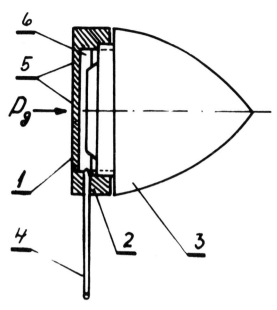

Figure 5. Speed capsule consisting of: 1, sensitive membrane; 2, frame; 3, flowmeter; 4, tube for compensation of hydrostatic pressure; 5, tensiotransformers built into the membrane; 6, chamber filled with water.

shows the propulsive forces during tethered swimming using the dolphin stroke, and Figure 9 illustrates the changes in the propulsive forces while performing the backstroke on a sliding sled.

This multiple approach increases considerably the possibilities for achieving greater knowledge about the complex swimming performance, but it is

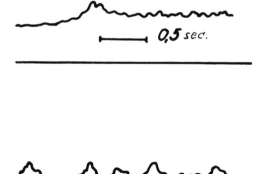

Figure 6. Recording of the speed in crawl swimming with legs only (upper) and coordination (lower).

Figure 7. Recording of maximal static effort in pose 90° from the body with the right hand, left hand, and both hands.

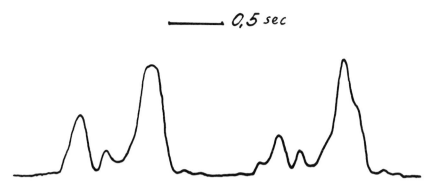

Figure 8. Recording of the force in tethered swimming using the dolphin stroke.

still not completely comprehensive. We have developed a tether stand which consists of a rotating steel disc, 3-mm pulley, and weights of 500 g each. This technique enables us to obtain gas analyses while the subject performs tethered swimming and thereby enables us to ascertain the intensity of the work during swimming.

Our future plans include a device for recording pulse rates and electrocardiograms. Then we will be prepared to obtain quantitative information on nearly all of the basic parameters that are vital to swimming performance. We shall then know the essence and the necessary characteristics for all styles of swimming and for all competitive distances. In addition, we will be able to

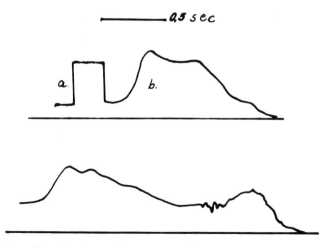

Figure 9. Recording of the force of the pulling stroke with both hands while on a sliding sled. *Upper curves a,* own weight; *b,* period of the dolphin stroke; *lower curves,* period of the backstroke.

ascertain the basic exercises which should be employed in the primary and secondary training of swimmers and the teaching methods to be used in achieving the desired goal. When we reach this stage, we will be able to recommend ways of modifying the training procedures in order to improve performances. This will mean that we shall be able to train swimmers so it will be possible for them to perform at an optimal level.

REFERENCES

Apsaliamov, T.M. 1964. Dinamičeskoe isledovanie tiagovih usilii pri plava nii krolem na grudi. Mat.načnoi met.konf. po plavanie,Gćolifk.

Aručev, A.A. 1962. Issledovanie deiatelnosti serdća s pomoštiu neprerivnoi registraćii častoti serdćebienii pri plavanii i nirianii. Teoria i praktika fizičeskoi kulturi (TPFK) 10: 36.

Astrand, P.-O. 1971. An aquatic swim-mill. In: L. Lewillie and J.P. Clarys (eds.), First International Symposium on Biomechanics in Swimming, pp. 197–198. Université Libre de Bruxelles, Brussels.

Bassan, L.B. 1967. Radiotelemetrische Untersuchungen der Herzfrequenz während des Schwimmens. Theorie und Praxis der Körperkultur (TuPdK) 7: 653.

Belokovskii, V.V. 1962. Električeskaia registraćia dvigenii plavća. Teoria i prakticafizičeskoi kulturi (TPFK) 8: 64.

Boičev, K.B. and P.I. Burzakov. 1969. Elektrotenzometrična aparatura za isledvane tehnikata na dviženiata pri pluvći v estestveni uslovia. Vapr.na fiz.kultura (VFK). 4:222.

Boičev, K., P. Barzakov, and D. Stoev. 1969. Elektronni ustroistva i aparatura za isledvane parametrite na dišaneto po vreme na rabota i počivka pri pluvći. VFK 10: 614.

Botnarenko, F.A. 1966. Radioinformaćia v trenirovke plovćov. TPFK 5: 68.

Čeburaev, V.S. 1967. Fotoelektričeskie metodi registraćii dvigenia sportsmenov. TPFK 3: 58.

Cureton, T.K. 1933. Observations and tests of swimming at the 1932 Olympic Games. J. Phys. Ed. (Y.M.C.A.). pp. 1–6.

Filcak, M. 1971. Application possibilities of the electrogoniographic method in swimming technique evaluation. In: L. Lewillie and J.P. Clarys (eds.), First International Symposium on Biomechanics in Swimming, pp. 73–80. Université Libre de Bruxelles, Brussels.

Gavriiski, V. 1962. Opit za prećeniavane sastoianieto na podgotvenost u pluvći. Trudove VIF, Sofia,t.V, str.237.

Gevlič, E.D. 1962. Eksperimentalnoe opredelenie sili davlenia vodi na ladon plavća pri grebke. TPFK 7: 71.

Glaser, R.M., J.R. Magel, and W.D. McArdle. 1970. A radiotelemetry transmitter for monitoring heart rate during swimming. Res. Quart. 41: 200–202.

Guminskii, A.A. and L.P. Makarenko. 1962. Issledovanie plavća metodom pneimodinamografii. TPFK 10: 68.

Ikai, M., K. Ishii and M. Miyashita. 1964. An electromiographic study of swimming Res. J. Phys. Educ. 7: 47–54.

Karpovich, P. and G. Karpovich. 1970. Magnetic tape Natograph. Res. Quart. 41: 119–122.

Kipke, L. 1966. Das electrografische Bild des am Train ingsgerat imiterten Armrudes der Freistilschwimmer. Med. Sport 6: 116—121.

Klećov, G.I. 1964. Metodika registraćii grebkovih dviženii,dihania i skorosti prodvigenia plovćof. TPFK 9: 33.

Koniar, M. 1967. Electrogoniographic studies about kinematic changes of structure of swimmers' movements inquiring and improvement of technics of swimming disciplines. Faculty Research Paper, Faculty of Physical Education and Sports, Bratislava.

Kovrigin, V.M. 1970. Trenirovačnii stanok dlia spećialnoi silavoi podgotovki plovćov na suše. TPFK 5: 69.

Kupper, K. 1960. Kinematografische Untersuchung Delphinbewegung. Theorie Praxis Korperkultur 11: 247.

Magel, J.R., W.D. McArdle, and R.M. Glaser. 1969. Telemetered heart rate response to selected competitive swimming events. J. Appl. Physiol. 26: 764—770.

Makarenko, L.P. 1965. Issledovanie dihania i serdečnoi deiatelnosti plavca vo vremia skorostnovo plavania. TPFK 8: 17.

Mitštein, V.M. and K.F. Slavoliubova. 1972. Vračebnie nabliudenia za avstraliiskimi plovćami. TPFK 8: 39.

Molinskii, K.K. 1961. Spidografia kak metod issledovania v plavanii. TPFK 7: 537.

Mosterd, W.L. 1961. Measuring of the propelling force and stroke analysis on trained swimmers. Doctoral Thesis, University of Utrecht Schotanus Sr.Jeus (Dutch and English Summary).

Mosterd, W.L. and J. Jongbloed. 1964. Analysis of the stroke of highly trained swimmers. Int. Z.Angew.Physiol. 4: 288—293.

Platonov, V.N. 1969. Ob intensivnosti i skorosti plavania i kriteriah oćenki intensivnosti. TPFK 6: 7.

Pugačev, P.V. 1966. Radiopriemnik dlia plavćov. TPFK 7: 57.

Ringer, L.B. and M.J. Adrian. 1969. An electrogoniometric study of the wrist and elbow in the crawl arm stroke. Res.Quart. 2: 353.

Sosin, I. 1965. Pribor dlia sročnoi informaćii v plavanie. TPFK 7: 56.

Stučinskii, M.A. 1966. Registraćii elektrokardiogrami vo vremia plavania. TPFK 5: 58.

Swegan and Thompson. 1970. Experimental research in swimming. Swimming Techn. 1: 8.

Volkov, N.I. and V.N. Čermisinov. 1970. Kislorodnii dolg v upražneniah različnoi mšnosti i prodolžitelnosti. TPFK 10: 17.

Volkov, N.I., S.M. Gordon, E.A. Širkovec, and V.S. Ivanov. 1968. Maximum aerobnoi i anaerobnoi rabotosposobnosti u plovćov. TPFK 10: 31.

Volkov, V.S. 1965. Elektronnii metod issledovania dihania. TPFK 4: 41.

Waltker, G. 1969. Neue gerate fur Verwirklichung der Schullen Information im Schwimmsport. Theorie Praxis Korperkultur 12: 1111.

Wanke, J. 1960. Moglichkeiten der Anwendung der Electronischen Schrittmachernlage zur Entwicklung des Zeitgefuhls bei Mittel und Langstreckensschwimmern. Theorie Praxis Korperkultur 11: 152.

Zaćiorskii, V.M. 1962. Naučnie isledovania za rubežom. TPFK 2: 53.

Zapnutdinov, P.K., Z.N. Usmanov, and I.S. Ureckii. 1968. Radioelektro kardiografia u plavćov i kunkobežćev v dinamike. TPFK 5: 15.

Zlatarev, V. and N. Gruev. 1965. Ustroistvo iizrabotvane s područni materiali na portativen aftomatičen lider pri pluvane. VFK 4: 220.

Response of the respiratory system to changes in pressure

J. Alexandrov and L. Petrov

In the aquatic environment, there is an increased pressure on the respiratory system of the swimmer. This resistance makes breathing during competition more difficult because of an increase in the requirements of ventilation. The work capacity of the respiratory system during competitive swimming depends on the physical capabilities of this system. The purpose of this study was to find a method for estimating the capabilities of the respiratory system for resisting water pressure during breathing.

METHODS

We constructed an apparatus based on the principles of the spirometer. Additional weights were employed to create pressure inside the bell of a spirometer. When these weights were applied with the spirometer opening to the atmosphere closed, the air pressure in the bell became greater than the atmospheric pressure. Likewise, the supplementary weights could also counterbalance the weight of the bell, thereby creating a smaller pressure than that of the atmosphere. This decreased pressure created a resistance to inhalation while a pressure greater than that of the atmosphere created a resistance to expiration. The volume of air inhaled and exhaled from the bell could then be calculated under these different pressure conditions.

During normal breathing vital capacity was measured with the pressure in the spirometer constant. The vital capacities of subjects were measured during inhalation and exhalation under lower and higher pressures, respectively. These capacities were compared with the vital capacity (VC) at atmospheric pressure. All results were converted to standard conditions of atmospheric pressure, temperature, and humidity.

RESULTS AND DISCUSSION

In this experiment, following a maximal exhalation, the subject inhaled air from the bell with the pressure decreased. This created a type of resistance because of the greater atmospheric pressure in the lungs during inhalation compared to that of the bell. When the subject inhaled air from the container with diminished pressure, it was not possible to attain the same pulmonary volume as that reached under atmospheric pressure conditions. On the *left side* of Figure 1, the mean levels of VC during inhalation with decreased pressures are presented in percent of the VC attained under atmospheric pressure conditions.

After maximal inhalation of air at atmospheric pressures, the subjects exhaled into the bell at pressures that were higher than those of the atmosphere. In order for expiration to take place under these conditions, the thoracic cage must be compressed, so that the pressure in the lungs becomes greater than that in the bell. Therefore, the VC for expiration diminished when the pressure in the bell was increased. This reduction, corrected in accordance with laws governing gases, is shown in *curve A* on Figure 1.

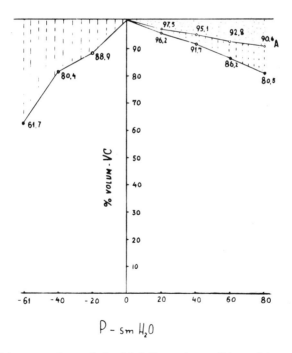

Figure 1. Pulmonary volumes during inhalation under conditions of decreased pressure (*left*) and during exhalation under increased pressures (*right*) expressed as percentages of corresponding pulmonary volumes under atmospheric pressure conditions.

Table 1. Mean pulmonary volumes during inhalation and exhalation under conditions of decreased and increased pressure

Pressure inferior to atmospheric	Maximum pulmonary volume during inhalation (cc)					Pressure greater than atmospheric	Maximum pulmonary volume during exhalation (cc)				
	N	M $\bar{X}$	S	$S_{\bar{X}}$	% of VC		N	$\bar{X}$	S	$S_{\bar{X}}$	% of VC
− 0	15	3693	623	161	100.0	0	15	3666	622	161	100
−20	15	3284	636	164	88.9	20	15	3525	613	158	96.2
−41	15	2969	638	165	80.4	40	15	3363	580	150	91.7
−61	15	2277	820	212	61.7	60	15	3160	564	146	86.2
						80	15	2951	459	123	80.5

During this study, we found a deviation from the theoretical curve. As the pressure of the bell was increased, the VC of subjects deviated more and more from the theoretical curve. This deviation and the corresponding decrease in the VC curve were caused by the increase in residual air. When a subject showed a higher level of expiration under conditions of increased pressure, he was also capable of inhaling a greater percentage of air and his pulmonary volume curve approached the theoretical *curve A*.

For each individual, different results for pulmonary volume at a given pressure were obtained. For the competitive swimmers, results for inhalation were better than those for individuals practicing other sports. For boxers, the expiration results were better. Using the same individuals, we determined the VC for different pressures during both inhalation and exhalation. We found a relationship between the ratio of VC for different persons under different conditions of pressure and the level of VC for atmospheric pressure (Table 1).

It may, therefore, be assumed that the percentage of decrease in the VC during expiration and inhalation in air under decreased or increased pressure conditions can be used to quantify the breathing capabilities of competitive swimmers while performing under the increased pressure imposed by the aquatic environment.

REFERENCES

Alexandrov, J. and L. Petrov. 1967. Questions de Culture Physique, Sofia, 12: No. 3, p. 171.
Hoa, B. P., C. Willa, and D. Fleisch. 1963. J. Physiol. 2: 55.
Klimt, F. Z. 1962. Kinderheilvund 87: 1—17.
Namur, M., D. Jandran, and J. M. Petit. 1960. J. Int. Physiol. Biochem. 68: 608—617.
Tins, I., S.K. Hong, and H. Rahn. 1960. J. Appl. Physiol. 15: 554—556.

Resistance, propulsion, and efficiency

Energetics of swimming in man

D. W. Rennie, D. R. Pendergast, and P. E. di Prampero

An analysis of swimming that quantitatively interrelates external mechanical power, over-all mechanical efficiency, total energy input, and the average velocity of progression has been hampered in the past by the absence of data on the over-all resistive forces (*i.e.,* form drag plus skin friction plus wave resistance) the swimmer must overcome during actual swimming. We shall refer to these resistive forces collectively as "body drag," D_b. With a knowledge of D_b, a quantitative analysis of swimming can be made to evaluate individual differences in performance and predict the energy cost of swimming.

When one swims at any steady state average velocity, the external power of swimming ($\dot{W}$) theoretically is related to velocity (v) and D_b as follows: $\dot{W} = v \cdot D_b$ (units = $kg \cdot m \cdot min^{-1}$). External power can also be expressed theoretically in terms of the over-all energy input ($\dot{V}_{O_2 \, net}$ for aerobic work) and the over-all mechanical efficiency of the swimmer (e): $\dot{W} = \dot{V}_{O_2 \, net} \cdot e$ (units = $kg \cdot m \cdot min^{-1}$ where 1 liter O_2 = 5 kcal = 2135 kgm).

Combining these expressions and rearranging terms:

$$\dot{V}_{O_2 \, net} / v = V_{O_2 \, net} / \text{distance} = D_b / e \qquad (1)$$

Thus the energy cost of swimming a given velocity or distance is seen from Equation 1 to be determined theoretically by the individual swimmer's ratio, "D_b/e."

D_b and e each can be influenced independently by many factors including body size and shape, body density, and the mechanics of the stroke (Adrian, Singh, and Karpovich, 1966; Alley, 1952; Counsilman, 1955, 1968; Karpovich, 1933, 1935; Karpovich and Pestrecov, 1939); and it seems important to be able to measure D_b and e independently in order to evaluate a swimmer's performance.

In this article a new method (di Prampero *et al.*, 1974) for determining D_b and e during actual swimming is described. The method has been applied to the freestyle performed by trained men and women swimmers of varying skill, swimming at velocities that do not exceed their maximal aerobic power.

Body drag was determined as illustrated in Figure 1 by adding known extra drag loads to swimmers moving at constant known speeds. The added drag (D_A) was related to the swimmer's steady state energy expenditure ($\dot{V}_{O_2\,net}$) as shown in Figure 2 to calculate the drag experienced by the free swimmer (D_b) and the mechanical efficiency (e).

Table 1, line 1, summarizes D_b as a function of v for all men and women. These values for D_b exceed those previously reported by others based upon towing or quick release of tethered subjects (Alley, 1952; Counsilman, 1955; Karpovich, 1933), presumably because of the motion of swimming. At any given velocity a wide range of D_b was observed in each group; however, D_b of men was significantly greater than that of women where the sample size was

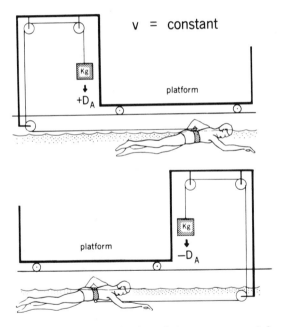

Figure 1. Method for measuring body drag. Swimmer was paced from observation platform moving at constant speeds about an annular pool 60 m in circumference. Expired gas was collected in a Douglas bag (not shown) during the 4th–6th min of exercise for determination of $\dot{V}_{O_2}$ by dry gas meter, O_2 meter, and CO_2 meter. Swimmer was connected to known weights (D_A) by pulleys so that the resulting force either increased (+D_A, *top*) or decreased (−D_A, *bottom*) the propulsive force the swimmer must provide to maintain constant speed. At least four successive 6-min periods were repeated with added drag and/or free swimming and the $\dot{V}_{O_2\,net}$ of each period was related to D_A as illustrated in Figure 2.

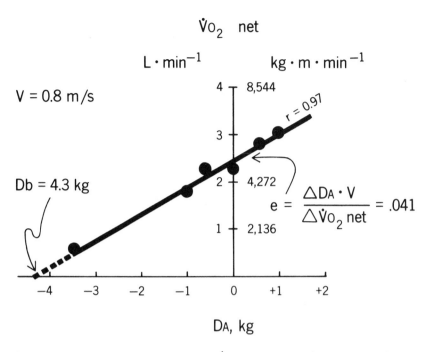

Figure 2. O_2 consumption above resting ($\dot{V}_{O_2}$ net, liters·min^{-1} or kg·m·min^{-1}) as a function of added drag (D_A) in one male subject swimming at a velocity of 0.8 m per sec. Extrapolation to $\dot{V}_{O_2}$ net = O gives D_b, in this case 4.3 kg. Because of the linear relationship between $\dot{V}_{O_2}$ net and D_A, the partial mechanical efficiency, e^P, equals the over-all mechanical efficiency, e; e.g., $e^P = e = \Delta D_A \cdot v / \Delta \dot{V}_{O_2} = 0.041$ in this example. Units are kg·m·min^{-1} where 1 liter O_2 = 5 kcal = 2.135 kg.

sufficiently large. When correction is made for surface area, this difference is no longer significant statistically.

Table 1, line 2, summarizes e as a function of v for all men and women. Again, differences between individuals in each group were very large at any given v, the highest values of e being associated with the most skilled swimmers. In each group, e rose as velocity increased to reach maximal values of 7.4 and 9.4 percent in men and women, respectively, at a velocity of 1.1–1.2 m per sec. A direct relation between e and v has been observed before (Klissouras, 1968), but the values for e reported here are 30–40 percent greater than those calculated from towing of passive subjects.

Table 1, line 3, summarizes D_b/e as a function of v for men and women, and line 4 summarizes the directly observed V_{O_2} net $/d$, which theoretically is equal to D_b/e as indicated in Equation 1. Values for V_{O_2} net $/d$ of other investigators are in this same range (Holmér, 1972; McArdle, Glaser, and Magel, 1971), and it is clear that the theoretical equality, V_{O_2} net $/d = D_b/e$ (Equation 1), agrees very closely with our empirical data on D_b and e. Note

Table 1. Body drag (D_b), mechanical efficiency (e), and O_2 consumption per kilometer (VO_{2net}/d) of men and women swimming the overarm crawl at velocities from 0.4 to 1.6 m per sec

Velocity (m per sec):	0.4–0.6			0.6–0.8			0.8		
	M ± SE	N	Range	M ± SE	N	Range	M ± SE	N	Range
1.									
Men, D_b (kg)	3.4 ± 0.3	10	2.3–4.7	5.2 ± 0.3	42	2.5–10.2	4.6 ± 0.3	15	3.1–7.1
Women, D_b (kg)	1.9 ± 0.2	9	0.8–3.3	4.2 ± 0.4	22	2.5–9.6			
p	< 0.05			< 0.05					
2.									
Men, e (%)	2.9 ± 0.2	10	2.1–4.0	4.8 ± 0.4	42	2.4–12.3	4.3 ± 0.4	15	2.5–6.6
Women, e (%)	2.7 ± 0.4	9	1.5–4.5	5.5 ± 0.8	22	1.9–21.2			
p	NS			NS					
3.									
Men, D_b/e (liters $O_2 \cdot km^{-1}$)	54 ± 1.6	10	46–63	50 ± 0.9	42	32–98	50 ± 1.2	15	41–72
Women, D_b/e (liters $O_2 \cdot km^{-1}$)	33 ± 0.4	9	24–47	36 ± 0.4	22	19–72			
p	<0.05			< 0.05					
4.									
Men, VO_{2net}/d (liters $O_2 \cdot km^{-1}$)	53 ± 2.5	12	34–62	51 ± 2.7	33	32–82	51 ± 2.3	10	40–62
Women, VO_{2net}/d (liters $O_2 \cdot km^{-1}$)	28 ± 2.1	6	21–35	39 ± 2.9	20	21–77			
p	< 0.05			< 0.05					

Velocity (m per sec):	0.9 M ± SE	N	Range	1.1–1.2 M ± SE	N	Range	1.6 M ± SE	N	Range
1.									
Men, D_b (kg)	6.9 ± 0.6	10	4.4–10.6	8.2 ± 0.9	4	6.2–10.2	12.1 ± 0.6	4	10.8–13.7
Women, D_b (kg)	3.5 ± 0.6	4	2.3–5.0	7.0 ± 0.7	5				
p	< 0.05			NS					
2.									
Men, e (%)	6.1 ± 0.7	10	3.5–10.5	7.4 ± 0.7	4	6.6–9.6	9.06 ± 0.8	4	7.5–11.2
Women, e (%)	3.7 ± 0.6	4	2.6–5.2	9.4 ± 1.4	5				
p	< 0.05			NS					
3.									
Men, D_b/e (liters $O_2 \cdot km^{-1}$)	54 ± 1.6	10	46–61	50 ± 0.5	4	47–68	63 ± 0.7	4	50–77
Women, D_b/e (liters $O_2 \cdot km^{-1}$)	45 ± 1.2	4	42–51	35 ± 0.4	5				
p	< 0.05			< 0.05					
4.									
Men, VO_2net$/d$ (liters $O_2 \cdot km^{-1}$)	53 ± 6.9	3	40–63						
Women, VO_2net$/d$ (liters $O_2 \cdot km^{-1}$)									
p									

that D_b/e does not change significantly up to a velocity of 1.2 m per sec and is significantly lower in the women.

The significantly lower ratio of D_b/e for women is due both to their lower D_b and their higher over-all mechanical efficiency. In a practical sense a lower D_b/e permits women to swim a kilometer at a net O_2 cost averaging 35 liters instead of 52 liters required by men. Expressed another way, it permits these women to achieve a 50 percent higher velocity than men for the same $\dot{V}_{O_2\,net}$. If women swimmers could develop a $\dot{V}_{O_2\,max}$ and a maximal anaerobic power comparable to that of men, they evidently could swim the overarm crawl at velocities exceeding that of men. In distance swims exceeding 10 km the higher D_b/e of women more than compensates for their lower $\dot{V}_{O_2\,max}$ and may account for their superiority at longer distances.

Reasoning that a person who floats more readily in the horizontal attitude would have a higher over-all mechanical efficiency (Karpovich, 1935; Counsilman, 1968), we have weighed a group of 32 men and 16 women underwater, as shown schematically in Figure 3. This method gives a direct measure of underwater foot weight (W_F), weight at the center of air (W_{ca}), and total body weight (W_{TB}) from which body density can be calculated as well as the torque ($T = W_F \cdot L$) that causes the lower body to sink. The $\dot{V}_{O\,net}/v$ and D_b/e for these same subjects were also measured independently at a velocity of 0.7 m per sec by the method described above.

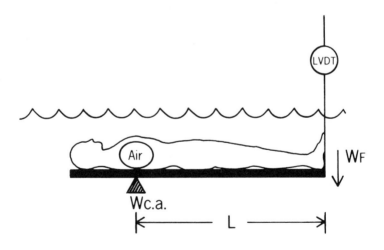

Torque = W$_F$ · L , kg · m

Figure 3. Method for determining underwater torque. The body, supported by tubular aluminum mesh frame, was treated as a beam having a moment of force, torque, about a fulcrum placed under the center of air. Weight at center of air and at feet was determined by linear displacement transducer. Torque = $W_F \cdot L$.

Table 2. Underwater weights of men and women measured as illustrated in Figure 3

	Weight$_{(TB)}$ (kg)	Weight$_{(ca)}$ (kg)	Weight$_{(F)}$ (kg)	Torque (kg·m)
Men (N = 32)	3.44 ± 0.20	2.32 ± 0.17	1.17 ± 0.03	1.44 ± 0.06
Women (N = 16)	1.72 ± 0.26	1.15 ± 0 20	0.585 ± 0.05	0.70 ± 0.05

Table 2 indicates that total body weight, weight at the center of air, foot weight, and torque were all significantly less in the women, presumably because of their greater depot of subcutaneous fat.

Figure 4 indicates the relationship between D_b/e or V_{O_2}/d and torque for these men and women. When the intergroup comparison is made, it appears that the greater D_b/e of men is related to greater torque leading to a more vertical attitude in water and a greater nonpropulsive energy cost (Karpovich, 1935) that reduces e and increases D_b.

In summary, the lower $\dot{V}_{O_2}/v$ of women swimmers is here related to their lower D_b/e, when D_b and e are measured independently by a new method. Their smaller D_b is due primarily to smaller surface area and their higher e to greater buoyancy.

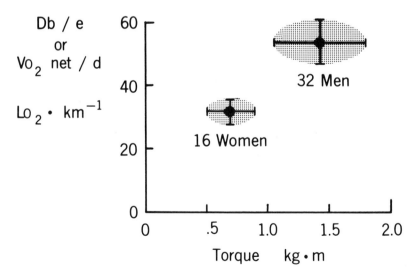

Figure 4. Net O_2 consumption at a velocity of 0.7 m per sec. (V_{O_2}/d), or its equivalent, D_b/e, is plotted as a function of underwater torque for 32 men and 16 women. Values are mean and 1 SD.

ACKNOWLEDGMENT

These studies were aided by Contract N00014-68-A-0216, (NR 101-722), between the Office of Naval Research, Department of the Navy, and the State University of New York at Buffalo.

REFERENCES

Adrian, M. J., M. Singh, and P. V. Karpovich. 1966. Energy cost of leg kick, arm stroke, and whole crawl stroke. J. Appl. Physiol. 21: 1763–1766.

Alley, L. E. 1952. An analysis of water resistance and propulsion in swimming the crawl stroke. Res. Quart. 23: 253–270.

Counsilman, J. E. 1955. Forces in two types of crawl stroke. Res. Quart. 26: 127–139.

Counsilman, J. E. 1968. The Science of Swimming. Prentice Hall, Englewood Cliffs, N.J.

di Prampero, P. E., D. R. Pendergast, D. W. Wilson, and D. W. Rennie. 1974. Energetics of swimming in man. J. Appl. Physiol. 37: 1–5.

Holmér, I. 1972. Oxygen uptake during swimming in man. J. Appl. Physiol. 33: 502–509.

Karpovich, P. V. 1933. Water resistance in swimming. Res. Quart. 4: 21–28.

Karpovich, P. V. 1935. Analysis of the propelling force in the crawl stroke. Res. Quart. 6: 49–58.

Karpovich, P. V. and K. Pestrecov. 1939. Mechanical work and efficiency in swimming crawl and back stroke. Arbeitsphysiol. 10: 504–514.

Klissouras, V. 1968. Energy metabolism in swimming the dolphin stroke. Arbeitsphysiol. 25: 142–150.

McArdle, W. D., R. M. Glaser, and J. R. Magel. 1971. Metabolic and cardiorespiratory responses during free swimming and treadmill walking. J. Appl. Physiol. 30: 733–738.

Body resistance
on and under
the water surface

J. Jiskoot and J. P. Clarys

Many reports of studies dealing with the water resistance of the human body can be found in the literature. The results of these studies, however, have been obtained by utilizing a towing device with a dynamometer attached (Alley, 1952; Counsilman, 1955, 1968; Karpovich, 1933; Schramm, 1958–1959), or a tethered swimming device with force transducers.

Most of the results in the existing literature were obtained with a small number of subjects. Experiments with a larger number of subjects, therefore, appeared to be justified. It seemed even more essential to use a number of different tests with the same group to provide for a more complete analysis.

PURPOSE

The purpose of this study was to determine the body resistance on the water surface and 60 cm under the water surface for a group of male subjects. It was assumed that under the water there is less resistance than on the surface (Schramm, 1958–1959) because the resistance of the waves is eliminated. The total resistance is the sum of the wave resistance, frictional resistance, and eddy resistance (Karpovich, 1933). The results of this study, therefore, might make it possible to distinguish the different resistance components (Clarys *et al.*, 1973). One must realize that resistance data obtained by towing bodies through the water are not the same as results from measurements of swimming as Alley (1952) found and as we have found in previous studies. But the results from towed bodies were required in order to-provide complete data and to make comparisons with actual swimming. Comparisons were also made with the earlier data reported by Schramm (1958–1959).

METHODS

Male physical education students (N=43) were selected for this investigation. They were average to good swimmers. Their individual freestyle swimming velocity ranged from 1.2 to 1.85 m per sec. The tests were carried out in the 200-m high speed towing tank of the Netherlands Ship Model Basin in Wageningen. The tank was filled with fresh water for this study. The apparatus consisted of an electrically driven towing carriage, a photoelectric cell system for velocity control, a telescopic towing device, force transducers, and an ultraviolet strip chart recording unit. A detailed description of this apparatus can be found in previously published studies (De Goede et al., 1971; Clarys et al., 1973). The apparatus is shown in Figure 1.

The pretest procedure was carried out with extreme body types in order to validate the procedures for the main investigation. The results of the pretest were presented by Clarys et al. (1974). The test conditions consisted of: a) measurements of the body resistance on the water surface at speeds ranging from 0.7 to 2.0 $m \cdot sec^{-1}$, at increments of 0.1 $m \cdot sec^{-1}$; b) measurements of the body resistance 60 cm under the surface of the water at speeds

Figure 1. Test apparatus at the Netherlands Ship Model Basin, Wageningen.

ranging from 1.5 to 1.9 m·sec^{-1}, in increments of 0.1 m·sec^{-1}. Both test conditions were repeated after some months. The water temperature during the first test series was 18°C, and at the time of the second test series it was 24°C. Comparisons between both types of tests were made at speeds of 1.5, 1.6, 1.7, 1.8, and 1.9 m·sec^{-1}. The body positions in the tests were similar. The subjects were taught to maintain a prone position, head between the arms (arms against the ears), legs extended and together, and feet in plantar flexion. They were instructed to hold their breath after a normal inhalation. The body position of all subjects was controlled by one of the examiners during the tests. Photographs were taken of all the subjects during the test to study the flow pattern of the water.

RESULTS AND DISCUSSION

The results of the tests and retests and the statistical treatment are shown in Table 1. The mean resistance of the tests and retests at specific speed ranges are presented in Figure 2. There was a relationship between the resistance curves on the surface and under the surface of the water as well as between the test and retests. There was a significant difference between the means of

Table 1. Mean, standard deviation, correlation coefficient of the total water resistance on and under the water surface (test and retest) (N=43)

Velocity (m/sec)	1.5	1.6	1.7	1.8	1.9
Mean resistance test on water surface (kg) (1)	7.019	7.958	8.835	9.886	11.005
SD	0.7673	0.9001	0.8931	0.9190	1.1265
Mean resistance retest on water surface (kg) (2)	6.581	7.391	8.361	9.253	10.616
SD	0.9103	0.9242	1.0431	1.1851	1.3146
Mean resistance test under water surface (kg) (3)	8.749	9.693	10.719	11.819	13.142
SD	1.1027	1.0754	1.0955	1.2561	1.3870
Mean resistance retest under water surface (kg) (4)	8.047	8.916	9.884	11.070	12.479
SD	1.0536	0.8893	0.9911	1.1277	1.4120
$r_{1,2}$	0.63	0.67	0.70	0.72	0.77
$r_{3,4}$	0.55	0.57	0.65	0.73	0.73
$r_{1,3}$	0.39	0.37	0.47	0.56	0.47
$r_{2,4}$	0.49	0.48	0.53	0.57	0.55

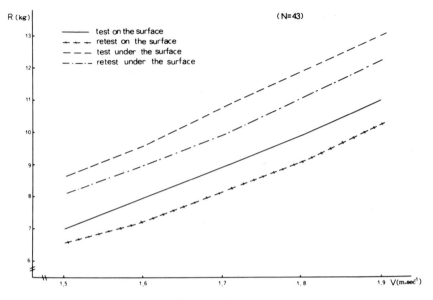

Figure 2. Mean total water resistance on tests and retests.

the data on the test and retest. This might have been the consequence of the different water temperatures. It is recommended that in the future the influence of the water temperature on body resistance be investigated as an experimental variable. The results indicated that the resistance under the water surface increased on the average about 21 percent in the test and 20 percent in the retest when the towing velocity was increased from 1.5 to 1.9 $m \cdot sec^{-1}$ (mean of increased resistance at the tested speeds, N=43). This result was in contradiction to the findings of Schramm (1958–1959), who concluded that the resistance under the water surface decreased about 11.5 percent (N=2) as speed increased. The body positions were similar in the two studies.

CONCLUSION AND REMARKS

Based on the hypothesis that in towing under the surface of the water, the resistance of the waves is for the most part eliminated, it might be possible to determine the frictional resistance plus the eddy resistance of the water. It appears that the total resistance while being towed under the surface of the water, consisting of the total frictional resistance plus the total eddy resistance, is higher than the total water resistance on the surface. The resistance on the surface consists of the sum of wave resistance, partial frictional resistance, and partial eddy resistance. This means that the additional combined frictional resistance and eddy resistance as a result of immersing the total body in the water are greater than the resistance afforded by the waves to a partially submerged body. Using the anthropometric data of all subjects, we intend to calculate the results in standard body dimensions, so that we might be able to derive a relationship between body form and water resistance. When applied to the practice of swimming, this means, as far as water resistance is concerned, it is preferable to swim on the surface instead of under the surface of the water.

REFERENCES

Alley, L. E. 1952. An analysis of water resistance and propulsion in swimming and crawl stroke. Res. Quart. 23: 253–270.

Clarys, J.P., J. Jiskoot, and L. Lewillie. 1973. A kinematographic, electromyographic and resistance study of waterpolo and competition front crawl. In: S. Cerquiglini, A. Venerando, and J. Wartenweiler (eds.), Biomechanics III: Medicine and Sport, Vol. 8, pp. 446–452. Karger, Basel.

Clarys, J. P., J. Jiskoot, H. Rijken, and P. J. Brouwer. 1974. Total resistance in water and its relation to body form. In: R. C. Nelson and C. A. Morehouse (eds.), Biomechanics IV, International Series on Sport Sciences, Vol. 1, pp. 187–196. University Park Press, Baltimore.

Counsilman, J. E. 1955. Forces in swimming two types of crawl stroke. Res. Quart. 26: 127–139.

Counsilman, J. E. 1968. The Science of Swimming. Prentice Hall, Englewood Cliffs, N.J.

De Goede, H., J. Jiskoot, and A. van der Sluis. 1971. Over stuwkracht bij zwemmers. Zwemkroniek 48: 78–90.

Karpovich, P. V. 1933. Water resistance in swimming. Res. Quart. 4: Oct., 21–28.

Rijken, H. 1971. Differences in resistance for the crawl stroke when applied as polo stroke or competition stroke. Wageningen, the Netherlands, N.S.M.B. Report no. 71 - 276 - 1 - HST.

Schramm, E. 1958–1959. Untersuchungsmethoden zur Bestimmung des Widerstandes, der Kraft und der Ausdauer bei Schwimmsportlern. Wiss. Z. Deutsch. Hochschule Körperkultur Leipzig: Heft 2: 161–180.

Total resistance of selected body positions in the front crawl

J. P. Clarys and J. Jiskoot

The effects of selected body positions on water resistance have been studied in previous experiments, using a series of existing standardized relationships from ship building model research (Clarys et al., 1974).

Form is an important factor influencing resistance, but body position changes must also be considered as factors that increase or decrease resistance. Karpovich (1933) and Schramm (1958–1959) reported that the supine streamlined position offered more resistance than a prone position. Hairabedian (1964), Schramm (1958–1959), Clarys et al. (1973), and De Goede et al. (1971) showed that resistance increased considerably when lifting the head out of the water from a streamlined prone glide. Total resistance also increases as the angle of inclination of the body to the water surface increases, especially at low velocities (Karpovich, 1933; Alley, 1952; Clarys et al., 1974).

In their research, Kent and Atha (1971) showed that greater resistance is created in four transient breaststroke body positions than in the glide position. Finally, Counsilman (1955), who examined the total drag of prone and side positions, stated that "less resistance is created in the prone than in the side position because the flow of the water against his feet tended to lift them and to streamline the body to a greater extent. The waterflow when the subject was being towed on his side did not elevate his feet as much, and consequently, the body was not as streamlined."

In all these studies a significant increase of total resistance was reported for all body positions (orientations) when compared with the glide or prone position.

All experiments were carried out using a towing device consisting of an electromotor, a pulley system, a tow line, dynamometer (spring scale and strain gauges), and transducer systems with kymograph or galvanometer recordings.

This study examined experimentally the total resistance (or drag) associated with two selected front crawl body positions at five different velocities.

The validity of the results obtained during towing has been shown to be a function of the resistance as described in previous studies. This study also sought to establish resistance values at selected speeds for the side position. Comparison is also made with data reported by Counsilman (1955).

METHODS

The apparatus used consisted of an electrically driven towing carriage, a photoelectric cell system for the velocity control, a telescopic towing device, force transducers, and galvanometer recording system which included a direct developing photostrip.

The device for the measurement of the forces acting on the moving body, the test environment and circumstances (Netherlands Ship Model Test Station, Wageningen) have been described in previous studies (De Goede et al., 1971; Clarys et al., 1973).

For this investigation, 43 male Caucasian subjects (mean age 19.06 years, body weight 76.15 kg, and height 177.9 cm) were selected from 96 individuals on the basis of anthropometric measurements. All subjects were good swimmers.

Resistance recordings were made at speeds ranging from 0.7 to 2.0 m per sec. In order to compare the results with those already reported in the literature, velocities of 1.5, 1.6, 1.7, 1.8, and 1.9 m per sec were analyzed statistically.

Data were recorded for each of the following positions: a) (streamlined) prone, drag, or gliding position; b) side position, one arm extended above the head, one arm against the body, legs straight and together, toes extended, and the head held so that the water level was approximately along the midline of the face. This side position was standardized for all subjects at an angle of approximately 45° by means of a pacing device controlled by one of the examiners.

RESULTS AND DISCUSSION

The results and the statistical treatment of the resistance measurements in the prone and side positions are shown in Table 1. The graphical presentation of these data are shown in Figure 1.

In addition to the statements concerning the ratio between speed and resistance previously mentioned by other researchers, we can describe the changes in resistance resulting from body position changes as follows:

1. With increasing velocity, there is an increase in the absolute resistance for

Table 1. Means, standard deviations. correlation coefficients, t-ratios and standard errors of the mean difference of the total resistance for two selected body positions in the front crawl (N=43)

Velocity (m/sec)	(1) Mean resistance at water surface (kg)	SD	(2) Mean resistance at 45° position (kg)	SD	$r_{1,2}$	$t_{1,2}$	SE_{diff}
1.5 (66.6sec/100m)	7.019	0.7673	6.521	1.0138	0.23	2.9139*	0.1708
1.6 (62.5sec/100m)	7.958	0.9001	7.542	1.0785	0.27	2.2650*	0.1838
1.7 (58.23sec/100m)	8.835	0.8931	8.670	1.2729	0.42	0.8944	0.1846
1.8 (55.55sec/100m)	9.886	0.9190	9.767	1.4395	0.52	0.6288	0.1886
1.9 (52.63sec/100m)	11.005	1.1265	11.165	1.5373	0.59	0.8390	0.1913

*Significant difference at 0.05 level.

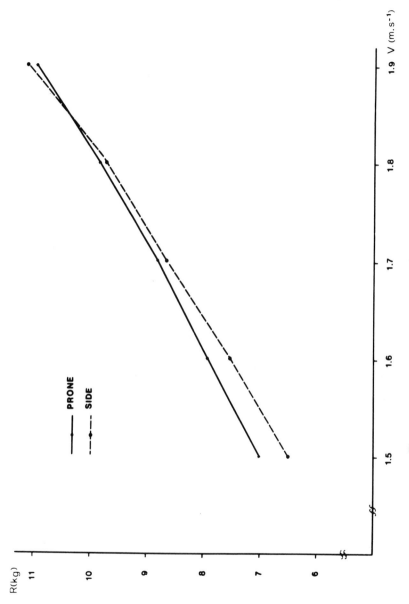

Figure 1. Mean resistance of prone and side positions (*N*=43).

both the prone and side positions (the absolute difference between means, however, decreases).

2. With increasing velocity, the increase in the prone position resistance is less than the increase in the 45° position drag. One should note that at lower speeds (1.5 and 1.6 m per sec) the prone position resistance is significantly greater than that for the side position. At 1.9 m per sec, the resistance of the side position is greater but not significantly different.

The prone position resistance was compared at identical velocities with the results of earlier studies. It was found that no significant differences existed between the resistances in the prone position obtained in this study and the results reported by Karpovich (1933), Alley (1952), Schramm (1958-1959) and the linear types of Clarys et al. (1974). The resistance values of Counsilman (1955) were significantly smaller at 1.5-1.9 m per sec, however. No comparison was made with the results of Kent and Atha (1971) because they only calculated resistances at velocities below 1.5 m per sec and because their investigation was concerned with the breaststroke. Since we assume that the head position was held higher on the water surface than in the crawl glide, we did not feel the results of the two studies were comparable. It was stated previously that the higher head position creates a significantly greater resistance (Schramm, 1958-1959; Hairabedian, 1964; Clarys et al., 1973; De Goede et al., 1971). All the findings of these studies are shown graphically in Figure 2.

The findings of this study contradict the findings of Counsilman (1955). His results showed the side resistance to be significantly greater than the drag created by a prone position at velocities of 1.5-1.9 m per sec (see Figure 3). In terms of swimming, this would mean that the rolling effect, especially in the transient side position in the front crawl, creates more resistance and thus it has a negative influence on the propulsion of the stroke. However, Counsilman tested only one swimmer in the side position. In our study, a small number of subjects showed results similar to those reported by Counsilman, but the majority (93 percent) displayed a resistance pattern as shown in Figure 1.

On the basis of our data it seems appropriate to assume that the transient side position decreases the total resistance in the front crawl at 1.5 and 1.6 m per sec velocities (67.0 sec to about 62.0 sec/100 m) and thus influences positively the propulsion forces. At velocities of 1.7 and 1.8 m per sec (approximately 58.5 to about 55.5 sec/100 m) the absolute resistance of the side position was still smaller and at 1.9 m per sec (52.6 sec/100 m) it was slightly greater than the prone resistance, but we assume this would have no effect on the total propulsion of the front crawl (no significant difference). This statement contradicts the findings of Counsilman (1955) based on only one swimmer.

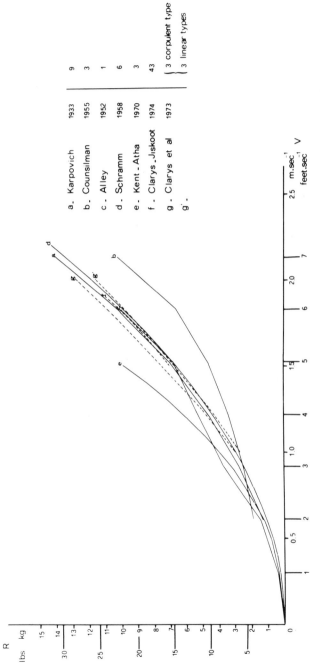

a.	Karpovich	1933	9	
b.	Counsilman	1955	3	
c.	Alley	1952	1	
d.	Schramm	1958	6	
e.	Kent - Atha	1970	3	
f.	Clarys - Jiskoot	1974	43	
g.	Clarys et al	1973	{	3 corpulent type
g'.			{	3 linear types

Figure 2.   Resistance (drag) of the prone (gliding) position at different velocities.

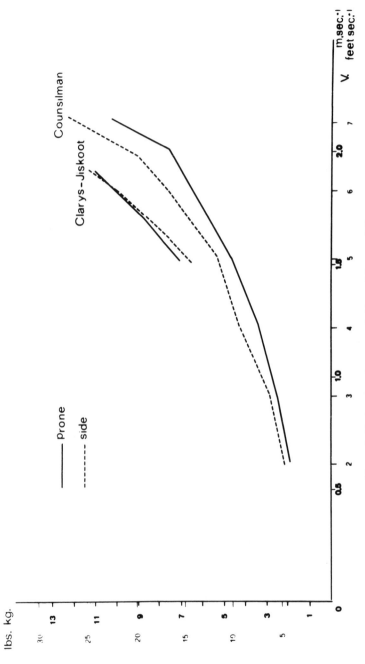

Figure 3. Resistance of prone and side positions at different velocities.

CONCLUSIONS

Significantly less resistance occurred for the side position as compared to the prone position for velocities of 1.5 and 1.6 m per sec. No significant differences were found at higher velocities. The results of this study appear to be valid since they compare favorably with the absolute resistance values of five other studies. The side position has less of a retarding effect on propulsion at lower speeds (1.5–1.6 m per sec) and has no influence upon the total propulsion at velocities higher than 1.7 m per sec.

ACKNOWLEDGMENT

This study is part of a research project, "Resistance of the Human Body in Water," supported by the Instituut voor Morfologie (Prof. P.J. Brouwer), Vrije Universiteit, Brussel.

REFERENCES

Alley, L.E. 1952. An analysis of water-resistance and propulsion in swimming the crawl stroke. Res. Quart. 23: 253–270.

Clarys, J.P., J. Jiskoot, and L. Lewillie. 1973. A kinematographical, electromyographical and resistance study of waterpolo and competition frontcrawl. *In:* S. Cerquiglini, A. Venerando, and J. Wartenweiler (eds.) Biomechanics III, Medicine and Sport Series, Vol. 8, pp. 446–452. Karger, Basel.

Clarys, J. P., J. Jiskoot, H. Rijken, and P. J. Brouwer. 1974. Total resistance in water and its relation to body form. *In:* R. C. Nelson and C. A. Morehouse (eds.), Biomechanics IV, International Series on Sport Sciences, Vol. 1, pp. 187–196. University Park Press, Baltimore.

Counsilman, J. 1955. Forces in swimming two types of crawl stroke. Res. Quart. 26: No. 2, 127–139.

De Goede, H., J. Jiskoot, and A. Van der Sluis. 1971. Over stuwkracht bij zwemmers. Zwemkroniek, 48: No. 4, 71–89.

Hairabedian, A. 1964. Kinetic resistance factors related to body positions in swimming. Doctoral thesis. Stanford University, Stanford, Calif.

Karpovich, P. V. 1933. Water resistance in swimming. Res. Quart. 4: 21–28.

Kent, N.R. and J. Atha. 1971. Selected initial transient body positions in breaststroke and their influence upon water resistance. *In:* L. Lewillie and J.P. Clarys (eds.), 1st International Symposium on Biomechanics in Swimming, pp. 53–58. Université Libre de Bruxelles, Brussels.

Schramm, E. 1958–1959. Untersuchungsmethode zur bestimmung des widerstandes, des kraft und der ausdauer bei schwimsportlern. Wiss. Z. Deutsch. Hochschule Körperkultur, Leipzig 1: 161–180.

A biomechanical model for swimming performance

P. R. Francis and N. Dean

This study is an attempt to develop a mathematical model involving those factors that govern maximal performance levels in freestyle swimming. Levels of athletic performance are determined by the interaction of three factors that govern all functions of the human organism. These factors may be classified as the mechanical, the physiological, and the psychological. It is logical to assume that any complete investigation of athletic performance must account for the effects of all three of these factors.

At the present time relatively sophisticated tools are available for the measurement of mechanical and physiological variables in the swimmer, but instruments designed to evaluate appropriate psychological variables are of questionable validity. Therefore, the present first approximation model incorporates both mechanical and physiological variables, while no attempt has been made to examine the influence of psychological factors. In an attempt to control the psychological variables, however, the present model was validated using world record performances for men and women swimmers. It was assumed that world record performances would be indicative of near maximal levels of motivation for the performers.

ASSUMPTIONS OF THE MODEL

Figure 1 illustrates the relationship between the model and previously unpublished data collected by students during biomechanics laboratory sessions at Iowa State University. Differences between the model and the data will be accounted for in the subsequent discussion.

The projectile phase

In the absence of significant air resistance the swimmer will have constant horizontal velocity during the parabolic trajectory of his dive. The dynamics

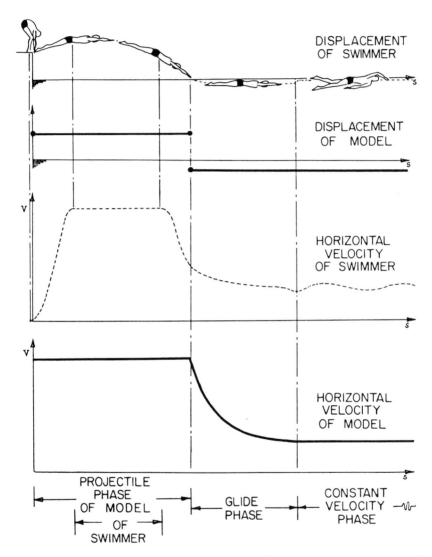

Figure 1. Comparisons between experimental data for a swimmer and the proposed model.

of the projectile phase of the model are therefore relatively simple. With an initial constant horizontal velocity V_o the body is displaced a horizontal distance d_p in a time t_p. Hence $d_p = V_o t_p$, and the energy expenditure per unit of mass is*

$$E_p = \frac{1}{2} V_o{}^2 \qquad (1)$$

The glide phase

The swimmer makes adjustments in his body form during the entry and subsequent glide; the adjustments are not accounted for in the model. Although swimming involves unsteady, turbulent flows, it is reasonable to assume that at the Reynolds numbers encountered, drag forces are proportional to the square of the velocity, V^2, of the swimmer. The retarding force per unit of mass can be equated to the acceleration of the body, and therefore $F_g = \dot{V} = -V^2/\lambda$ where λ = a drag coefficient. This equation can be integrated with the boundary conditions $V = V_o$ at $t = 0$; $V = V_s$ at $t = t_g$ (time lapsed during glide) to yield

$$t_g = \lambda(1/V_s - 1/V_o) \qquad (2)$$

$$d_g = \lambda\log(V_o/V_s) \qquad (3)$$

It is assumed that no energy is expended during the glide and that the body is allowed to decelerate until the horizontal velocity is precisely equal to that velocity which the swimmer can maintain for the remainder of the race. (The swimmer from whom the data in Figure 1 were compiled did not, however, accomplish this.)

The constant velocity phase

The basic assumption of the model is that the energy available to the swimmer should be completely used up at the completion of the desired distance. Further, the swimmer is assumed to maintain constant velocity throughout the swimming phase. (The swimmer from whom the data in Figure 1 were compiled appeared to accelerate and decelerate about a mean constant swimming velocity.) If the effects of turns are neglected,

$$E_o + \sigma t_s = F \times d_s \qquad (4)$$

where E_o = the total stored energy available for anaerobic metabolism; σ = the rate of energy conversion during aerobic metabolsim; t_s = the time during

*This and all subsequent energy values are assumed to be the product of the actual energy value and some, as yet undetermined, efficiency constant. The overall effect of this simplification is to alter the magnitudes of physiological and mechanical parameters, but does not affect the relationship of these parameters to one another.

which the swimmer swims at constant velocity; d_s = the distance traveled at constant swimming velocity, where $V_s = d_s/t_s$; F = the resultant retarding force exerted by the water upon the swimmer. Assuming that the retarding force is proportional to the square of the velocity of the body, $F = V^2/C^3$ where C is a constant. Then Equation 4 becomes $E_o + \sigma t_s = d_s^3/C^3 t_s^2$ and it follows that $d_s = Ct_s (\sigma + E_o/t_s)^{1/3}$. For a long race $E_o \ll \sigma t_s$ and the expression in parentheses can be expanded as a Taylor series to yield

$$d = Ct_s \sigma^{1/3} (1 + E_o/3\sigma t_s + \dots$$

$$= C\sigma^{1/3} t_s + (C\sigma^{(1/3-1)}/3 E_o \dots$$

For a race sufficiently long that starting effects are negligible and that $t \gg \tau$ (*i.e.*, the race is basically aerobic)

$$d \simeq V_\infty (t_s + \tau) \tag{5}$$

where $V_\infty = C\sigma^{1/3}$ and $\tau = E_o/3\sigma$. One may interpret V_∞ as that velocity at which the swimmer could swim forever were it not for local muscle fatigue and other factors such as the need for sleep and diminished motivation; τ is the amount of time for which the energy initially available for anaerobic metabolism would suffice to swim at this rate. The distance, d_s, and time, t_s, for the constant velocity phase are determined by $d_s = V_s t_s = D - d_p - d_g$, and the energy per unit of mass expended is equal to the work done by the swimmer in overcoming the retarding resistance.

$$E_s = Fd = V_s^2 d/\lambda \tag{6}$$

PROCEDURES

Under the assumptions just stated, the distance covered, the time required, and energy expended in each of the three stages of a swimming race can be calculated. The optimal performance for any given competitor will be achieved if the speed during the constant velocity phase is such that the total energy available is expended at precisely the same time that the desired distance has been covered. In order to find the minimal total time, $T = t_p + t_g + t_s$ for the swimmer to cover a distance $D = d_p + d_g + d_s$ without prematurely exhausting his energy supply, we must find the value of V_s for which

$$E_p + E_s = E_o + \sigma T \tag{7}$$

Equations 1 through 7 define the model precisely in terms of the five unknown constants t_p, V_o, λ, E_o, and σ. The implicit equations cannot be solved algebraically so an iterative numerical solution technique must be used. The determination of the best values for the parameters was accomplished using a standard nonlinear functional minimization program, originally written for phenomenological studies in high energy physics, and was carried out on the Iowa State University High Energy Physics Group's PDP 11/45 computer.[†] Validation of the model was accomplished by determining the values of the five unknown parameters which produced the best agreement with available data and subsequently evaluating whether that agreement was satisfactory. If the model were qualitatively wrong, no values of the parameters would produce a good agreement at all distances.

RESULTS AND DISCUSSION

The best fits obtained, using 1973 world freestyle records for men and women, are shown in Table 1, and the values of the parameters leading to these fits are given in Table 2. Agreement in all cases is within 2.47 percent and for most distances is substantially better. Furthermore, it may be noted that a part of this error can clearly be ascribed to a systematic difference between long course (meters) and short course (yards) records. (The latter have been converted to meters in Table 1, e.g., 100 yards = 91.44m.) The former are uniformly slower (negative error) whereas the latter are generally faster (positive error).

The parameters to which the model is most sensitive are $V_\infty = (\sigma \lambda)^{1/3}$ and $\tau = E_0/3\sigma$. Examination of the data generated by the program reveals that women have a value of V_∞ which is only 5 percent less than that for men (1.38 m per sec vs. 1.45 m per sec), but that their energy reserve time τ is 33

[†]We are grateful to the Ames Laboratory of the U.S. Atomic Energy Commission and to Professor W.J. Kernan for making the computer available for this research.

Table 1. Comparison of model results with input data

Distance (m)	Men's records (sec)			Women's records (sec)		
	Fit	Data	Error (%)	Fit	Data	Error (%)
45.72	20.16	20.23	−0.34	Not used		
91.44	45.23	44.41	1.61	51.85	51.60	0.48
100.0	50.23	51.22	−1.93	57.42	58.59	−1.99
182.9	100.2	98.35	1.85	112.2	110.5	1.57
200.0	110.8	112.8	−1.76	123.6	124.4	−0.60
400.0	235.2	238.2	−1.24	257.6	258.1	−0.18
457.2	271.0	264.5	2.47	294.7	292.5	0.75
1500.0	925.6	935.4	−1.05	996.8	1014.0	−1.71
1509.0	931.1	926.5	0.50	1003.0	996.6	0.62

Table 2. Best values of parameters

Parameter	Men's values		Women's values	
RMS* error, %	1.56	1.58	1.17	1.23
V_∞, m/sec	1.454	1.454	1.378	1.381
τ, sec	23.13	23.31	15.32	14.78
λ, m	0.1523	0.04 (fixed)	0.03916	0.25 (fixed)
E_O, (m/sec)^2	1400.0	5373.0	3070.0	467.1
σ, m^2/sec^3	20.18	76.85	66.82	10.53
V_O, m/sec	5.022	4.936	10.14	10.20
t_p, sec	0.08468	0.09 (fixed)	0.08935	0.09 (fixed)

*Residual mean square.

percent less (15.32 sec vs. 23.13 sec). The faster times for men thus reflect a greater capacity for muscular storage of energy, rather than a more efficient metabolizing process. The remaining parameters are less critical to the model as a whole and are far more dependent upon small details of the model. The values of the remaining parameters can be varied over a considerable range, in a correlated manner, without significant effect on the quality of the fit. They are consequently determined here only to the order of magnitude. To illustrate this point by an example, Table 2 shows a fit in which λ and t_p were fixed, the value of λ was somewhat removed from the best fit value. The quality of the fit, and the values of V_∞ and τ, were not significantly affected by this change, although changing λ did change E_0 and σ, drastically.

The same is not true of V_∞ and τ, which are closely determined by the model. To extract values of the physiological parameters E_0 and σ from them, however, requires accurate knowledge of λ. There are problems associated with direct determinations of drag forces on swimmers using the towing method of Kent and Atha (1971). Drag forces exerted by steady flow conditions must be assumed to differ significantly from those exerted during the unsteady flows encountered in swimming. However, indirect determination of λ could be accomplished by supplying the model with more data in the short distance range which is most sensitive to λ, V_0, and t_p. This would necessitate the use of world class performers to produce "record" times for distances between 10 and 50 m.

For purposes of comparison the present calculational program was applied to the data on world records for running. Appropriate changes were made to describe an initial acceleration phase in the manner employed by Keller (1973). That author proposed that maximal performances would necessitate that a performer decelerate over the final few meters of a race, but this suggestion was regarded as being unrealistic and omitted from the present program. Retarding forces which were quadratic, linear, and constant with respect to the runner's velocity were used, and the fits were carried out varying all four of his parameters simultaneously (rather than one at a time as

Keller did). In general, the results are in agreement with Keller's, but the best fits were obtained for an air resistance proportional to the square of the velocity. The most pertinent comparison is between the computed values of the ratio E_o/σ. For mens' swimming records $E_o/\sigma = 3 \tau = 69.4$ sec whereas for mens' running records Keller found $E_o/\sigma = 57.9$ sec. Assuming that E_o is the same for world record holders in both swimming and running, the computed value of σ for swimming is 83 percent of the value of σ for running. This observation is in apparent agreement with the findings of Holmer (1972), who reported that the highest oxygen uptake during swimming averaged 89 percent of the maximal value of the oxygen uptake for nine subjects in running.

REFERENCES

Holmer, I. 1972. Oxygen uptake during swimming in man. J. Appl. Physiol. 33: 4.

Keller, J. B. 1973. A theory of competitive running. Physics Today. September.

Kent, M. and J. Atha. 1971. Selected critical transient body positions in breaststroke and their influence upon water resistance. In: L. Lewillie and J.P. Clarys (eds.), Proceedings of the First International Symposium on Biomechanics in Swimming, pp. 119–125. Université Libre de Bruxelles, Brussels.

Intracycle kinematics and body configuration changes in the breaststroke

M. R. Kent and J. Atha

Developing high quality competitive performance in swimming, as in any other skilled activity, requires more than intensive and intelligently directed practice: it requires information. At best this information will include details of the way in which the many different movements of the swimmer produce changes in his swimming speed.

In this investigation an attempt was made to provide a detailed description of the intracycle kinematics of one top class breaststroke swimmer and to associate these with the body configuration changes which accompanies them.

METHODS

A British Olympic swimmer who was the country's current men's 100-m and 200-m breaststroke champion acted as the subject. After warm-up and a period of familiarization with the test procedures, he performed two separate one-length (25-yard) maximal speed sprints from a push start. During these sprints, which were performed in the Loughborough College Pool, underwater films were taken of his performance and recordings made of his instantaneous swimming velocity. The films and the velocity recordings were carefully synchronized using a trigger pulse that operated an event marker and a signal lamp, simultaneously (Figure 1).

The camera employed was a tripod-mounted Bolex H16, 16-mm triple turret motion picture camera with an integral self-governing shutter. It was operated by an external 24 volt D.C. supply. Kodak Tri-X reversal film was used throughout, and the film was force processed.

Swimming velocity was measured using a specially designed instrument, the swim speed recorder (SSR) (Kent and Atha, 1975). The recorder was

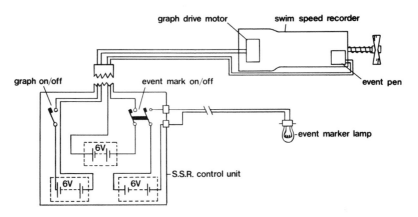

Figure 1. Swim speed recorder and control unit.

switched on at the start and remained on for the duration of the sprint. The paper drive speed required less than 1 sec to achieve its constant recording speed of 15.5 mm sec^{-1}.

The SSR was calibrated immediately prior to testing by means of a constant speed towing device. The camera frame speed was also check-calibrated immediately before and after filming with the use of a Venner electronic stop clock.

The velocity records obtained were digitized with a D-Mac graph plotter, then rescaled and redrawn on I.C.L. 1904A computer. The films were analyzed on a modified Bell and Howell Uniscop focal projector.

RESULTS

A sample 7 sec of a typical recording of instantaneous velocity are shown in Figure 2. The original recording (*upper trace*) and its recalibrated and re-drawn analogue (*lower trace*) illustrate the marked variations that are a characteristic of the breaststroke. A consistent pattern comprising a trough separating two peaks may be seen in these traces. Although interesting minor variations between the different cycles are clearly discernible, there appears to be no variability in the inevitable interpeak plummet to zero velocity.

In Figure 3 a single stroke cycle is presented. It is illustrated at selected critical points in the cycle with filmed images of the associated body configurations of the swimmer recorded at those moments.

By combining the results of ten such stroke cycles obtained during two separate one-length sprints, a mean pattern of stroke velocity was constructed. From this composite record the following data were extracted.

Taking the start of the stroke cycle to be that moment when the hands preparatory to the arm pull first begin to turn, it was determined that the

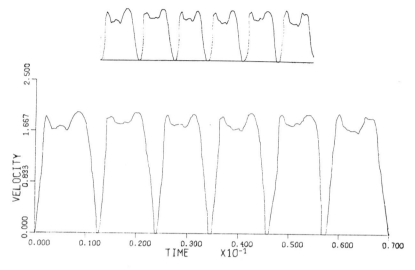

Figure 2. SSR trace and calibrated computer reproduction. First filmed sequence.

prestart glide velocity of the subject was 1.76 m sec^{-1}. At that moment there was virtually zero acceleration and the swimmer appeared to be traveling with more or less constant velocity. Some irregular fluctuations could be seen, but these were apparently associated with minor corrections of body inclination (which decreased by some 5° during the glide), body balance, and streamline adjustments.

As the glide ended and the arm pull started, the head began to lift. This resulted in a slight initial loss of velocity, which quickly gave way to a rapid gain as the main pull phase was attained. However, even at their most effective moment the maximal acceleration achieved by the arms was only 1.0 m sec^{-2}, recorded 190 msec after the start. Peak arm velocity (1.95 m sec^{-1}) was attained 50 msec later, by which time the arms were inclined at 50° ($\pm$ 5°) to the water surface. Despite the low accelerative forces generated, this peak velocity exceeded that subsequently produced by the much more powerful leg drive.

During the following 300 msec the legs began their preparations for the drive, bending at the knees into a tightly flexed position and at the hips less completely. During this leg recovery phase the swimmer decelerated at a rate that reached a maximum of 8.15 m sec^{-2}, eventually stopping absolutely. The leg drive began with a fast rebound catch on the water while the arms were straight and parallel with the surface. At this moment 640 msec had passed and 59 percent of the stroke had been completed.

The leg drive proceeded and produced an acceleration which within 150 msec had reached a maximum of 9.25 m sec^{-2}. At the moment of maximal acceleration the hips and knees had extended to 135° and 100°, respectively.

128   Kent and Atha

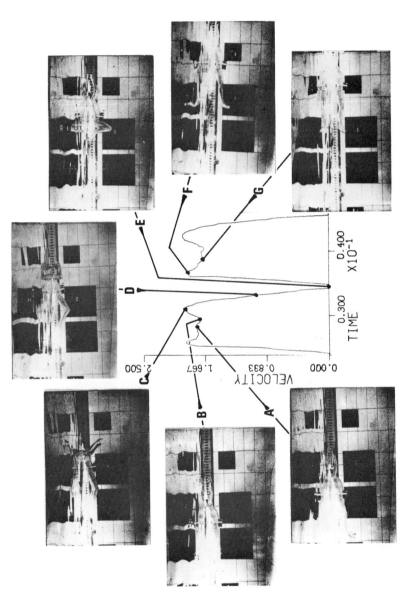

Figure 3. The relationship between posture and instantaneous velocity of a top class swimmer.

Only an additional 50 msec were required to carry the legs through to the limit of the kick, by which time the leg peak velocity of 1.85 m sec^{-1} had been attained.

After the leg drive the body remained extended for 140 msec. During this phase exhalation took place and velocity slowly fell back to the prestart glide velocity of 1.76 m sec^{-1}.

The full stroke cycle lasted 1.080 sec, during which time the swimmer had moved 1.53 m.

DISCUSSION

The results presented here are but one example of the kinematics of breaststroke as performed by a top class breaststroke swimmer. It is hoped that the insights provided by such an analysis may be of general interest and lead to more generalized studies of the stroke which has so far been somewhat neglected.

Accurate empirical data of the kind presented could, of course, also provide an effective coaching tool. For instance, it would probably be possible to introduce variants into a swimmer's stroke pattern and then to measure the accelerative effects that are no doubt initially unpredictable and transient. If promising results were produced, then they could be pursued with persistence and confidence, until such time as the level of skill required to exploit them had been developed.

REFERENCE

Kent, M. R. and J. Atha. 1975. A device for the on-line measurement of instantaneous swimming velocity. *In:* L. Lewillie and J.P. Clarys (eds.), Swimming II. International Series on Sports Sciences, Vol. 2, pp. 58–63. University Park Press, Baltimore.

Efficiency of breaststroke and freestyle swimming

I. Holmér

In most studies of efficiency of man during swimming (Karpovich and Pestrecov, 1939; Adrian et al., 1966; Klissouras, 1968; Holmér, 1972) the calculation of the propulsive forces is based on drag measurements of the body in an outstretched, passive, prone or supine position. Drag during swimming is presumably higher than drag during passive towing of the body mainly because of the movement of head, trunk, and limbs within the stroke cycle. Kent and Atha (1971) reported significantly higher drag values in selected transient body positions in the breaststroke than in the prone glide positions, and di Prampero et al. (1974) applied a new method to determine the actual drag experienced by man during swimming and found it was about twice as high as that of the passively towed swimmer. The data of di Prampero and his associates (1974) will probably produce a reasonably accurate measure of propulsion efficiency, while others should be considered underestimations. In the present study, the method described by di Prampero et al. (1974) was applied and data were collected on drag during breaststroke and freestyle swimming.

SUBJECTS

Three highly skilled male swimmers participated in this study. Subject HL (age 25 years, height 175 cm, weight 79 kg) was a medley specialist with a maximal $\dot{V}O_2$ during swimming of 4.99 liters per min. Subjects AN (17, 179, 63) and TW (16, 188, 84) were breaststroke swimmers. Maximal $\dot{V}O_2$ during swimming was 4.05 and 5.19 liters per min for AN and TW, respectively. The swimming results for each of the three subjects are given in Table 1.

Table 1. Swimming results and efficiency of three subjects

Subject	Swim, 200 m (min:sec)	Leg kick 0.5	Leg kick 0.7	Arm stroke 0.8	Arm stroke 0.5	Arm stroke 0.7	Arm stroke 0.9	Whole stroke 0.7	Whole stroke 0.9
HL									
Breaststroke	2:31.2		3.3	3.0	5.9	5.8		5.7	5.1
Freestyle	1:58.3	2.4				7.7	7.3	6.6	6.1
AN									
Breaststroke	2:31.1		2.9	3.8	4.3	3.6		4.7	4.4
Freestyle	2:12.0	1.3				4.6	5.1	6.0	5.9
TW									
Breaststroke	2:33.4		2.4	2.9	3.1	3.0		4.2	3.8
Freestyle	2:09.2	2.3				4.0	4.2	5.6	5.8

(Efficiency (%); Velocity (m/sec))

METHODS

All experiments were performed in a swimming flume, allowing the subject to swim in the same spot in water flowing at a given, predetermined rate (Åstrand and Englesson, 1972). The average drag experienced by the subject during swimming was calculated according to the method described by di Prampero et al., (1974). At a physiological steady state, the essential principle is that changes in body drag during swimming at a constant speed are met by corresponding changes in energy consumption. Net $\dot{V}O_2$ (oxygen uptake − resting oxygen uptake) turns out to be a linear function of added (or subtracted) drag (D_A) (see Figure 1). Extrapolation of the regression line for the net $\dot{V}O_2/D_A$ relationship to zero net $\dot{V}O_2$ (Figure 1) will give the average drag exerted upon the swimmer at that swimming speed (D_{sw}). This should be interpreted so that D_{sw} is the drag force which, if exerted upon the swimmer in a forward direction, would result in "idle swimming," i.e., with no extra oxygen uptake above resting. For a detailed description and discussion of the method the reader is referred to di Prampero et al. (1974). Passive drag (D_p) was measured with a strain gauge force transducer and recorded on a Honeywell amplifier and recorder.

Expired gas was collected in Douglas bags. Volume was determined by a balanced spirometer and the gas sample was analyzed for O_2 and CO_2 by the Haldane technique. Respiratory rate and swimming stroke rate were counted.

Efficiency was calculated from the equation:

$$\text{Efficiency} = \frac{D_{sw} \times v \times 60}{\text{net } \dot{V}O_2 \times 4.9 \times 427} \times 100 \, (\%) \qquad (1)$$

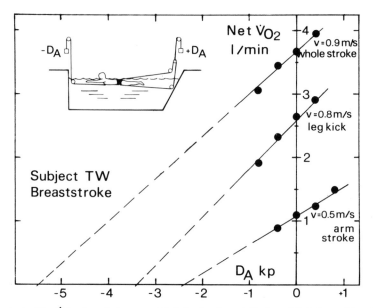

Figure 1. Net $\dot{V}O_2$ in relation to added (and subtracted) drag (D_A) for subject TW. Regression line is extrapolated to net $\dot{V}O_2 = 0$, which gives the average drag experienced by the swimmer at that velocity (D_{sw}). The insert illustrates the experimental set-up.

D_{sw} is the drag during swimming (kp), v is swimming velocity (m per sec), net $\dot{V}O_2$ in liters per min (4.9 kcal per min are equivalent to an oxygen uptake of 1 liter per min), and 1 kpm = 1×427^{-1} kcal.

PROCEDURE

Resting oxygen uptake was measured with the subjects lying motionless in the swimming flume. In the experiment the subject swam for about 20 min at a given submaximal velocity. At approximately every 5 min, the drag of the swimmer was either increased or decreased by adding ($+D_A$) or subtracting ($-D_A$) given loads to the swimmer. This was obtained by hanging known weights (0.4 or 0.8 kg) from a system of lines and ball bearing pulleys exerting a horizontal force on the swimmer in the direction of movement (see Figure 1). These lines did not interfere with normal stroke mechanics. At each velocity, swimming started with one or two 5-min periods with subtracted drag ($-D_A$), followed by another period of swimming without any load, and completed with two or one period of added drag ($+D_A$). Each experiment provided four different values of drag (added or subtracted) at a given velocity. Within each period steady state $\dot{V}O_2$ was determined, as described by Holmér (1972). None of the work periods demanded an oxygen uptake greater than approximately 80% of the subjects' maximal $\dot{V}O_2$. Within both breaststroke and freestyle, the subjects swam in different experiments with the stroke as a whole, with the arms only (legs supported by a cork plate), or using only the legs (arms supported).

Passive drag (D_p) was determined with the subject lying outstretched in the flowing water. He was connected via a handle and the line pulley system to the force transducer. D_p was calculated as the mean value during 30 sec. D_p was also measured with first the legs and then the arms supported by a cork plate, imitating the body position during arm swimming and leg kicking.

RESULTS AND DISCUSSION

D_p at a given water flow rate varied with body size and body position (Figure 2). D_p was approximately 0.5 kp less when legs were supported by a cork plate at a given speed. A more horizontal body position is established when the legs are lifted, which is favorable from the point of view of water resistance. D_p was, within the velocities examined, slightly increased or unchanged when the arms were supported by a cork plate.

During swimming with the whole stroke as well as with the arms only D_{sw} was 1½ to 2 times higher than D_p at a given velocity (Figure 2). Leg kicks in freestyle produced slightly lower D_{sw}, while D_{sw} of the breaststroke leg kick was slightly higher than D_p.

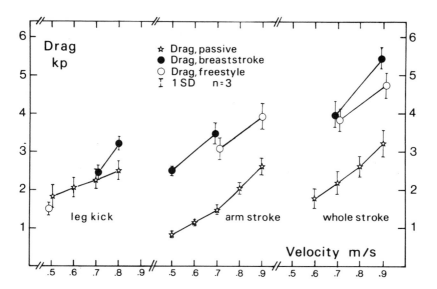

Figure 2. Mean values and SD for passive drag and drag during swimming with leg kicks, arms only, and the whole stroke.

The method for determination of D_{sw} applied in this study has been described and discussed in detail by di Prampero *et al.* (1974). These authors stated that the speed oscillations at the low velocities they examined, are negligible when calculating the mechanical work, at least for the crawl stroke. Furthermore, they concluded that the extrapolation of the net $\dot{V}O_2/D_A$ relationship to net $\dot{V}O_2 = 0$ (Figure 1) was justified, since it could be assumed that energy not spent for propulsion was negligible or directly proportional to total energy consumption. The latter would be the case with respiratory and cardiac work and changes in stroke mechanics. However, not all mechanical energy is useful in overcoming drag. Part of it is lost in the creation of turbulence, and in vertical and lateral displacement of water. The ratio of mechanical power output to drag power is unknown. Theoretical calculations resulted in an estimated efficiency of 30 to 40 percent for freestyle swimming (Seireg and Baz, 1971). The basic assumption in utilizing this method is that this ratio is not substantially altered by changes in swimming velocity. However, these conditions remain to be proven.

Efficiency calculated according to Equation 1 for the subjects and the different styles and strokes are given in Table 1. The values are higher than most of the results reported by other researchers. di Prampero *et al.* (1974) calculated an average efficiency of 5.24 percent for ten swimmers in the freestyle at a velocity of 0.9 m per sec. The reason for the differences in most cases is that the previous investigators have used passive drag values when calculating efficiency. As mentioned before, D_{sw} was about 1½ to 2 times higher than D_p for the subjects in this study and also in the study by di Prampero *et al.* (1974). Efficiency calculated from D_p values results in a considerable underestimation. Another source of variation in efficiency is the swimming technique of the subjects. Although they were highly skilled swimmers, the subjects in this study demonstrated rather great interindividual differences. The high values for efficiency in the breaststroke reflect the fact that the three swimmers were very skilled and trained in this stroke. The efficiency of the freestyle stroke is only slightly higher than that of the breaststroke. Body attitude and limb movements in the breaststroke are more unfavorable than in freestyle, from the point of view of water resistance and consequently, higher drag values are expected. These drag values were also measured in this study. However, two of the subjects were not especially trained in freestyle swimming, which restricts the value of a comparison between the styles.

Efficiency of swimming with arm strokes only in freestyle was for the medley swimmer 7.3 to 7.7 percent, while the leg kick in freestyle demonstrated a poor efficiency, 1.3 to 2.3 percent. Over longer distances, leg kicking is too expensive and should be reduced considerably. Data support the common opinion among coaches that the major contribution to the propulsion in freestyle is derived from the arms. The main objective in the leg kick is to balance the body and lift the legs, so water resistance can be kept low.

The leg kick in the breaststroke was more efficient than in the freestyle. Recovery of the legs in the breaststroke produces high water resistance (Kent and Atha, 1971), but, on the other hand, the backward kick works under more favorable conditions than the up and down kick in freestyle. Propelling force of the breaststroke leg kick is also higher than that of the leg kicks used in the crawl and butterfly strokes (Magel, 1970). In conclusion, the increase in propulsive force seems to be better in the breaststroke kick.

The arms in both the breaststroke and the freestyle pull and push in a backward movement, with a relatively great surface area exposed perpendicular to the direction of movement. The angle of attack, however, is favorable to producing propulsive forces. Consequently, efficiency of arm work, especially in the freestyle, is high. The longer arm stroke cycle and the more continuous work by the arms will result in more efficient propulsion than the equilateral, short arm pull in the breaststroke in which the recovery phase is in the water.

It should be emphasized that efficiency discussed in this study does not reflect the true ratio of chemical energy expenditure to mechanical energy output in the muscle during swimming movements. As mentioned, the amount of energy lost in turbulence is unknown. Only the work performed by the propulsive forces in the direction of progression was determined. However, from the point of view of swimming technique the ratio of propulsive force to total energy consumption should yield a useful measure of the efficiency of different strokes and styles, various swimmers, and the effects of swimming training. It is obvious that the efficiency of propulsion of different strokes varies as does the efficiency among swimmers. The main objective for each swimmer should be to develop those strokes which contribute the most propulsion. Attention must then be paid to the swimmer's anatomical features and physiological capabilities.

Efficiency was studied at clearly submaximal swimming velocities, and the range of velocities examined does not allow any conclusions of the relation between efficiency and swimming velocity. This study presents one way of studying swimming technique. The method is indirect and has a relatively great methodological error. With a larger sample of swimmers and further development of the method, it will be possible to draw more general conclusions on man's efficiency in swimming.

ACKNOWLEDGMENTS

The author is indebted to Stenberg-Flygt AB, Solna, for providing the swimming flume. The study was supported by Grant 73:13 from the Research Council of the Swedish Sports Federation.

REFERENCES

Adrian, M. J., M. Singh, and P. V. Karpovich. 1966. Energy cost of leg kick, arm stroke, and whole crawl stroke. J. Appl. Physiol. 21: 1763–1766.

Åstrand, P.-O. and S. Englesson. 1972. A swimming flume. J. Appl. Physiol. 33: 514.

Holmér, I. 1972. Oxygen uptake during swimming in man. J. Appl. Physiol. 33: 502–509.

Karpovich, P. V. and K. Pestrecov. 1939. Mechanical work and efficiency of swimming crawl and backstrokes. Arbeitsphysiol. 10: 504–514.

Kent, M. R. and J. Atha. 1971. Selected critical transient body positions in breaststroke and their influence upon water resistance. *In:* L. Lewillie and J. P. Clarys (eds.), First International Symposium on Biomechanics in Swimming, pp. 119–125. Université Libre de Bruxelles, Brussels.

Klissouras, V. 1968. Energy metabolism in swimming the dolphin stroke. Int. Z. Angew. Physiol. 25: 142–150.

Magel, J. R. 1970. Propelling force measured during tethered swimming in the four competitive swimming styles. Res. Quart. 41: 68–74.

di Prampero, P. E., D. R. Pendergast, D. W. Wilson, and D. W. Rennie. 1974. Energetics of swimming man. J. Appl. Physiol. 37: 1–5.

Seireg, A. and A. Baz. 1971. A mathematical model for swimming mechanics. *In:* L. Lewillie and J. P. Clarys (eds.), First International Symposium on Biomechanics in Swimming, pp. 81–103. Université Libre de Bruxelles, Brussels.

Maximal oxygen uptake rate during swimming and bicycling

N. H. Secher and I. Oddershede

The biomechanics of humans while swimming is unique in one aspect. Most locomotory performances, *e.g.*, walking, running or bicycling, are established by means of leg movements; however, the arms are the most important factor in front crawl swimming. This fact was reported by Magel (1970) and is also demonstrated in this study (Figure 1).

The dominance of arm performance in front crawl swimming has profound consequences for the physiology of swimming and the evaluation of physiological parameters of swimmers (Secher *et al.*, 1974). The present investigation was carried out in order to determine the influence of arm fitness on maximal oxygen uptake during swimming.

METHODS

Ten healthy young male subjects were chosen so that marked interindividual differences with regard to swimming experience were represented.

Swimming was performed in a swimming flume as described by Åstrand and Englesson (1972). Selected arm and leg strokes were performed as in front crawl swimming. This swimming style was also used for comparisons with determinations of $\dot{V}_{O_2 max}$ made during cycling. $\dot{V}_{O_2 max}$ was determined after a 10-min warm-up period. The subjects then performed six to seven 30-sec bursts at maximal speed (or load) interspersed with 10-sec rest intervals. Gas analyses were performed as described in Secher *et al.* (1974). Maximal swimming speed (m per sec) and power (kpm per min) were calculated as the average of the values obtained during the six to seven bursts of exercise. In contrast, metabolic parameters represented the period of maximal oxygen uptake.

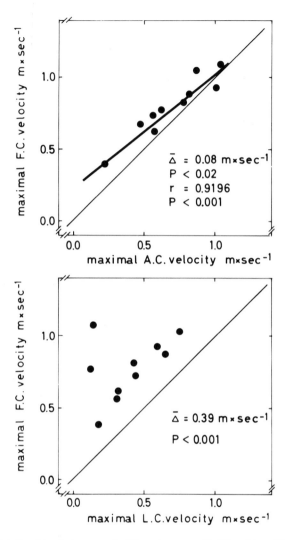

Figure 1. Relationships between velocities using arms (*A.C.*) and legs (*L.C.*) alone and front crawl velocity (*F.C.*).

RESULTS AND DISCUSSION

The type of subjects selected was reflected in the calculated $\dot{V}_{O_2 \, max}$ values: four of the five trained swimmers had higher $\dot{V}_{O_2 \, max}$ during swimming than when bicycling (Figure 2). The best trained swimmer had the highest $\dot{V}_{O_2 \, max}$ value during the leg crawl. In contrast to this the five recreational swimmers had their highest $\dot{V}_{O_2 \, max}$ values during bicycling.

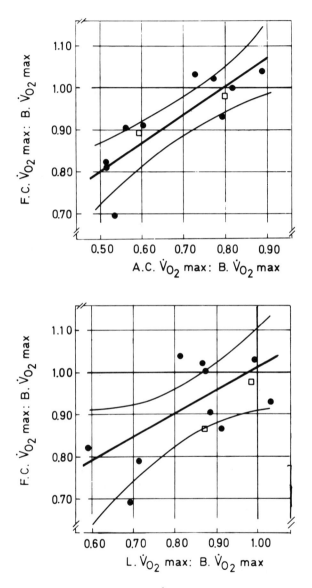

Figure 2. Relationships between ratios of $\dot{V}_{O_2\,max}$ during swimming and bicycling *Upper,* $\dot{V}_{O_2\,max}$ front crawl/bicycling vs. $\dot{V}_{O_2\,max}$ arm stroke/bicycling. *Lower,* $\dot{V}_{O_2\,max}$ front crawl/bicycling vs. $\dot{V}_{O_2\,max}$ leg stroke/bicycling.

Table 1. Maximal oxygen uptake rate during swimming and cycling or running in subjects trained for swimming (T) and recreational swimmers (UT)

	Type of leg exercise	Sex	N	$\dot{V}_{O_2max}$ STPD		Swimming $\dot{V}_{O_2max}$ (% of leg $\dot{V}_{O_2max}$)	
				Swimming	Leg work	T	UT
Åstrand et al. (1963)	Cycling	fm	22			92.5	
Åstrand and Saltin (1961)	Cycling	m	6	3.79	4.36		86.5
Dixon and Faulkner (1971)	Running	m	6	4.05	4.26	95	
Foglia et al. (1973)	Running	m	15		4.05	93	
		m	15	3.48	4.12		84.6
Holmér (1972)	Running	m	9	3.82	4.19	89.0	
		fm	12	2.96	3.17	93.4	
Holmér and Åstrand (1972)	Cycling	fm	1	3.36	3.44	97.5	
		fm	1	2.71	3.13		86.5
Magel and Faulkner (1967)	Running	m	17	3.83	3.32	115	
Secher and Oddershede (present study)	Cycling	m	5	3.24	3.50	92.5	
		m	5	3.59	4.08		87.9

The results of the comparisons of maximal oxygen consumptions during swimming and either cycling or running seem typical. In Table 1 the literature has been summarized. It appears that subjects trained for swimming have oxygen consumptions during swimming of more than 89 percent of their running or cycling $\dot{V}_{O_2 max}$. Recreational swimmers, however, show values during swimming of less than 88 percent of their maximal oxygen uptake during running or cycling.

The influence of selected arm and leg conditioning exercises associated with training for swimming on the ratio $\dot{V}_{O_2 max}$ swimming/bicycling is demonstrated in Figure 2. The relative arm fitness was positively correlated to relative swimming fitness ($r = 0.85, p < 0.005$) as was the relative leg fitness ($r = 0.64, p < 0.02$).

Although swimming $\dot{V}_{O_2\,max}$ was correlated to leg ($r = 0.74, p < 0.05$) rather than to arm $\dot{V}_{O_2\,max}$ ($r = 0.55, p > 0.05$), the more sensitive relative values do stress the importance of arm fitness for swimming performance.

It is of special interest that the maximal oxygen consumptions of the very best swimmers are rather low, less than 4 liters per min; however, their swimming oxygen consumption was 15% above their running $\dot{V}_{O_2\,max}$ (Magel and Faulkner, 1967). A similar value was noted for two Danish subjects, during arm cranking compared with cycling (Secher *et al.*, 1974).

It has been claimed previously that $\dot{V}_{O_2\,max}$ is statistically unchanged when arm work is added to bicycling work (Åstrand and Saltin, 1961; Secher *et al.*, 1974; Stenberg *et al.*, 1967). However, $\dot{V}_{O_2\,max}$ is increased when arm

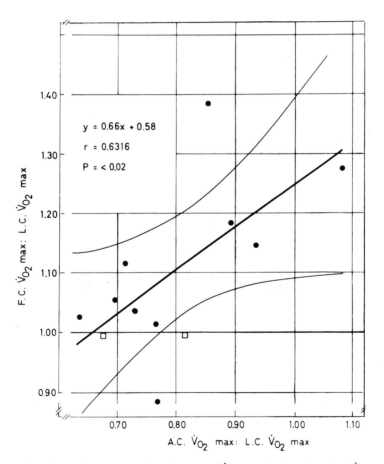

Figure 3. Relationship between selected ratios of $\dot{V}_{O_2\,max}$ during swimming. ($\dot{V}_{O_2\,max}$ front crawl/leg stroke vs. $\dot{V}_{O_2\,max}$ arm stroke/leg stroke.)

work is added to isolated leg exercise, in proportion to the subjects' fitness for arm cranking (Secher *et al.,* 1974). The last result was confirmed in the present study as shown in Figure 3. Although these results do not profoundly challenge the "heart limitation theory" for $\dot{V}_{O_2 \, max}$, they indicate that both heart and local muscle factors are contributing to the limitation.

ACKNOWLEDGMENT

This study was supported in part by Idrættens Forskningsråd.

REFERENCES

Åstrand, P.-O. and S. Englesson. 1972. A swimming flume. J. Appl. Physiol. 33: 514.

Åstrand, P.-O., L. Engstrøm, B. Erickson, P. Karlberg, I. Nylander, B. Saltin, and C. Thoren. 1963. Girl swimmers—with special reference to respiratory and circulatory adoption and gynaecological and psychiatric aspects. Acta Paediat. Supp. 147.

Åstrand, P.-O. and B. Saltin. 1961. Maximal oxygen uptake and heart rate in various types of muscular activity. J. Appl. Physiol. 16: 977–981.

Dixon, R. W., Jr. and J. A. Faulkner. 1971. Cardiac output during maximum effort running and swimming. J. Appl. Physiol. 30: 653–656.

Foglia, G. F., J. R. Magel, B. Gatin, and W. D. McArdle. 1973. Effects of training in swimming on maximum oxygen uptake (abstract). Med. Sci. Sports 5: 61.

Holmér, I. 1972. Oxygen uptake during swimming in man. J. Appl. Physiol. 33: 502–509.

Holmér, I. and P.-O. Åstrand. 1972. Swimming training and maximal oxygen uptake. J. Appl. Physiol. 33: 510–513.

Magel, J. R. 1970. Propelling force measured during tethered swimming in the four competitive swimming styles. Res. Quart. 41: 68–74.

Magel, J. R. and J. A. Faulkner. 1967. Maximum oxygen uptake of college swimmers. J. Appl. Physiol. 22: 929–933.

Secher, N. H., N. Ruberg-Larsen, R. A. Binkhorst, and F. Bonde-Petersen. 1974. Maximal oxygen uptake during arm cranking and during combined arm plus leg exercise. J. Appl. Physiol. 36: 515–519.

Stenberg, I., P.-O. Åstrand, B. Ekblom, I. Royce, and B. Saltin. 1967. Hemodynamic response to work with different muscle groups, sitting and supine. J. Appl. Physiol. 22: 61–70.

Analysis of swimming techniques

A model for upper extremity forces during the underwater phase of the front crawl

R. K. Jensen and B. Blanksby

The research of Ringer and Adrian (1969) showed that elbow flexion and extension occur during the underwater phase of front crawl swimming. The thrust from the upper extremity action was estimated by Seireg and Baz (1971), but their model did not allow for the relative motion of the segments of the upper extremity. Gallenstein and Huston (1973) used Hanavan's human body model (1964) to analyze a number of swimming actions, but did not investigate the upper extremity movements for the front crawl stroke. The purpose of the present study was to develop equations of motion for a model of the upper extremity during the underwater phase of front crawl swimming and to use these equations to demonstrate the effect of elbow flexion and extension on the forces acting on the upper extremity segments.

SYSTEM

The upper arm (segment 1) and forearm (segment 2) were each considered to be a frustrum of a right circular cone (Hanavan, 1964). The hand (segment 3) was modeled on a circular plate with dimensions which allowed for hand length, breadth, and depth, and for the relaxation of the hand during the swimming action. Standard formulas were used to calculate the volume (V_i), radius from the proximal axis to the centroid (r_i), and mass moment of inertia $(\bar{I}_i)$. Segmental buoyancy (B_i), mass (m_i), and weight (W_i) were calculated from the volume and the relevant density (Dempster, 1955). The segments were considered to be rigid bodies and connected by pins.

145

SEGMENT KINEMATICS

It was assumed that the motion of the system was restricted to a single plane. Displacements, velocities, and accelerations for the proximal and distal ends and for the centroid of each segment were expressed in terms of an $X - Y$ inertial reference frame. The coordinates for the distal axis in relation to the proximal axis for segment i are given by (see Figure 1):

$$x_{i+1} = x_i + s_i \cos \theta_i \tag{1}$$

$$y_{i+1} = y_i + s_i \sin \theta_i \tag{2}$$

where s_i is the segment length. Differentiating with respect to time yields velocity

$$\dot{x}_{i+1} = \dot{x}_i - s_i \sin \theta_i \dot{\theta}_i \tag{3}$$

$$\dot{y}_{i+1} = \dot{y}_i + s_i \cos \theta_i \dot{\theta}_i . \tag{4}$$

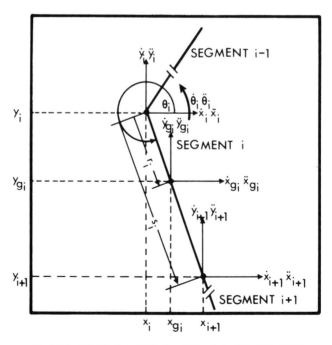

Figure 1. Kinematics of the three-segment upper extremity.

Differentiating a second time provides acceleration

$$\ddot{x}_{i+1} = \ddot{x}_i - s_i\cos\theta_i\dot{\theta}_i^2 - s_i\sin\theta_i\ddot{\theta}_i \tag{5}$$

$$\ddot{y}_{i+1} = \ddot{y}_i - s_i\sin\theta_i\dot{\theta}_i{}^2 + s_i\cos\theta_i\ddot{\theta}_i . \tag{6}$$

In similar fashion, the equations for the coordinates of the centroid,

$$x_{gi} = x_i + r_i\cos\theta_i \tag{7}$$

$$y_{gi} = y_i + r_i\sin\theta_i \tag{8}$$

can be differentiated to obtain velocity and acceleration. Velocity normal to the segment axis and through the centroid is given by

$$v_{ni} = \dot{y}_{gi}\cos\theta_i - \dot{x}_{gi}\sin\theta_i . \tag{9}$$

SEGMENT KINETICS

Free body diagrams of the three segments while underwater are presented in Figure 2. The forces acting on each segment are weight, buoyancy, drag, muscle forces, and joint reaction forces. Other forces are regarded as negligible. In accordance with Dillman (1971), the muscle forces can be idealized as a single resultant and replaced by an equivalent force and couple at the joint axis. Equations can then be written for the resultant force components at the joint and the moment of force about the joint.

The x component of the resultant is given by

$$R_{xi} = m_i\ddot{x}_{gi} + D_i\sin\theta_i + R_{x(i+1)} \tag{10}$$

and the y component by

$$R_{yi} = m_i\ddot{y}_{gi} - D_i\cos\theta_i - B_i + W_i + R_{y(i+1)} . \tag{11}$$

The moment about the proximal axis is given by

$$M_i = \bar{I}_i\ddot{\theta}_i + m_i\ddot{y}_{gi}r_i\cos\theta_i - m_i\ddot{x}_{gi}r_i\sin\theta_i - D_ir_i - B_ir_i\cos\theta_i + W_ir_i\cos\theta_i$$

$$+ M_{(i+1)} - R_{x(i+1)}s_i\sin\theta_i + R_{y(i+1)}s_i\cos\theta_i \tag{12}$$

where $R_{x(i+1)}$ and $R_{y(i+1)}$ are the resultant force components and $M_{(i+1)}$ is the moment for the $(i+1)$ segment. These terms are zero in the case of the nth segment.

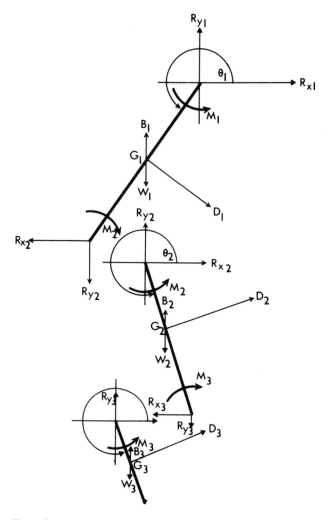

Figure 2. Free body diagrams of the arm segments while under water.

Drag forces normal to the segment axis and through the centroid have been estimated by Gallenstein and Huston (1973). In order to use drag coefficient curves (Hoerner, 1958), the hand was modeled on a flat circular plate, and the remaining segments were considered mean diameter cylinders. Drag, based on the normal velocity, is given by

$$D_i = \tfrac{1}{2} C_D A_i \rho v_{ni}^2 \qquad (13)$$

where C_D is the drag coefficient and A_i is the frontal area of the segment.

ANALYSIS OF MOTION

A program based on the above equations was written in the FORTRAN $\overline{\text{IV}}$ G language. Body segment measures were taken on an 11-year-old swimmer in accordance with Hanavan (1964) and the kinematic equations were based on the mean velocity over 40 m($\overline{V}_{xi}$) and the estimated period (τ) for the upper extremity cycle. A set of sinusoidal curves was used to describe the motion. The horizontal velocity of the shoulder axis was given by

$$\dot{x}_1 = \overline{V}_{x1} + \Delta V_{x1} \cos \left(\frac{2\pi t}{\tau}\right) \tag{14}$$

where t is time. The equation was integrated to yield displacement and differentiated to obtain acceleration. The change in velocity (ΔV_{x1}) was estimated from the experimental results of Miyashita (1971). Vertical displacement was assumed to be zero. Upper arm angular displacement was given by

$$\theta_1 = \overline{\theta}_1 - \Delta\theta_1 \sin \left(\frac{2\pi t}{\tau} + \frac{3\pi}{4}\right) \tag{15}$$

where $\overline{\theta}_1$ and $\Delta\theta_1$ are the mean displacement and the change in displacement for the segment, respectively. The underwater movement of the segment was considered to be 2π radians. The angular displacement of the forearm in relation to the upper arm was

$$\theta_2' = \overline{\theta}_2 + \Delta\theta_2 \sin 4\pi \frac{t}{\tau} \tag{16}$$

and was added to θ_1 to give the angular displacement, θ_2. The curve was based on the experimental evidence of Ringer and Adrian (1969). First and second order derivatives of Equations 15 and 16 are the angular velocity and acceleration. The relative motion between the forearm and hand was considered to be zero.

RESULTS AND DISCUSSION

The movement of the upper extremity generated by the equations of motion is presented in Figure 3, and the drag forces for the three segments are graphed in Figure 4. It is evident that the drag forces about the upper arm are comparatively small. The size of the drag force for the hand as compared to the forearm is readily apparent. The importance of these observations can be seen from Figure 5. Most of the horizontal force was developed at the wrist

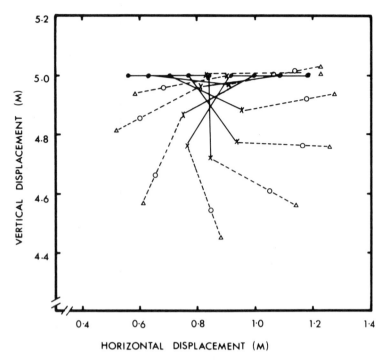

Figure 3. Underwater motion of the arm as generated by equations of motion.

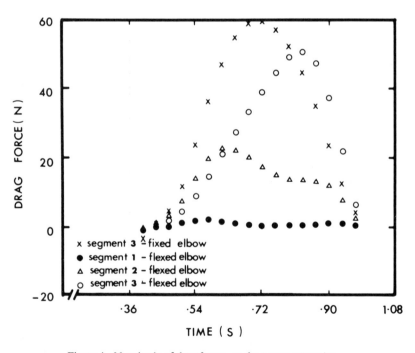

Figure 4. Magnitude of drag forces on the upper extremity.

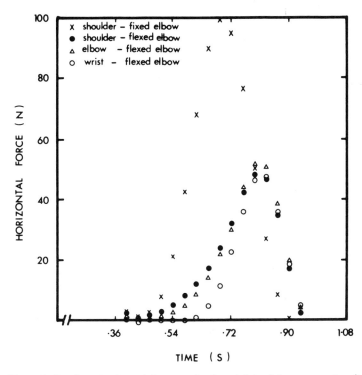

Figure 5. Resultant horizontal forces at the three joints of the upper extremity.

with a limited upper arm contribution during the initial phase of the action. The moments of force produced by action of the upper extremity (Figure 6) were similar in magnitude to the experimentally obtained moments of Jensen and Bellow (1974). The moment for the wrist fixed the hand in relation to the forearm, and the moment for the elbow produced the rotation for the forearm and hand. The curve of the moment for the shoulder featured a second step due to the elbow extension action.

Figures 3 to 6 can also be used to compare the forces for the fixed elbow angle with the flexed elbow stroke. It is evident that flexing the elbow had the effect of skewing the curves from a symmetrical position. The reaction force components and the moments about the joints were less, indicating that smaller muscle forces would be needed with the flexed arm stroke, and thus the swimming efficiency would be increased.

SUMMARY

A three-segment model of the upper extremity during the underwater phase of front crawl swimming was developed and used to calculate reaction force

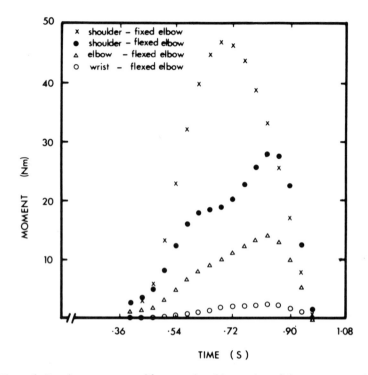

Figure 6. Resultant moments of force produced by motion of the upper extremity.

components and moments. These results demonstrated the relative contributions of the segments to propulsion and were used to compare a fixed elbow stroke with the flexed elbow stroke.

REFERENCES

Dempster, W. T. 1955. Space requirements of the seated operator (WADC-TR-55-159,USAF). Wright Patterson AFB, Dayton.

Dillman, C. J. 1971. A kinetic analysis of the recovery leg during sprint running. In: J. M. Cooper (ed.), Selected Topics on Biomechanics. The Athletic Institute, Chicago.

Gallenstein, J. and R. L. Huston. 1973. Analysis of swimming motions, Hum. Factors 15: No. 1. 91–98.

Hanavan, E. P. 1964. A mathematical model of the human body (AMRL-TR-64-102,USAF). Wright Patterson AFB, Dayton.

Hoerner, S. F. 1958. Fluid Dynamic Drag. Hoerner, New Jersey.

Jensen, R. K. and Bellow, D. G. 1974. Impulse and work output curves for swimmers. In: R. C. Nelson and C. A. Morehouse (eds.), Biomechanics IV, International Series in Sport Sciences, Vol. 1, pp. 197–202. University Park Press, Baltimore.

Miyashita, M. 1971. An analysis of fluctuations of swimming speed. *In:* L. Lewillie and J. P. Clarys (eds.), First International Symposium on Biomechanics in Swimming, pp. 53–58. Université Libre de Bruxelles, Brussels.

Ringer, L. B. and M. J. Adrian. 1969. An electrogoniometric study of the wrist and elbow in the crawl arm stroke. Res. Quart. 40: 353–363.

Seireg, A. and A. Baz. 1971. A mathematical model for swimming mechanics. *In:* L. Lewillie and J. P. Clarys (eds.), First International Symposium on Biomechanics in Swimming, pp. 81–104. Université Libre de Bruxelles, Brussels.

Three-dimensional spatial hand patterns of skilled butterfly swimmers

K. M. Barthels and M. J. Adrian

Underwater observations of the motion of the hands during the butterfly arm stroke have led to the hypothesis that both hydrodynamic lift and drag forces created by the hands are involved in the propulsion of the body (Barthels, 1974; Brown and Counsilman, 1970; Counsilman, 1971). There are few objective scientific data, however, to support this hypothesis.

PURPOSE

The purpose of the investigation was to identify the three-dimensional underwater motion of the hand with respect to still water during the performance of the butterfly stroke, with and without the kick, and to relate this hand motion to the horizontal motion of the swimmer's body.

PROCEDURES

Simultaneous front and side view motion pictures were taken of three male and three female intercollegiate swimmers skilled in the butterfly stroke. Each subject swam two trials without the kick and two trials with the kick.

The films of two battery-powered 16-mm cameras were synchronized with respect to time by means of an underwater light bulb flashed at specified intervals. Each camera was set to provide a film transport speed of approximately 44 frames per sec. A timing light unit on the side view camera was used to determine exact speeds.

An L & W stop-action motion analyzer and computerized graphic tablet system, described by Owen and Adrian (1974), were utilized for the film analysis. The distal end of the middle finger of the right hand in both the front and side views was used to represent the hand, and a point on the right hip on the side view film was used to represent the body in its sagittal plane of motion. Point displacement data were taken from the films and used with computer programs (Barthels, 1974) to provide output of frame-by-frame displacement and velocity values for the right hand in the x, y, and z directions and for the hip in the x and y directions. Forward and backward motion was represented on the x-axis; upward and downward motion, on the y-axis; and lateral motion, on the z-axis. Graphic output was obtained from a Calcomp plotter. The spatial displacement patterns of the right hand as viewed from the front, side, and top of the swimmer were reproduced from the plotter output for inclusion in this report.

RESULTS AND DISCUSSION

Figure 1 presents the patterns observed from each view for the three female subjects, D, C, and L, performing with and without the kick. Figure 2 shows the patterns of the three male subjects, J, T, and B. These illustrations show that the subjects displayed similar patterns, specific to the view (common pattern), although each subject exhibited his (her) own path characteristics ("signature"). The signature of each subject shown for each of the three views (front, side, and top) when the kick was used had the same characteristics as did the corresponding signature during the no-kick stroke. No differences were observed which could be identified as being characteristic of male or female patterns.

To provide more descriptive information about the hand motion, the underwater stroke was divided into four phases: 1) the reach (forward movement of the hand following entry), 2) the outsweep (outward movement at the beginning of the stroke), 3) the insweep (inward movement following the outsweep), and 4) the push (backward movement following the insweep). Because the motion of the hand always occurred in more than one direction within each phase, further subdivision was required to more accurately describe the three-dimensional course of the hand through the water. Directional displacement paths were defined according to the x, y, and z directions: motion in the x direction was denoted by F (forward) or B (backward); in the y direction, by D (downward) or U (upward); and in the z direction, by O (outward from the midsagittal plane of the swimmer) or I (inward toward the midsagittal plane). For example, the directional path of the hand traveling backward, downward, and inward during the insweep phase was denoted by BDI.

From an inspection of the films, the orientation of the palmar surface of the hand relative to the water was observed and related to the directional

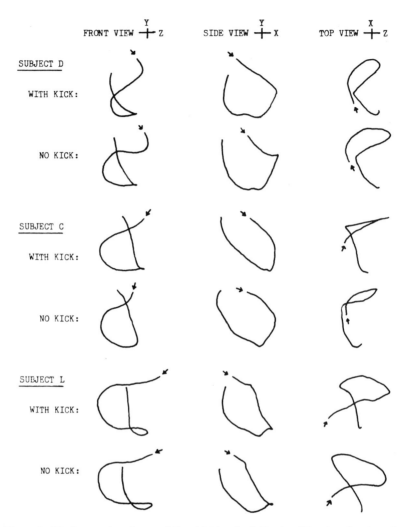

Figure 1. Displacement patterns of the right hand relative to still water, female swimmers. *Arrow* indicates entry into water; *line* shows path of hand.

path of the hand. Measurement of the actual angle of attack of the palmar surface to the direction of flow past the hand could not be obtained from the films. It was observed that the leading edge of the hand, relative to flow, changed as the hand changed direction. The movements of the hand were such that the palmar surface was encountering the flow at some angle other than the perpendicular during the entire stroke. The smallest angle of attack appeared to be present during the FDO path in the outsweep and the BDI or BUI path in the insweep phase. The angle of attack in the BUO path appeared

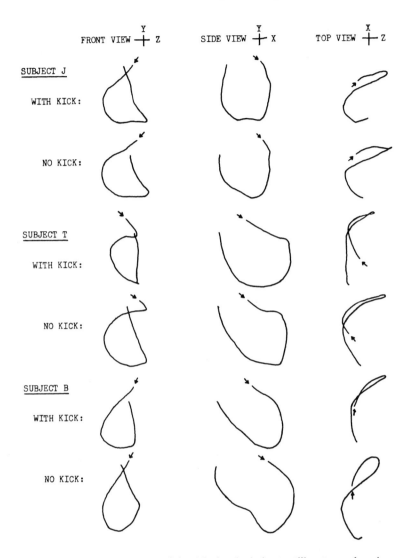

FRONT VIEW $\stackrel{Y}{+}$ Z   SIDE VIEW $\stackrel{Y}{+}$ X   TOP VIEW $\stackrel{X}{+}$ Z

SUBJECT J

WITH KICK:

NO KICK:

SUBJECT T

WITH KICK:

NO KICK:

SUBJECT B

WITH KICK:

NO KICK:

Figure 2. Displacement patterns of the right hand relative to still water, male swimmers. *Arrow* indicates entry into water; *line* shows path of hand.

initially to be almost normal to the flow, but it decreased progressively as the hand moved through this path and was small by the time the hand was being withdrawn from the water.

To determine the propulsive role of the observed hand movements, average horizontal body acceleration was determined for the time period corresponding to each directional hand path during the stroke without the kick. Table 1 presents the directional paths and corresponding body accelera-

Table 1. Average hip acceleration within each path and during the arm recovery phase (m per sec²)

Subject	Trial	Reach FDI	Outsweep FDO	Outsweep BDO	Insweep FDI	Insweep BDI	Insweep BUI	Push BDO	Push BUO	Arm recovery phase
Females										
D	1	-3.59*	0.06*	0.66		1.48			0.25	-1.34
	2	-7.30*	0.48*	0.00		1.53			0.59	-1.39
C	1		0.76*			0.51	2.02		1.18	-1.94
	2		0.46*	2.32		1.06	0.83		1.28	-2.27
L	1		0.14*		-0.40	4.85		-0.58	1.91*	-2.10
	2		-0.13*		-0.53	2.29		1.95	0.56*	-1.48
Means		-5.45	-0.30	1.00	-0.47	1.96	1.42	0.69	0.97	-1.75
Males										
J	1		0.15*			5.16	-0.24		-2.51	-0.84
	2		-0.60*	-1.53		4.29	-2.93		-0.61	-1.25
T	1	5.45*	0.88*	-3.35		0.77	3.32		-0.16	-2.80
	2	0.84*	1.77*	-1.26		1.51	1.67		1.84	-1.95
B	2		1.66*	1.07*		3.60	1.72		1.14	-2.53
Means		3.14	0.77	-1.27		3.07	0.71		-0.06	-1.87
All Subjects										
Means		-2.30	0.51	-0.30	-0.47	2.47	0.91	0.69	0.50	-1.80

*Downbeat of legs was observed in part or all of the path and acceleration was not related to hand motion.

tions for all trials. Component hand velocities in the x, y, and z directions also were determined for each directional path and, with consideration being given to the pitch of the hand relative to flow, were related to the body acceleration which occurred. High hand velocity in the z direction, transverse to the direction of body travel, was characteristic of the outsweep and insweep phases of the arm stroke while high backward and upward hand velocities characterized the push phase of the stroke. The greatest average body accelerations occurred during the insweep phase (BDI or BUI paths) for all trials except trial 2 of subjects C and T. The large body accelerations during the insweep were attributed to lift forces produced by the hand which was in the most favorable position to create thrust in the direction of body travel. The small or negative body accelerations in the outsweep phases, which occurred in spite of the high lateral hand velocities, were attributed to the unfavorable orientation of the hand with respect to direction of body travel; *i.e.*, the palmar surface was directed more toward the bottom of the pool than it was directed backward. As Table 1 indicates, appreciable body accelerations occurred during the push phase of the stroke in some trials. The results of analysis indicated that during the initial part of the BUO path the backward hand velocity was the greatest and the hand position during this time was such that the flow was almost normal to the palmar surface. These conditions suggested that the hand produced a drag force for body acceleration. Toward the end of the BUO path, however, as the flow direction became more oblique to the palmar surface, the upward, and in some cases the outward, hand velocity increased and the backward component decreased. These changing hand velocity components and the changing angle of attack of the hand suggested that the final portion of the BUO path contributed more life than drag force.

Horizontal body velocity during the times in which body acceleration occurs is an important factor involved in the amount of resistance to be overcome. Average body velocity in the early portion of the underwater stroke was found to be less than it was at the end of the underwater stroke. Perhaps one reason why the maximal body acceleration occurred during the insweep phase for most subjects was that the body was moving at a relatively low velocity at that time. Thus there was less resistance to acceleration than during the push phase, when the average body velocity was near maximum. Although the lift force of the hand was effective when the body encountered relatively low resistance, the same lift force might not be as effective when the body has a greater velocity and more resistance must be overcome.

SUMMARY AND CONCLUSIONS

The true underwater motion of the hand during the butterfly stroke can be more accurately described when it is analyzed in terms of its three-dimensional characteristics. A common pattern appears in each of the three views for skilled butterfly swimmers, male and female, and individual variations within the common pattern characterize the stroke signature of each swimmer. Interpretation of the hand displacement patterns, observation of the orientation of the hand relative to flow direction, and analysis of corresponding body acceleration data led to the inference that the hand was capable of producing both lift and drag forces useful for horizontal acceleration of the body.

REFERENCES

Barthels, K. M. 1974. Three dimensional kinematic analysis of the hand and hip in the butterfly swimming stroke. Unpublished doctoral dissertation, Washington State University, Pullman.
Brown, R. M. and J. E. Counsilman. 1970. The role of lift in propelling the swimmer. *In:* J. M. Cooper (ed.), Selected Topics on Biomechanics, pp. 179–188. The Athletic Institute, Chicago.
Counsilman, J. E. 1971. The application of Bernoulli's principle to human propulsion in water. *In:* L. Lewillie and J. P. Clarys (eds.), First International Symposium on Biomechanics in Swimming. pp. 59–71. Université Libre de Bruxelles, Brussels.
Owen, M. G. and M. J. Adrian. 1974. Versatile uses of a computerized graphic tablet system. *In:* R. C. Nelson and C. A. Morehouse (eds.), Biomechanics IV. International Series on Sports Sciences, Vol. 1, pp. 491–495. University Park Press, Baltimore.

The division of swimming strokes into phases, based upon kinematic parameters

K. Wiegand, D. Wuensch, and W. Jaehnig

Physical educators, coaches, and athletes should have objective criteria for the determination of the development of swimming strokes, *i.e.,* those factors and basic parameters that establish the structural fundamentals of top class performances. One of the main prerequisites for accomplishing this is, among others, the quantitative assessment of swimming strokes to make them *comparable* with each other. It will be possible to determine the essentials of swimming strokes only by analyzing them quantitatively. Such an approach will lead to an understanding of the laws of swimming techniques including their hydromechanical aspects. The authors believe that the distribution of swimming strokes into phases based upon objective criteria is of major importance.

Several investigators have divided the swimming stroke into phases such as pulling, pushing, supporting, main phase, dipping phase, etc. with a wide variety of applications. Such a procedure is of limited value in scientific investigations because of the difficulties encountered in accurately quantifying the stroke phases.

It seems necessary, therefore, to establish criteria for clear identification of phases so that comparative investigations of swimming strokes can be made. The procedure must provide for comparison of *every* movement in a stroke regardless of the quality of their execution and any interdependence among them. These conditions are satisfied sufficiently by including the comparison of velocity parameters into the distribution criteria, for the motor task of a competitive swimmer is to cover a given distance in the water in the shortest possible time.

A main function of the arm strokes, for example, is to produce propulsion. This development of propulsion can be measured by the horizontal velocity of the hips. An objective system of relationships can thus be established for the distribution of phases by corresponding measurements of the velocity of the hand and hip joint.

PROCEDURE

A 16-mm camera was used in underwater filming for purposes of determining these parameters. The test area is shown in Figure 1. To determine the exact camera speed, a transistorized light spotter was utilized. Points at all of the joints of primary importance of the swimmers were marked.

Male and female swimmers from all the performance categories executing all types of strokes were included in our study. Several trials were made at different swimming velocities. We are quite aware of the limitations of kinematic methods; however, they did not appreciably influence our findings.

Processing of parameters

The film negative was used to measure the real camera speed, while a positive cinegram of the movement was projected on a suitable film analyzer. The average velocities of the wrist joint and hip joint movements were determined

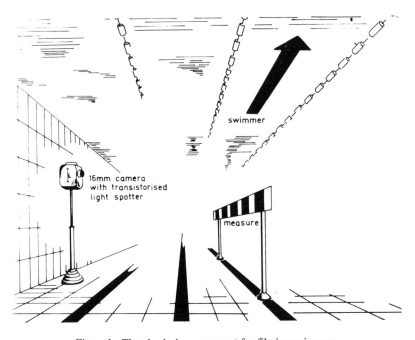

Figure 1. The physical arrangement for filming swimmers.

between two adjacent cinegram spots, respectively. The others were calculated by using the coordinates of all the cinegram spots. In doing so, the direction of movement of the body points was taken into consideration.

It seemed to be useful to find out the relative horizontal velocity $(vx'm)$ of the wrist joint movement in relation to the hip joint spot by subtracting the absolute horizontal hip velocity (vxf).

$$vx'm = vxm - vxf.$$

The parameters vxf and $vx'm$ were the basis for our distribution of phases (see Figure 2).

Distribution of phases

It is suggested that propusion can be created mainly if the swimmer's hand moves faster backwards than his/her trunk. That is the condition for the *propulsive phase,* calculated by

$$|vx'm| \geqslant |-vxf|.$$

Included in this condition is the case, $|vx'm| = |- vxf|$, because our measurement spot for $vx'm$ was marked at the wrist. Thus, the distal parts of the hand move at a velocity greater than that of the wrist joint.

The *introductory phase* occurs before the propulsive phase (related to time), provided

$$|-vxf| > |vx'm| > 0.$$

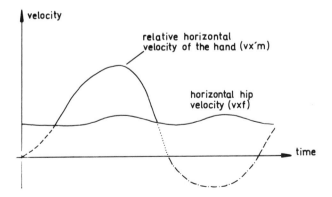

Figure 2. A cinegram of a typical stroke cycle. − −, introductory phase; ——, propulsive phase; · · ·, transitional phase; −·−, preparatory phase.

In this phase the hand moves more slowly backwards than the trunk moves forward. Thus no propulsion can be created in the introductory phase. Nevertheless, that phase is necessary because the hand reaches a horizontal relative velocity of 0 m·sec^{-1} at the front return point of arm stroke cycle. The introductory phase is defined as the time from that point up to the point where the relative horizontal hand velocity equals the swimming velocity.

After the propulsive phase there follows the *transitional phase*. Here the same condition is valid as for the introductory phase. It must exist in any case, too, for it represents the period between $|vx'm| = |- vxf|$ and the rear return point of the arm stroke cycle, when

$$vx'm = 0.$$

The period between the transitional phase and the introductory phase is called the *preparatory phase*. It comprises that period during which the hand moves forward in the direction the swimmer is moving. With the exception of the breaststroke the hand movements are executed during that phase almost exclusively out of the water. Here the following condition is valid

$$vx'm \leqslant 0.$$

During the preparatory phase the hands are moved into the starting position to begin a new stroke cycle (see Figure 2 for description of all four phases).

In our study of the crawl, the dolphin, and the backstroke we could only determine the time of the preparatory phase but not the velocity since only the underwater movements of the swimmers were recorded cinematographically.

FUNCTION OF THE PHASES

A distinct purpose can be attributed to each phase of the swimming cycle. General functions can be identified as well as those specific to the stroke performed. Only the general functions of each phase will be emphasized here.

Introductory phase

During this phase essential preliminary movements for the production of propulsion are created. The effective propulsive segments of the hand and forearm are moved into a favorable position to create propulsion (elbow-front-position); optimal water resistance is sought (catching the water); the application of force and velocity of pulling through are brought to an optimal level in preparation for the propulsive phase which follows.

Propulsive phase

Direct propulsion by the arm stroke is created mainly during this phase. The main function of the phase is to optimize the backward-directed components of distance, velocity, and force. The main strength efforts should be made during this phase, and the greatest horizontal pulling-through-velocity should be achieved.

Transitional phase

This phase immediately precedes the recovery of the arms out of the water. The relative horizontal movement of the arm opposing the propulsive direction comes to an end during this phase.

Preparatory phase

Preparation for the next arm movement is accomplished at this time. This phase provides for recovery of those muscles that have been participating in the work of the previous phases. The arm is moved forward in a relaxed manner while the completion of the movement provides for prestretching of important muscle groups.

RESULTS

Average velocities of the extremities and the over-all swimming performances can be measured for each of the phases as described. Thus the point in the cycle during which the swimming velocities decrease can be identified. Furthermore, the time when maximal velocity occurs within each of the phases can also be found. The time of the cycle as well as stroke frequency can be calculated from the times of single phases. Interesting conclusions can be drawn from changes in phase times and partial velocities that occur with changes in stroke frequencies (see Figure 3). For example, in the case where high hand velocities during the propulsive phase produce no noticeable increase in over-all swimming velocities, it is concluded that either the hand or forearm positions are incorrect and therefore do not produce optimal pressure against the water.

The phases analyzed here pertaining to arm movements can also be applied to the breaststroke kick. However, the kicks of the other three strokes require other criteria for division into phases. The reason for this is that the main direction of the movement lies in the vertical plane and therefore the relative horizontal velocities of the feet do not always reach the value of the swimming velocity.

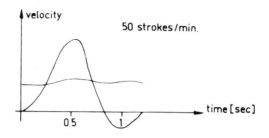

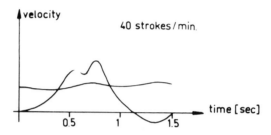

Figure 3. Cinegrams for stroke frequencies of 40 and 50 strokes per min.

CONCLUSION

The division of swimming strokes into clearly defined phases has proved to be a useful method of quantification. The four phases described exist independently of the swimming velocities and the level of swimming performance. Consequently, all four phases can be quantified even with beginners, and teachers and coaches are provided with an effective means to assess the development of the swimming technique provided they know the structure of these phases.

Arm action in the crawl stroke

M. Miyashita

It is generally agreed that the arms provide 70 to 85% of the total thrust in the crawl stroke (Faulkner, 1966; Armbruster, Allen, and Billingsley, 1973). Water resistance is proportional to the square of the velocity according to fluid mechanics. Therefore, the movement velocity of the hand in the water is an important factor in swimming fast. Since the hands are moved alternately in the crawl stroke, the stroke time is related to the movement velocity of the hand.

This study consisted of three experiments. The first concerned the stroke time in the crawl in relation to age and performance (experiment 1). Stroke time is maintained by contraction of the arm and shoulder muscles. Little data have been published on the strength of swimmers, and a definitive study on the strength requirements of swimming has not been made (Faulkner, 1966).

The second experiment involved the relation between arm-pull strength and speed of swimming with arms alone (experiment 2).

Thirdly, the oxygen requirement for swimming 25 m with arms alone was determined for four swimmers with different levels of muscular strength and swimming technique (experiment 3).

PROCEDURES

Experiment 1

The subjects were 10 highly trained swimmers (aged 16 to 24 years), 9 age group swimmers (aged 12 to 14 years), and 10 beginners (aged 7 to 12 years). The number of strokes and lap times for the first 50 m of the official 100-m races were measured for the highly trained and age group swimmers. The same factors were measured for the beginners when they tried to swim 25 m as fast as possible.

The average stroke time (*Pt*), the average distance covered in one stroke (*Pd*), and average swimming speed (*V*) were calculated using the following equations:

$$Pt = \frac{\text{lap time for 25 or 50 m}}{\text{number of strokes}}$$

$$Pd = \frac{25 \text{ or } 50 \text{ m}}{\text{number of strokes}}$$

$$V = \frac{25 \text{ or } 50 \text{ m}}{\text{lap time for 25 or 50 m}} = \frac{Pd}{Pt}$$

Experiment 2

The subjects were 30 highly trained male swimmers (age 18 to 22 years), 35 highly trained female swimmers (aged 14 to 20 years), and 5 male nonswimmers (aged 20 to 24 years). Arm-pull strength with the elbow joint slightly flexed was measured for right and left arms, respectively. Arm-pull strength was obtained with the subjects lying in a prone position on a desk. In addition, the maximal swimming speed with arms alone was measured.

Experiment 3

The male subjects employed were one highly trained sprint swimmer (20 years old), one highly trained long distance swimmer (19 years old), and two poor swimmers (20 years old). They were asked to swim 25 m with arms alone, as fast as possible without breathing. The highly trained swimmers were tested twice, but the poor swimmers were tested only once. The number of strokes during swimming and the times were measured, and the expired gas was collected for 45 min immediately after swimming. The oxygen requirement for swimming 25 m was determined.

RESULTS

Experiment 1

The results of the first experiment are illustrated in Figure 1. In the case of the highly trained and age group swimmers, there is a positive relationship between swimming speed (*V*) and age. The increase in speed depends mainly

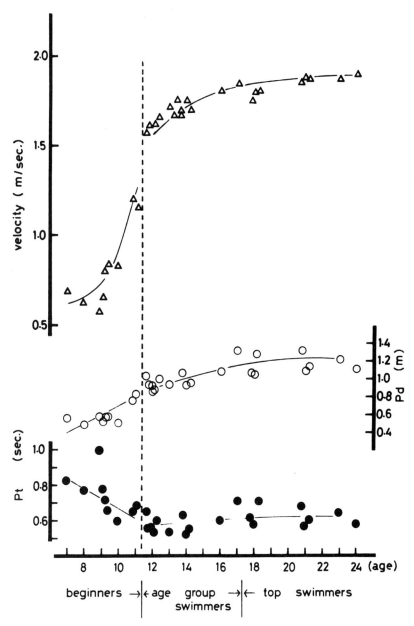

Figure 1. Swimming speed, distance covered in one stroke (*Pd*), and stroke rate (*Pt*) in relation to age. △, swimming velocity (*V*); ○, stroke distance (*Pd*); ●, stroke rate (*Pt*).

on the increase in the distance covered during each stroke (*Pd*). Therefore, the stroke time (*Pt*) remained almost constant (603 ± 55 msec) over a large age range (from 12 to 24 years). In the case of beginners, both factors (the distance covered per stroke and the time per stroke) had an effect on the increase in swimming speed. These results suggest that the temporal pattern (rhythm) in swimming is obtained in the earlier stages of swimming practice.

Experiment 2

The results for experiment 2 are shown in Figure 2. There was a high positive correlation between arm-pull strength and swimming speed with arms alone among both male and female highly trained swimmers. It is apparent, however, that nonswimmers cannot swim fast even though they possess adequate arm strength.

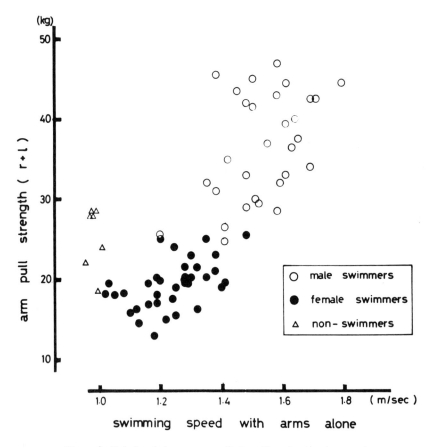

Figure 2. Relation between arm-pull strength and swimming speed.

Experiment 3

The results of the third experiment are shown in Table 1. The energy requirement per stroke tended to increase in proportion to the swimming speed. Comparing the sprint swimmer and the long distance swimmer, the former had a greater muscular strength, consumed more calories, and swam faster. But the long distance swimmer consumed more calories and swam faster than the poor swimmer, though both had similar muscular strength. Therefore, it can be said that the poor swimmer uses his strength less efficiently in water, while muscular strength becomes a decisive factor for swimming fast among highly trained swimmers.

DISCUSSION

Since swimming is an ontogenic type of human movement, no individual can swim without some practice. Consequently, well trained age group swimmers can usually swim faster than typical adults. Also some of the world's top female swimmers can swim faster than the majority of trained male swimmers. These facts suggest that swimming technique can be a decisive factor in fast swimming. On the other hand, Astrand et al. (1963) and Miyashita, Hayashi, and Furuhashi (1970) have already pointed out that there is a significant correlation between aerobic work capacity and swimming performance among the trained swimmers. Taking those phenomena into consideration, the author hypothesizes that, in general, swimming performance (speed) is equal to the products of technique in swimming and physical resources. Therefore, each hyperbolic curve shows the same performance (or speed) as is shown in Figure 3.

Table 1. Swimming performance and physical response to swimming 25 m without breathing

		Mean swimming speed (m/sec)	Number of strokes (strokes/25 m)	Calories per stroke (cal)	Arm-pull strength (kg)
Sprint	I	1.86	23	0.99	r.25.5
swimmer	II	1.85	24	1.01	1.25.0
Long distance	I	1.72	26	0.88	r.17.0
swimmer	II	1.68	25	0.85	1.17.0
Poor swimmer A		1.37	34	0.77	r.18.0
					1.17.5
Poor swimmer B		1.49	34	0.70	r.16.0
					1.15.5

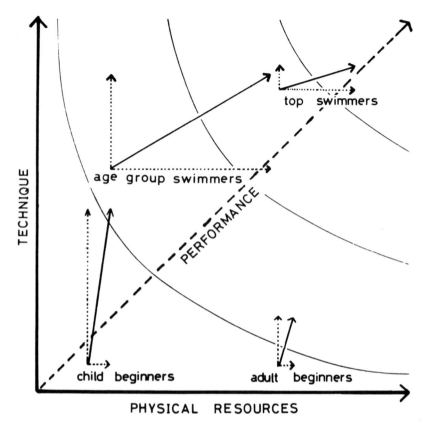

Figure 3. Hypothetical relationship among performance, technique, and physical resources in swimming.

Muscular strength of the arms can be representative of physical resources in the case of swimming 25 or 50 m with the arms alone. Therefore, the results obtained in this study (experiment 2) show a high positive correlation between swimming speed and muscular strength. However, adult nonswimmers do not fit this relationship. The correlation between swimming performance and physical resources (muscular strength) becomes significant, if the subjects have similar swimming techniques. This fact is supported by the results obtained in experiment 3, whereby a clear difference in the swimming speeds of highly trained long distance swimmers and poor swimmers was observed even though they had the same muscular strength. Therefore, an adult person who wants to learn swimming improves his performance mainly through the improvement of technique in swimming. However, it may be difficult for adults to acquire efficient technique without having had swimming experience in childhood.

On the other hand, young people (under 10 years of age), are able to swim at a certain speed as a result of their great improvement in swimming technique despite their relatively limited physical resources. This hypothesis may be supported by the results obtained in experiment 1, namely, that young beginners improve their swimming performance by rapid acquisition of the temporal pattern of arm action.

As for the age group swimmers (teenagers), their swimming performance is greatly improved year by year with swimming practice in addition to natural growth and development as shown in Figure 3. To the contrary, the swimming performance of the top adult swimmers is dependent only on the improvement of their physical resources through hard training such as weight training, interval training, etc. This supports the fact that there is a significant correlation between swimming performance and muscular strength (experiment 2) and/or maximal oxygen intake (Astrand *et al.*, 1963; Miyashita *et al.*, 1970).

REFERENCES

Armbruster, D. A., R. H. Allen, and H. S. Billingsley. 1973. Swimming and Diving, p. 53. The C. V. Mosby Company, Saint Louis.

Astrand, P. O., *et al.* 1963. Girl swimmers with special reference to respiratory and circulatory adaptation and gynaecological and psychiatric aspects. Acta. Paediat. Suppl. p. 147.

Faulkner, J. A. 1966. Physiology of swimming. Res. Quart. 37: 41–54.

Miyashita, M., Y. Hayashi, and H. Furuhashi. 1970. Maximum oxygen intake of Japanese top swimmers. J. Sports Med. Phys. Fitness 10: 211–216.

An analysis of arm propulsion in swimming

G. W. Rackham

Observation of the current methods of arm propulsion in the front crawl, back crawl, and butterfly strokes shows quite clearly a factor common to all strokes; *i.e.*, during the pulling phase, the hand deviates from a straight line track (when viewed from above).

The purpose of this investigation was to observe this arm pull deviation from a straight line and to decide a) why it occurs, b) whether or not any advantage is obtained from its use, c) if it is advantageous, what mechanical principles are involved, and d) what influences if any could it have on training methods?

PAST BELIEFS

When swimming front crawl, it was the accepted practice in the past to pull the hand through the water in a straight line parallel with the line of progression. This straight pulling technique was taught to swimmers at all levels and was generally accepted as the obvious and most efficient method of propulsion. It was often said that, "the shortest distance between two points is a straight line and any deviation from this line results in inefficiency." The term "feathering" was given to any hand pull that departed from the so-called normal straight line limb track.

For many years feathering in front crawl was considered a common fault and was thought to be due to weakness of the arm and shoulder muscles. It was likened to a falling leaf slipping sideways through the air in alternate directions taking the easiest path to the ground.

Corrections for feathering

Swimmers guilty of feathering were often advised to shorten the lever by bending the arm at the elbow so that less strength was needed. In some cases opening the fingers was advised to reduce the effective resistance of the "paddle," and in some instances the swimmer was advised to pull slower to lessen the resistance at the hand. It was assumed that, as the swimmer gained in strength, the arm could be straightened and/or the fingers closed or the stroke rate increased as the case may be, the main aim being to comply eventually with the "correct" straight line limb track.

It was taken for granted that all top grade competitive swimmers used the straight pulling technique in all strokes.

A champion's analysis

In 1963, John Devitt, the reigning Olympic 100-m men's freestyle champion, wrote "In my view, any tendency to 'water feather,' that is, the waver that the hand and arm experiences owing to the resistance of the water, is wrong and the straighter the pull with just a slight bend the more power exerted." This view was shared by most coaches and swimmers of that period.

Underwater observation

With the advent of slow motion cine film taken through underwater observation windows, it became apparent that top grade swimmers *did not* pull straight back. There was one other factor common to all swimmers observed; *i.e.,* they were all obviously strong and fit. It was hardly likely, therefore, that they feathered through weakness.

The opportunity to study strokes under water showed that, because of water refraction and the general disturbance of the water surface when swimming, it was not possible to observe a stroke accurately from *above* the surface.

CURRENT BELIEFS

The deviation in the pull, clearly demonstrated by champions, could obviously not be called feathering and classed as a fault. It was eventually given the name "S pull' and was accepted as being the swimmer's attempt to solve many of the individual difficulties inherent with propulsion in water.

Many swimming publications show the individual wavering limb tracks of many world class swimmers in an attempt to find a common technique to be copied and used when teaching the strokes.

It is now generally accepted that the bent arm pull is the technique used by world class swimmers in front crawl, back crawl, and butterfly strokes. The S pull is sometimes thought to be the result of pulling with a bent arm. The swimmer's hand enters the water at a point usually in front of his shoulder. He then moves the hand inwards toward his center line in order to pull below his center of gravity. The hand must then be moved outward again to clear the hip for the recovery.

EXPERIMENTAL EVIDENCE

The results of tests with competent freestylers swimming at different speeds seem to suggest that the hand tends to deviate more as the speed is *reduced.* Most swimmers found it easier to pull straight back with the hand when it was moving relatively fast through the water than when moving slowly. When swimmers were asked to swim *slowly* and also keep the hand following a straight line, they found it difficult. When asked why, they said it was difficult to get a "grip" of the water at slow speeds.

Those swimmers who swam slowly and did manage to employ a straight line pull found that their speed dropped considerably. Their hands seemed to go *through* the water without gaining purchase.

A sampling of freestyle swimmers employing an S pull were asked whether they pulled straight back or deviated. They all replied that they pulled straight back. When asked to watch their hands on the next swim, they found it difficult to believe what they saw.

Paddle propulsion

There are two methods of propelling in water: a) the paddle and b) the screw. The paddle was for many years the obvious and only method of propelling boats in water. All animals and web-footed birds such as the duck use the paddle method, in which the propelling member pulls back in a straight line from front to back, *i.e.,* in a direction opposite and parallel with the direction of travel. The oar used in rowing boats and later the paddle wheel used in larger boats were designed by man to exploit this principle.

Screw propulsion

The screw principle was developed later than the paddle and proved far superior to the paddle as a means of propelling boats in water. The screw propellor differs from the paddle and paddle wheel in one important aspect, the blade of the propellor (screw) rotates in a direction at *right angles* to the direction of travel.

This principle is often difficult for the layman to understand. Propulsion is achieved by angling the blades of the propellor so that water at the front edge of the angled blade is forced to the back edge of the blade, and as a result the propellor (and boat) moves in the *opposite* direction.

Screw propulsion using an oar

It is possible for a person to propel a boat using only one oar operated from a rowlock in the stern with the oar in line with the boat's direction of travel. By moving the oar sideways, alternately left and right, *i.e.,* in a direction at right angles to the direction of travel, the boat will move forward. It is usually called sculling.

Screw propulsion—fish

A fish swims by using its tail in the same way, only more efficiently. The fish's tail presses sideways at an angle against the water causing the water to move backward and sideways slightly with the result that the fish's body moves forward through the water.

The principle is that of the screw. Whereas the blade of the screw is able to revolve continuously in the same direction, the fish is only able to move its tail through a restricted range and therefore has to reverse the angle of its tail and move it in the opposite direction. It is an oscillating movement at *right angles* to the direction of travel and much more efficient than the paddle method used by the duck.

Sculling

This same action can be employed by a swimmer lying on his back and moving his hands outwards and inwards from the hips; this is termed sculling. This can also be performed starting with the arms extended beyond the head. In such a situation, it is aptly termed "propeller."

It can also be performed lying face down in the water with the arms parallel, at right angles to the body, and beneath the surface of the water, palms facing the rear. By moving the hands sideways alternately inwards and outwards at right angles to the direction of travel, it is possible to set the body in motion headfirst. The swimmer will usually automatically rotate the palms slightly at the wrist so that the palms are angled, *i.e.,* thumbs to the rear when moving outwards and little fingers to the rear when returning the hand inwards.

Sculling pulls

The swimmer may also swim by pulling both hands downwards slowly from the face-down forward glide position until the arms are by the sides. The arms bend at the elbow and the hands move forward close to the body to the forward extended position and the action is repeated. If the swimmer pulls his hands downward in a straight line from front to back (when viewed from above) he will move forward very slowly. It will be found that a strong swimmer invariably will scull as he pulls; this will enable him to gain a greater purchase on the water and as a result he will move through the water *farther* for each arm pull.

Synchronized swimming

All synchronized swimmers develop the sculling pull automatically when swimming slowly in their routines. This is seen when swimming front crawl, back crawl, breaststroke, and butterfly. In certain variations of the front crawl the recovering arm remains above the surface for long periods and in consequence the propelling hand is seen to scull vigorously to prevent the hand from moving backwards too much.

MECHANICS OF SWIMMING

To propel a body in water, the propelling members must apply a force in a direction opposite to the intended direction of travel (*i.e.*, push backwards against the water to go forwards). To gain effective propulsion, the resistance of the body must be reduced to a minimum and the resistance of the propelling members increased to a maximum. The faster the body (or hand) moves through water, the greater the resistance it creates. The resistance increases with the square of the speed, *i.e.*, *doubling* the speed increases the resistance approximately *four* times. Therefore, the faster the arm moves backwards in the front crawl, the greater the resistance created at the hand and the more efficient the propulsion, *i.e.*, the farther the body moves forward compared with the distance the hand travels backward.

CONCLUSIONS

The deviation technique is an attempt by the *strong* swimmer to gain additional purchase on the water. It is not to be confused with "feathering" (slipping) demonstrated by *weak* swimmers.

   The technique is a skillful combination of pulling (paddle action) and sculling (screw action). The competent swimmer, providing he is strong enough, will *scull* with his hand as he pulls through the water, thereby creating greater resistance at the hand so that the hand is propelling for a longer period of time during the stroke cycle (*i.e.*, the stroking rate is reduced).

   Often the swimmer is not consciously aware of what he is doing. It is a technique that may develop naturally. The hand, instead of being a passive paddle, becomes a sensitive propulsive instrument seeking to obtain more effective methods of creating greater resistance as it is moved through the water.

It would seem that sculling skills could be introduced into the training program in order to strengthen the muscle groups concerned. With knowledge of the reason for the S pull, a new insight into propulsion is realized, enabling the swimmer to acquire improved results from his training.

REFERENCE

Devitt, J. 1963. Modern trends in freestyle swimming. Swimming Times 40: No. 2.

The influence of the leg kick and the arm stroke on the total speed during the crawl stroke

W. Bucher

Not all instructors in swimming have the same opinion about the importance of the leg kick in the crawl stroke. Some believe that the leg kick is very important for propulsive power; others think that it is only needed for stabilization of the body. Furthermore, opinions vary about the number of leg kicks required per arm stroke. This problem has been the subject of many investigations in which a variety of methods have been used. Counsilman (1968) used a towing apparatus to measure the actual influence of the leg kick. Swimmers performed the leg kick while being towed through the water at various speeds. Thus the forward push or the braking effect could be measured. The results showed that in general the leg kick supports the forward push at speeds of less than 1.5 m per sec. At speeds above 1.5 m per sec the leg kick did not increase the towing speed, but on the contrary produced a retarding effect.

The purpose of this investigation was to evaluate the relative effectiveness of the leg kick and arm stroke on the speed of crawl stroke swimmers.

METHOD

The subjects selected were swimmers of both sexes of various ages representing different levels of performance. The best performers were taken from participants at: a) the regional youth competition, 1972, b) the training of the water polo team from Zug, national category B, c) some top Swiss swimmers during their altitude training in preparation for the Olympic games in Munich, d) the training of talented youngsters at ages 8 to 12 in the Vevey Swimming Club, and e) a 1972 course for instructors in swimming of the IVSCH. On the basis of their performance, the 76 selected subjects were divided into three groups: G_1 = (N=28) good swimmers ($\bar{V}$ = 1.55 m per sec), G_2 = (N=35) average swimmers ($\bar{V}$ = 1.30 m per sec), and G_3 = (N=13) poor swimmers ($\bar{V}$ = 0.99 m per sec).

The test was conducted under three conditions: a) 15-m leg kick, b) 15-m arm stroke, and c) 15-m crawl (arms and legs). The 15-m distance had to be covered as quickly as possible. The take-off was performed in the water without a command by pushing off from the wall. After a starting distance, A, the highest speed was attained at C. The speed was controlled during the test distance, B, from point C to point C' (see Figure 1).

The subjects covered the test distance using three different methods; a) legs alone with arms stretched out in front (leg kick), b) arms alone with legs dragged through water (arm stroke), and c) legs and arms combined (crawl). They were encouraged to minimize breathing when swimming through the test area.

RESULTS

Table 1 contains the means and standard deviations for the three groups. Also included are the percentages of leg kick velocity vs. crawl and arm stroke vs. crawl.

Comparison of the crawl and arm stroke times

Figure 2 illustrates the relationship between the times for the total crawl stroke and for the arms alone over the 15-m distance. If the subject swam equally fast with the arms alone as with the whole body movement, the coordinate point would be exactly on the diagonal, d. It is most interesting to note that nearly all swimmers—good, average, and poor alike—are on a straight line; $i.e.$, in all three groups the arm stroke contributed the same proportion of effectiveness to the total crawl stroke.

Comparison of the crawl and leg kick times

The points for all three groups in Figure 3 are significantly further from the diagonal than in the previous figure. This is due to the fact that propulsive force of the legs is considerably less than that of the arms. Again it should be noted that all groups are similar with regard to differences between total stroke and leg kick times. Variabilities in 15-m times when using the legs only were comparatively large within the individual groups as compared to the variabilities of the group times when utilizing the arms by themselves.

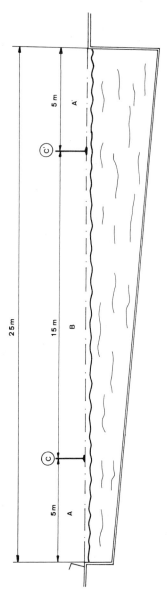

Figure 1. Illustration of the test situation.

Table 1. Means and standard deviations for the three test groups*

Test group	15-m arm stroke with pullboy			15-m leg kick without swimming aid			15-m crawl, complete stroke		100-m best time
	t_a (sec)	S_A (m/sec)	SA/S_{15m} (%)	t_L (sec)	S_L (m/sec)	S_L/S_{15m} (%)	t_{15m} (sec)	S_{15m} (m/sec)	t_{100m} (sec)
Good swimmers (N=28) $\bar{X}$	10.77	1.40	91.30	16.51	0.93	60.40	9.75	1.55	1.06
S	0.99	0.35	2.30	1.72	0.39	2.81	0.78	0.33	
Average swimmers (N=35) $\bar{X}$	12.90	1.17	90.50	19.89	0.77	58.90	11.59	1.30	1.19
S	1.11	0.32	2.61	1.67	0.32	2.68	0.75	0.24	
Poor swimmers (N=13) $\bar{X}$	17.73	0.89	90.10	26.00	0.61	61.70	15.36	0.99	
S	2.16	0.40	3.05	2.63	0.36	2.79	1.87	0.44	

*t_a, t_L, t_{15m}, and $t_{100}m$ represent times for arms alone, legs alone, both arms, and legs at 15 m, and best time for 100 m, respectively. S_A, S_L, and S_{15m} represent average velocities in m per sec using arms alone, legs alone, and the complete stroke over the 15-m test distance. SA/S_{15m} and SL/S_{15m} are expressed as percentages and depict the contribution of the arms alone and legs alone to the total stroke.

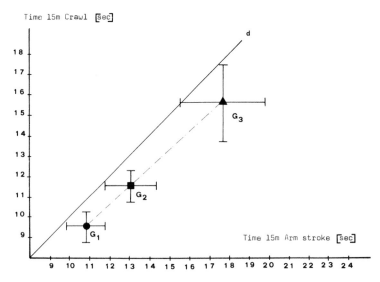

Figure 2. Relationship between crawl and arm stroke times (group means and standard deviations).

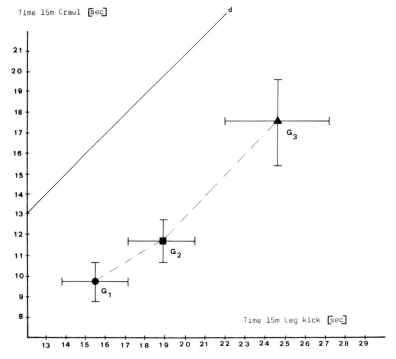

Figure 3. Relationship between times for the total stroke and the leg kick alone (mean values and standard deviations).

Comparison of leg kick and the arm stroke times

To show in more detail the differences between the leg kick and arm stroke times, individual performance values are presented in Figure 4. The arm stroke results clearly separate the three groups, with the best swimmers having lower times. The differences are less apparent for leg kick times. (Note: Not all data for the poor group were included because of some extremely high times.)

Sixteen subjects were selected for the analysis presented in Figure 5. The results show the wide variation among subjects with respect to the partial effects of arms and legs on the total crawl stroke time.

Genetti and Ballif, two top Swiss swimmers, required only 8.7 sec to crawl the test distance. They were asked before the experiment how important was their leg kick in the crawl. Genetti was convinced that his arm stroke was the most important and thought that his leg kick was not very effective, whereas Ballif believed that his leg kick was of considerable importance. The results of the performances are presented in Figure 6. The results indicate that both men were correct in their subjective evaluations. It is interesting to note that even though these two swimmers are very similar in performance over 100 m (Genetti 57.9 sec, Ballif 57.5 sec) they are quite different in terms of the relative contribution of arms and legs to the total movement.

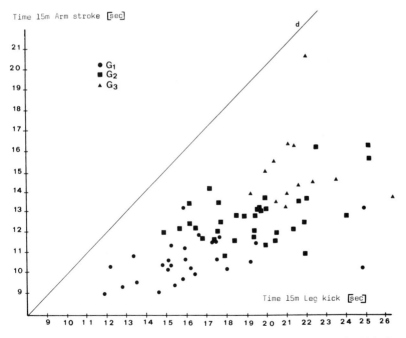

Figure 4. Relationship between the 15-m times for the arm stroke and the leg kick alone (individual values for arms and legs).

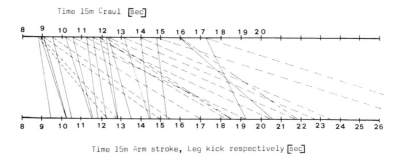

Figure 5. Relationship between total stroke time and times using the arms and the legs alone. ——, connects times for crawl stroke and for arm stroke; − −, connects times for crawl stroke and for leg stroke.

Relationship between times over 15 and 100 m

Figure 7 shows the relationship between the test results for group G_1 subjects over 15 m and their best times in the 100-m crawl in 1972. A high positive relationship ($r=0.99$) existed between these two performance times. This indicates that their rankings of the subjects in their test swims were quite similar to their performances under competitive circumstances.

SUMMARY

This study attempted to determine relative contributions of the arm stroke and leg kick to the total speed of crawl stroke swimming. The results showed that for the average of the groups: a) the arm stroke alone enabled good

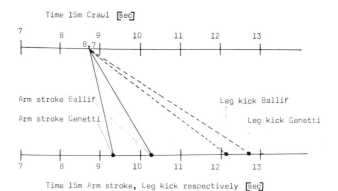

Figure 6. Relationship of total stroke time to times using arms and legs alone of two top swimmers. ——, connects times for crawl stroke and for arm stroke; − −, connects times for crawl stroke and for leg stroke.

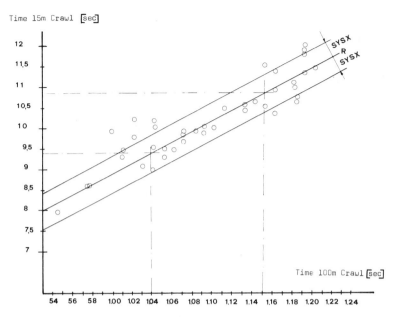

Figure 7. Relationship between the times for the test distance of 15 m and for 100 m. *R* = line of linear regression; *SYSX* = average deviation from linear regression.

swimmers to obtain 91.3 percent, average swimmers 90.5 percent, and poor swimmers 90.1 percent of their crawl stroke speed; b) the leg kick alone enabled good swimmers to obtain 60.4 percent, average swimmers 58.9 percent, and poor swimmers 61.7 percent of their swimming speed using the total stroke. These small differences in the percentages lead to the conclusion that most swimmers, regardless of ability, do not show great deviations in the performance of partial movements. In order to determine the actual share of leg kick and arm stroke in relation to the total speed, it would be necessary to measure them during the performance of the crawl. Measuring the two components separately produces speeds which when combined do not equal the speed observed in the complete movement.

REFERENCE

Counsilman, J. 1968. The Science of Swimming. Prentice Hall, Englewood Cliffs, N.J.

Changes in breaststroke techniques under different speed conditions

T. Bober and B. Czabanski

Training in different sport events has the realization of a definite set of aims. Generally, these purposes can be divided into tasks for developing skill, technique, or tactics. However, these elements are interdependent and each task, although it has a specific purpose, will indirectly influence the other aspects of the competitor's preparation. This is caused by the motoric nature of man, who realizes the aims of his activity by using a definite movement form which is consistent with his physical skill. Similarly, in swimming, training programs contain various degrees of emphasis upon skill, speed, strength, and endurance. It is known that swimming under different speed conditions causes changes in movement frequency (East, 1970). However, it can be expected that changes also occur in the technique of movement, especially in rhythm of the swimming cycle. In this study an attempt was made to characterize the interdependence of the breaststroke technique and the speed of swimming. It is hoped that the awareness of the side effects of the exercises utilized by coaches may improve the effectiveness of the teaching and coaching process.

METHOD

An investigation was carried out on a former Polish national record holder in breaststroke who was not competing then but retained his well established technique. He swam several times over a distance of 25 m at different speeds with the start performed in the water. In the investigation we utilized a speedometer (Miyashita, 1971), recorder, and film. The speedometer contained a photoelectrical converter consisting of a photoelement, bulb, and measuring block with apertures which let in the light from the bulb. The turning of the measuring block produced by movement of the swimmer caused the light to fall on the photoelement. The velocity was proportional to the speed of the turning of the block and created an electrical impulse which was registered at the recorder. The synchronization of the speedometer with the film enabled us to identify the speedogram curve and divide the swimming cycle into phases.

RESULTS

Since our interest in the technique dealt mainly with the analysis of the swimming cycle, we used as a point of reference the mean time of the cycle in a given trial in preference to the time needed to cover the entire distance. The swimmer performed tasks with the following mean cycle times:

Trial	No. of strokes	Stroke times (sec)
1	18	1.256 ± 0.062
2	8	1.675 ± 0.076
3	9	$1.92 \ \pm 0.103$
4	6	2.356 ± 0.044
5	5	2.616 ± 0.100

In the speedogram the following four phases of the swimming cycle were identified: a) the arm pull (t_1), b) leg recovery (t_2), c) leg kick (t_3), and d) completion of arm recovery and glide (t_4) (see Figure 1). We did not attempt any further differentiation of arm recovery because according to Counsilman (1968) this movement occurs simultaneously to a great extent

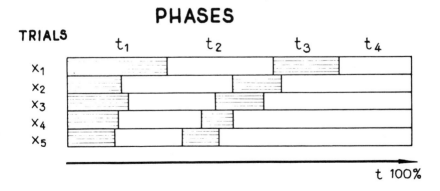

Figure 1. Time of the particular phases in percentage of the cycle time.

with the leg recovery phase. On the other hand, it was possible to identify a dividing line between phases t_4 and t_1 of the next cycle, which Chudzik (1974), using the same method, treated as a single phase.

We observed that the changes in the cycle duration were accompanied frequently by disproportionate changes in the duration of particular phases. In the absolute values there exist no statistically significant time differences among phases t_1, t_2, and t_3 between the given tasks (t-ratio was below the 0.05 significance level) but with the longer cycle time a distinct prolongation of the duration of the phase t_4 occurred (see Table 1).

The division of the swimming cycle included both the arm recovery and the glide. However, it must be remembered that the glide occurs mainly in slower swimming. According to Counsilman (1968), in the 100-m distance, with some swimmers this glide does not appear at all. Because of this alteration and the changes in the duration of the whole cycle, a very important element of the movement coordination, that is, the rhythm, is altered. This can be observed in Figure 2. We note that the time of the leg kick and the arm pull is similar under different speed conditions. The proportion of time of leg kick to arm pull in all trials is about 1 to 1.5, whereas the relation of the time of leg kick to the time of glide changes proportionally to the time of the cycle duration. The correlation coefficient between glide time and total stroke time is 0.96 and the regression equation is: $Y = 3.34t - 2.92$ where Y represents the number of times that phase t_4 is longer than phase t_3 and t is the time for the stroke cycle. The proportion of the time for the propulsive phases (phases t_1 and t_3) to the drag phases changes accordingly. In trial 1, the proportion is almost 1 to 1, while in trial 5 (slow swimming) 1 to 3. The regression equation is as follows: $Z = 1.4t - 0.4$ where Z stands for the number of times that the restraining phases are greater than propulsive phases.

In the reference points of the velocity curve $V_1, \ldots_4$ (see Figure 1) the momentary speed was measured (see Table 2). The lowest velocity was observed at the completion of the leg recovery (V_3) and the highest at the completion of the leg kick (V_4). These two velocities, minimum and maxi-

Table 1. Means and standard deviations of times in cycle phases (sec)

Trial	Phases of stroke			
	t_1	t_2	t_3	t_4
1	0.363 ± 0.041	0.385 ± 0.052	0.241 ± 0.048	0.263 ± 0.067
2	0.263 ± 0.082	0.542 ± 0.081	0.225 ± 0.048	0.645 ± 0.089
3	0.355 ± 0.077	0.482 ± 0.065	0.257 ± 0.040	0.825 ± 0.116
4	0.357 ± 0.051	0.573 ± 0.063	0.213 ± 0.015	1.213 ± 0.052
5	0.376 ± 0.081	0.504 ± 0.067	0.276 ± 0.022	1.46 ± 0.068

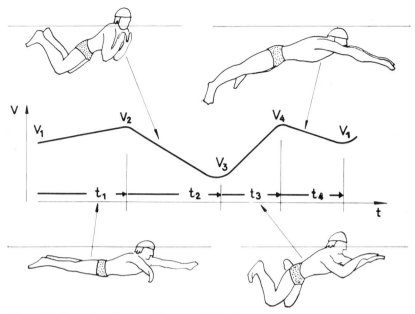

Figure 2. Example of a speedogram of the breaststroke cycle. $t_1, \ldots_4$, phases; $V_1, \ldots_4$, reference points of velocity.

mum, were not subject to the uniform changes in the swimming speed, expressed by the mean cycle time. All of the differences were statistically nonsignificant on the basis of t-tests ($p > 0.05$). However, a clear relationship was observed between the time of the cycle and the velocity at the end of the arm pull. This relationship is expressed by the correlation coefficients of: -0.94 for velocity V_1 and -0.90 for V_2 (see Figure 3).

In the swimming cycle two propulsive phases have been differentiated: arm pull (t_1) and leg kick (t_3). Measurement was made of the mean acceleration for these phases which is the tangent of an angle formed by the time and velocity lines. The mean acceleration of the arm pull was 1.09 m per sec^2 and, excluding trial 1 which had the shortest cycle time and an acceleration of

Table 2. Means and standard deviations of momentary velocities at the reference points of the cycle (m/sec)

Trial	V_1	V_2	V_3	V_4
1	1.20 ± 0.089	1.49 ± 0.081	0.45 ± 0.071	1.53 ± 0.073
2	1.02 ± 0.073	1.38 ± 0.033	0.48 ± 0.053	1.60 ± 0.063
3	0.83 ± 0.036	1.20 ± 0.074	0.34 ± 0.030	1.58 ± 0.192
4	0.85 ± 0.031	1.26 ± 0.033	0.45 ± 0.086	1.62 ± 0.060
5	0.72 ± 0.050	1.14 ± 0.068	0.24 ± 0.050	1.45 ± 0.033

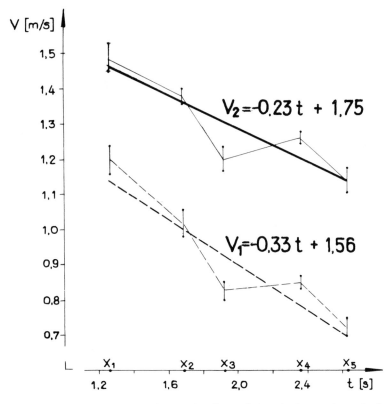

Figure 3. Empirical and theoretical regression lines of the velocity vs. the cycle time. – –, velocity at the end of the glide V_1; ——, velocity at the end of the arm pull V_2.

0.8 m per sec², in the other trials there were no significant differences. Accordingly, no greater differences were observed between the succeeding trials in the acceleration of the leg kick. The mean acceleration in that phase was 4.9 m per sec². The drag is the greatest in leg recovery in the trial with the maximal speed and is expressed by the negative value, −2.68 m per sec², while in the remaining trials it is contained within the limits of −1.4 to −1.8 m per sec².

A distinct relationship of the drag to cycle time was observed only in the glide phase. The longer the time of the cycle in that phase the less drag and therefore lower negative accelerations. The correlation coefficient for these parameters was −0.98. Maintaining a high swimming speed is related not so much to strength and increase of the momentary maximal velocities as to keeping up the high mean speed of the cycle by avoiding decreasing velocities in some phases. This is in agreement with the views of some authors (Czabanski, 1969) who state that emphasis in training should be on reducing the drag during certain phases and increasing the endurance of the swimmers.

CONCLUSIONS

The change in speed during the breaststroke expressed by the time for the stroke cycle is related mainly to the change in time of the glide phase. The slower the swimming, the longer the glide. Prolonging the glide duration alters the rhythm of the stroke cycle which changes the ratio of time of leg kick to time of glide and the relationship between propulsive and drag phases. In the breaststroke the maximal and minimal velocities are not subject to greater changes under the condition of speed alteration within the investigated range of speeds, whereas the decrease in swimming speed is accompanied by lower velocities achieved through the arm pull and at the end of the glide phase. The longer glide in slow swimming is characterized by lower mean negative acceleration than in fast swimming.

REFERENCES

Chudzik, A. 1974. Proba zastosowania spidografu do charakterystyki techniki plywania. Sport Wyczynowy 5: 15—18.
Counsilman, J. E. 1968. The Science of Swimming. Prentice Hall, Englewood Cliffs, N.J.
Czabanski, B. 1969. Teoria techniki plywania sportowego. WSWF we Wroclawiu, Wroclaw.
East, D. J. 1970. Swimming: an analysis of stroke frequency, stroke length and performance. New Zealand J. Health, Phys. Educ. Recr. 3: 16—27.
Miyashita, M. 1971. An analysis of fluctuation of swimming speed. In: L. Lewillie and J. P. Clarys (eds.), First International Symposium on Biomechanics in Swimming, Proceedings, pp. 53—57. Université Libre de Bruxelles, Brussels.

Use of light trace photography in teaching swimming

G. Hoecke and G. Gruendler

In the past few years considerable effort has gone into the study of the learning process, including physical activities found in physical education. The aim of these efforts has been to reduce the time of learning and enhance the development of skilled movements. As a result new knowledge has been obtained concerning the phases of the learning process and the most effective organization of physical education lessons. Providing information to the student is an important aspect of learning. Consequently, it is important to know what is the most effective type, time, and intensity of information to be given to students in various stages of the learning process. Only some preliminary information concerning this process can be provided at the present time.

In the initial phases of learning, visual information is of particular importance (Meinel, 1960) in developing and refining motor concepts. This knowledge, confirmed by research in different types of sports (Leirich, 1973), is also of great importance for training in swimming. Besides the traditional application of visual information such as the demonstration by the teacher or other pupils of exercises to be learned and the use of films or pictures, the investigators sought to find other methods for recording significant parameters of the motor process and for using them as an aid in the teaching and coaching of swimming.

This study was based on the following assumptions: a) In the initial phases of motor learning, information on the special aspects of movement is particularly important. Therefore, it seemed appropriate to obtain a demonstration of the motor process in which the curves of selected body points are indicated. b) It is appropriate for explanations and corrections to have, in addition to pictures of the motor process to be learned, records of the skill level reached on which concrete and clear suggestions for correction can be based.

According to the results reported by Gutewort (1969), it appeared that light trace photography would be particularly suitable. On the basis of the experiences of Counsilman (1971) and Clarys and Lewillie (1971) in recording light traces of movements in the water, we developed a simple method for our investigations to record the actual level of motor development in the different learning phases and to use it for feedback in learning. The light traces obtained, although without time marks, proved to be adequate since only movement parameters relating to space were required.

PROCEDURE

Three endoscope lamps, fed by a waterproof battery, were fixed at selected points on one side of the body: at the ankle (malleolus lateralis), at the hip joint (trochanter major), and at the top of the middle finger. A camera was positioned either at an underwater window or in a waterproof box with its optical axis at a right angle to the path of the swimmer at a distance of about 7 m.

The camera, which utilized black and white film (27 DIN), was set at an F/stop of 5.6 and operated at the bulb position (shutter opens and closes under control). Although illumination of the pool was kept as low as possible, the swimmers were able to monitor their position by sight. The subjects swam a distance of about 40 m at a nearly constant speed. The middle section of the distance was within the optical field of the camera.

RESULTS

Suitable light traces for the four strokes—freestyle, butterfly, backstroke, and breaststroke—were obtained (Figure 1). As shown in Figure 1, the possibilities of interpretation are different for the individual strokes. In all four examples the curve of movement of the marked point at the hip joint can be clearly seen. On the basis of its movements in the total curve, it is possible to derive some findings concerning the hip position during a cycle of movements.

In the example selected for freestyle (Figure 1a) a very stable position of the hip can be observed which is scarcely influenced by arm pulls and respiration. The curve of the hip joint in butterfly (Figure 1b) reveals the connection between hip movements and the butterfly stroke, because a quick stroke of the legs always corresponds to a short movement of the hip joint, and a slower leg stroke is always associated with a long hip movement. In backstroke swimming (Figure 1c) the entrance of the arms causes a cor-

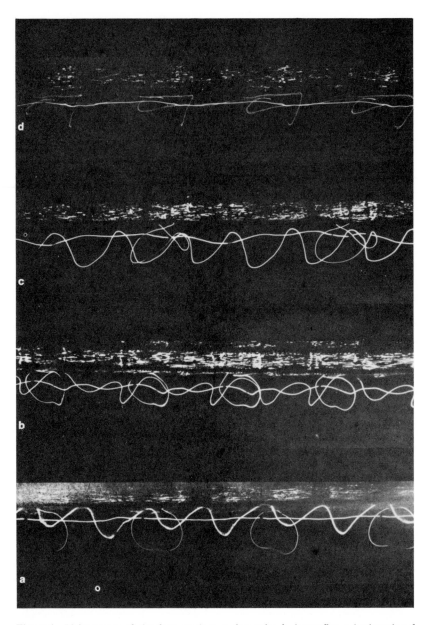

Figure 1. Light traces of the four strokes. *a*, freestyle; *b*, butterfly; *c*, backstroke; *d*, breaststroke.

responding turn of the hip. In the example selected, this hip turn remains low because of the effect of an even leg stroke and a good state of relaxation of the shoulder girdle. Also in the breaststroke (Figure 1d) the position of the hip can be followed clearly.

For the leg stroke in freestyle (Figure 1a), in butterfly (Figure 1b), and in backstroke (Figure 1c) essential information can be derived from the light trace produced by the lamp at the ankle joint. This concerns particularly the results for movement width; the regularity of movements; the frequency of strokes in one swimming cycle; and, to some degree, the findings on speed. (Steep vertical movements indicate quick movements.)

The light trace marking the curve of the hand produced by a lamp at the middle finger provides, for the three strokes mentioned, suitable findings on the structure of the movement phases; implementation of the entering phase; and transition into the working phase when the hands are leaving the water.

For breaststroke (Figure 1d) the analysis of the movement curves of the hand and leg points is much more difficult, because curves are resulting from a swimming technique which is difficult to record with the camera position selected. The remarks which follow, therefore, are limited to the two swimming strokes where particularly good possibilities for interpretation exist, namely, freestyle and butterfly. In Figure 2 the movements of two freestyle swimmers are shown. The first example (Figure 2a, 2b) shows a swimmer with a very stable position in the water, with even leg strokes (4-beat kick) and even arm pulls without a long entering phase. The picture of the movements hardly changes even when the subject swims at maximal speed (Figure 2b). The second swimmer shows a clear hip turn depending upon the rhythm of the arm pulls, an uneven leg stroke (6-beat kick) and at slow swimming (Figure 2c) a long entering phase in the arm pull. In swimming at maximal speed (Figure 2d) the entering phase is reduced, the leg stroke becomes more flat and faster, the foot is breaking through the water surface, and the oscillation of the hip is also reduced.

In Figure 3 examples of different leg movements are presented. The different kinds include the 4-beat kick already mentioned (Figure 3a), a very clearly expressed 6-beat kick (Figure 3b), a 6-beat kick with an emphasized movement, less emphasized movements of the marked leg (Figure 3c), and a small movement of the extended leg, where no rhythm in the swimming cycle can be seen (Figure 3d).

Various kinds of arm movements in freestyle swimming can be seen in Figure 4. In the first (Figure 4a) and fourth (Figure 4d) examples, the hand has a short entering phase and goes deep into the water. The interruption in the middle part of the curve indicates that the hand in the working phase is going down under the center of the body. In the second example (Figure 4b) it is assumed from the even light trace that a rectilinear arm movement is performed with a short horizontal working path. The arm pull in the third

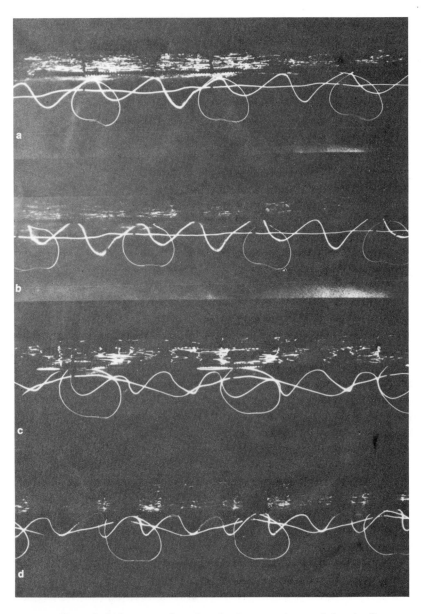

Figure 2. Light traces of crawl strokes by two swimmers (*a,b* and *c,d*).

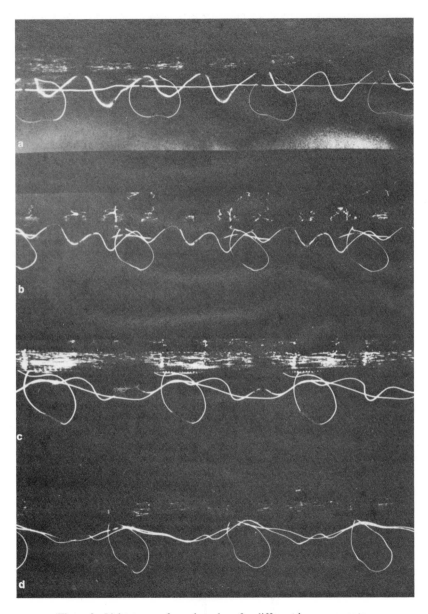

Figure 3. Light traces of crawl strokes: for different leg movements.

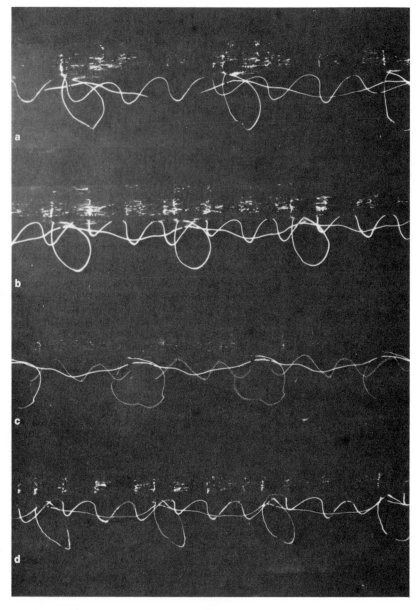

Figure 4. Light traces of crawl strokes: for different arm strokes.

example (Figure 4c) has a long entering phase, a rapid downward movement of the hand associated with a repeated bringing forward before the transition into the very long working phase.

Also in the butterfly some varieties of movements can be observed on the basis of light trace photography as shown in Figure 5. The upper light trace (Figure 5a) depicts a swimmer with relatively large butterfly movements, which are very even according to the speed of the upward and downward strokes. His arm pull is characterized by a long entering phase and by a long horizontal working distance. In the second example (Figure 5b) both leg strokes, belonging to one swimming cycle, are a little more differentiated in their realization. A quick downward movement is followed by a long, wide upward motion and a not so wide, balanced slow second stroke. The entering phase in the arm pull is relatively short, the hands are moved down deeply underneath the surface of the water until the working movement starts.

In the third example (Figure 5c) the generally very plain butterfly movement has a basic structure similar to that in Figure 5b (a quick and a slow stroke). The three arm pulls in the figures are relatively different. The emphasis on the downward movement of the hands and the short working phase in the second pull indicates that the swimmer inhaled, thus causing a disturbance in the expression of the movements.

In the fourth example (Figure 5d) we find a clear butterfly movement in each swimming cycle connected with wide kicking of the feet above the water surface. The arm movement is awkward in the transitions between these phases. This indicates a lack of motoric flow and leads to braking effects which should be avoided.

Figures 6 and 7 contain selected movement curves in freestyle and butterfly of swimmers in different stages of the learning process. The following characteristics can be observed: a) A consistent movement pattern is already developed in the initial learning stage. This indicates that ineffective and incorrect movements have become relatively fixed with respect to their spatial characteristics (see Figures 6b, 6c, 7a, 7b). b) In spite of the clearly defined movements in space, the swimmers have difficulty producing a propulsive force because of the incomplete dynamic pattern.

The upper light trace in Figure 6 shows a swimmer in the initial stage of freestyle swimming (Figure 6a). The arm pull is still not divided into phases. The leg movements with a small stroke amplitude are very quick and are produced by a strong movement in the knee joint. The body is turning excessively and awkwardly around the longitudinal axis according to the rhythm of the arm movements. As a consequence the propulsive effect is minimal.

In the second example (Figure 6b) an improvement can already be seen in the execution of the movements. The first beginnings of a phase structure can be seen in the arm pull. The turning movement of the hip is reduced and the

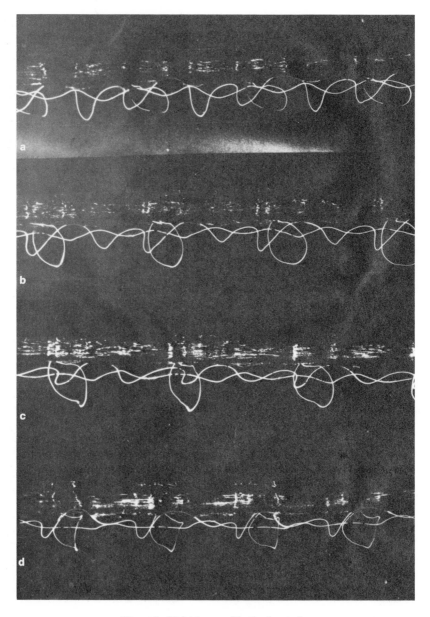

Figure 5. Light traces of butterfly stroke.

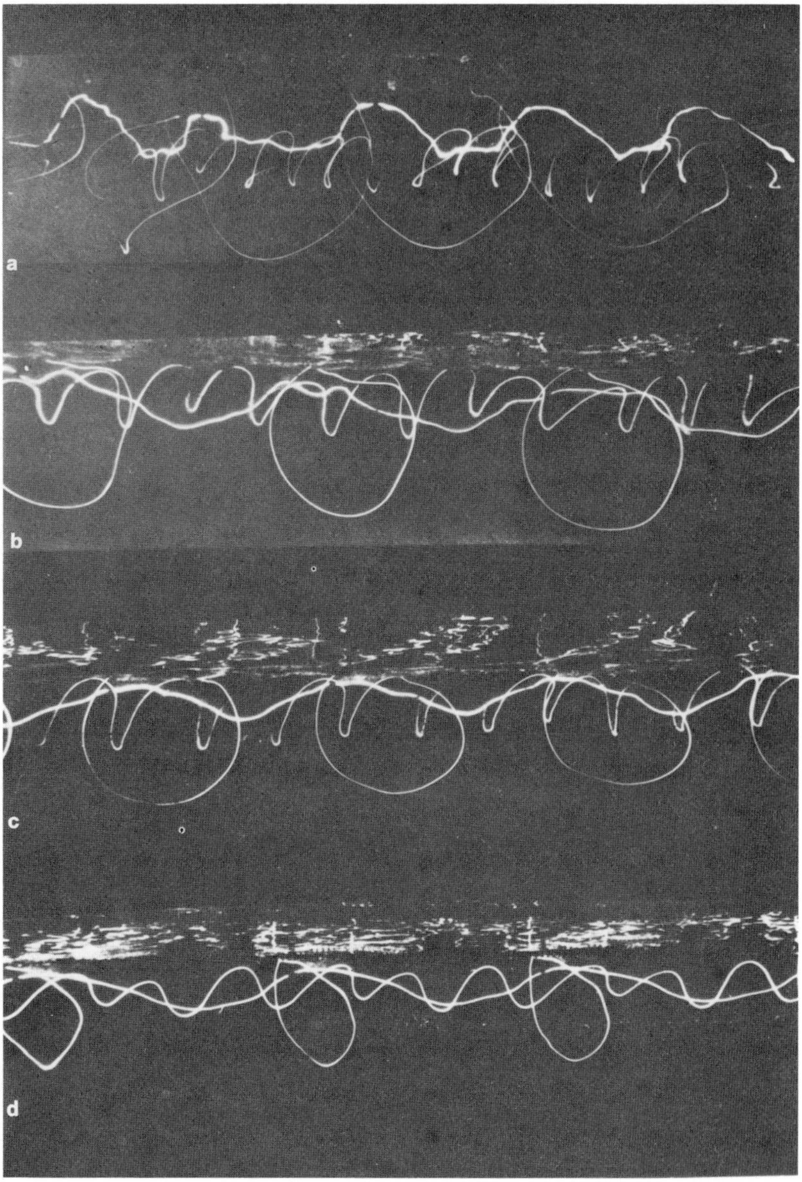

Figure 6. Examples for freestyle by swimmers in different stages of learning.

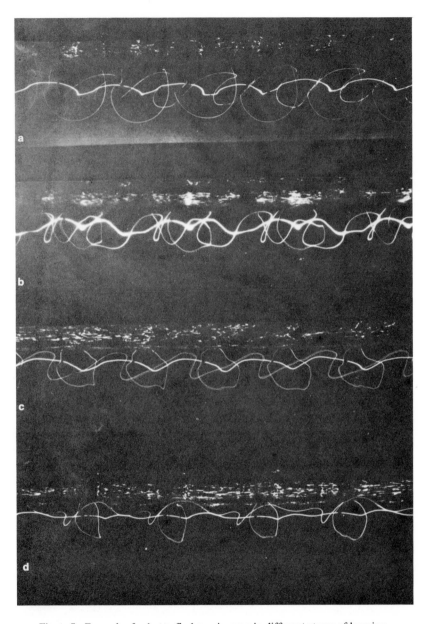

Figure 7. Examples for butterfly by swimmers in different stages of learning.

leg stroke is more even. A propulsive effect is now present during each swimming cycle.

Figure 6c shows another stage of the motor development. Typical for this stage is the extension of the horizontal part in the working phase of the arm pull and the smooth transition to the working phase. In comparison to the former example, the leg movement changed very little.

In Figure 6d a further development of leg stroke can be observed. The motor picture reached here corresponds in general with the objective of training, namely, proper execution of the movement. In the examples for learning butterfly, similar tendencies can be found (Figure 7). The regularity of leg movements, already seen in the initial stage of coordination between butterfly stroke and arm pull, is remarkable (Figures 7a, 7b, 7c). It is the result of a methodologically conditioned, longer special training of the dolphin kick.

Figure 7a shows a swimmer in the initial stage of coordination of arm and leg movements. From the path of the ankle joints it is clear that the leg stroke is performed with a strong bending of the knee joint. Further, the quick ineffective arm pulls lead to an awkward hip movement.

In the second example (Figure 7b) clear deviations from the normal course can be identified, but the movements in general have a propulsive effect. This is the result of two factors: a) in entering the water the arms are making a strong waving movement, which leads to a big delay in time and to a braking effect, before the transition into the working phase is accomplished, and b) the leg strokes are adapted to the delayed arm movement. This results in a wide movement with a longer pause at the deepest point, followed by a very quick upward and downward movement with the feet breaking through the water surface.

The third example (Figure 7c) is characterized by a very even leg movement with a quick downward stroke and slow upward movement. The arm pulls are clearly divided into phases with awkward transitions between them.

In the fourth example (Figure 7d) the leg movement has only a stabilizing function. This is indicated by the connection between a small, quick stroke followed by a long oscillation movement of the extended legs and the small hip movement. The hands go deeply downward following entry and are drawn inward under the body into the working phase.

SUMMARY

By means of light trace photography, pictures on the curve of selected body points in freestyle, butterfly, backstroke, and breaststroke swimming were obtained. From these tracings useful information on motor technique could be derived, particularly in freestyle and butterfly swimming.

Pictures of the motor performance in the various stages of the learning process can be used as a means of obtaining information for developing motor concepts, for methodological instructions, and for the correction of movement errors.

REFERENCES

Clarys, J. and L. Lewillie. 1971. The description of wrist and shoulder motion of different waterpolo shots using a simple light trace technique. *In:* L. Lewillie and J. P. Clarys (eds.), First International Symposium on Biomechanics in Swimming, Proceedings, pp. 249–256. Université Libre de Bruxelles, Brussels.

Counsilman, J. E. 1971. The application of Bernoulli's principle to human propulsion in water. *In:* L. Lewillie and J. P. Clarys (eds.), First International Symposium on Biomechanics in Swimming, Proceedings, pp. 59–71. Université Libre de Bruxelles, Brussels.

Gutewort, W. 1969. Fotografische Aufnahmeverfahren der biomechanischen Kinemetrie. II. Theor. Praxis Korperkultur Berlin 18: 444.

Leirich, J. 1973. Bewegungsverstellungen und motorischer Lernprozess. Korpererziehung, Berlin 23: 13.

Meinel, K. 1960. Bewegungslehre. Volk und Wissen Volkseigener Verlag, Berlin.

Asymmetry of the lower limbs in breaststroke swimming

B. Czabanski

Performance of the breaststroke is comprised of simultaneous, symmetrical motions, executed by the lower and upper limbs. Subjective observations of breaststroke swimmers reveal that many individuals demonstrate marked asymmetry and therefore contradict the basic principles of synchronized movements. The difficulties that arise in the execution of symmetrical motion of the legs in swimming undoubtedly reflect a problem of greater scope, namely, the functional laterality of human beings.

PURPOSE

This study involving the investigations of the causes of asymmetrical kicks during breaststroke swimming should be of initial value to teachers and coaches. The results will also contribute to the knowledge in the general area of laterality as it relates to human movement. Although the study is concerned with asymmetry of limb motion in the breaststroke kick, the findings may provide insight into the general problem of asymmetrical motion.

METHODS

Subjects for this investigation were 60 students at the Academy of Physical Education in Wroclaw who were divided into experimental and control groups. The 30 subjects comprising the experimental group were selected from among breaststroke swimmers who exhibited severe asymmetries to the point of being disqualified in competition. A control group of 30 subjects was comprised of swimmers with no detectable asymmetry in their kicking motions. The subjects were filmed during execution of the kick so that an accurate quantification of the asymmetrical deviations could be made. Illuminated points on the heels were used to identify the path of leg motion. The extremity (heel) was selected under the assumption it would reveal most clearly the magnitude of the deviations from the desired path.

The initial evaluation of the subjects in the experimental groups indicated that 63 percent had asymmetrical motions of the left limb, 18.5 percent had asymmetry of the right limb, and 18.5 percent had incorrect movement patterns with both legs (see Figures 1 to 4). Based on the results of film analysis, the errors can be classified into: a) asymmetry shown by the different traces of separate limbs, b) differences due to nonsimultaneous initiation of the limb motion, and c) asymmetry resulting from incorrect motion of one or both limbs. The reasons for these mistakes cannot be determined exactly. The assumption is that athletes in training know what motion they have to execute and attempt to perform it correctly.

In general the reasons for errors can be resolved into: a) those of a functional nature, b) those due to structural problems, c) those of psychological nature, and d) those resulting from use of the wrong pedagogical procedures in teaching the execution of the precise motion during the initial phase of instruction.

One of the first hypotheses was the assumption that beginners may have muscles that are too weak to overcome the density of water and therefore are unable to execute the motion correctly. In order to test this assumption, the strengths of the lower limb muscles were measured in the experimental group and in the control group (Table 1). The strengths of the extensor muscles of the left and right legs were obtained as well as the strength of the adductor muscles. Upon examination of these test scores, it was ascertained that in both groups the extensor and adductor muscles of the right leg were stronger than the same muscles of the left leg. In spite of their functional differences,

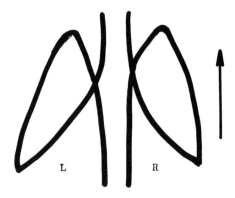

Figure 1. An example of a symmetrical breaststroke kick.

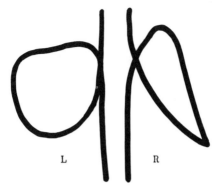

Figure 2. An example of an asymmetrical breaststroke kick. Incorrect motion rhythm of the left leg.

the difference between the muscle strength of the right and left limbs of the experimental group when compared to the control group was not statistically significant. It is interesting to note that, contrary to the initial hypothesis, the subjects of the experimental group had higher mean strengths of the lower limbs than did the subjects of the control group (Table 2). Therefore, it seems that lack of strength is not a fundamental characteristic of swimmers with asymmetrical breaststroke kicks. The lack of relationship between the lower limb strength and the motion asymmetry is not particularly surprising since the errors generally occur first in the initial phase of the motion, or at the time of the free unconstrained preparatory movements of the legs. At the

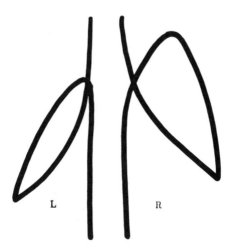

Figure 3. An example of an asymmetrical breaststroke kick. Errors in the movement pattern of the left leg.

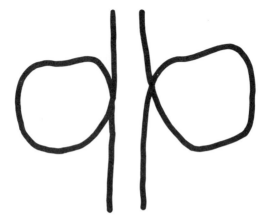

Figure 4. An example of an asymmetrical breaststroke kick. Incorrect motion rhythm in both legs.

time of this initial motion, the resistance afforded by the water is small, and therefore the movements can be executed without great physical effort. Consequently, it can be concluded in this particular situation that the asymmetrical breaststroke kick is not the result of dynamic asymmetry.

The morphological lateralization may also be the cause of the functional asymmetry. To test this hypothesis, the length and circumference of the lower limbs of all subjects were measured in both groups (Table 3). In both groups, the left limb was slightly longer than the right one. But this difference was not statistically significant. In both groups the largest and the smallest circumferences of the lower leg were greater in the right legs than in the left legs. There was no statistically significant differences in these circumferences between the experimental and the control group. It may be assumed that the wrong or inconsistent motion can be caused by faults in body structure that, during swimming, may result in leg motions which attempt to compensate for these faults.

Table 1. Differentation of the muscular strength of the right and left legs

Muscles	Experimental group (N=30)			Control group (N=30)		
	Left leg mean (kg)	Right leg mean (kg)	t-ratio	Left leg mean (kg)	Right leg mean (kg)	t-ratio
Extensor	104.27	107.60	0.75	93.40	97.73	2.99
Adductor	72.00	78.20	1.78	63.33	66.00	0.48

Table 2. Differentation of the strength of the lower limb muscles of experimental and control group

	Experimental group (N=30)	Control group (N=30)	t-ratio
Left leg			
Extensor muscles	104.27 ± 10.68	93.40 ± 4.49	3.50*
Adductor muscles	72.00 ± 8.87	65.33 ± 4.15	2.55†
Right leg			
Extensor muscles	107.60 ± 12.81	97.73 ± 3.02	2.80†.
Adductor muscles	78.00 ± 9.58	66.00 ± 3.12	4.53*

*Significant at 0.01 level of probability.
†Significant at 0.05 level of probability.

Next, the curvatures of the spine were examined by means of the Iwanowski Spherosomatometre (1968) (Table 4). Based on the examination of these results, one might assume that the persons in the experimental group were characterized by smaller curvatures. In both groups we did not observe any appreciable lateral deviations of the spine. Therefore, the morphological examinations did not provide an explanation for the asymmetry of the lower limb motions during breaststroke swimming.

The attempt to find the causes of the asymmetrical motions in breaststroke swimming also included the psychological reasons. It was assumed that perhaps when exercising, individuals may not remember the motions because their motor memories are unsatisfactory. Therefore, Talyszew's (1963) and Boigey's (1939) tests were given to both groups. The results of independent t-tests revealed no statistically significant differences between the means in

Table 3. Length and circumference of the lower limbs

	Experimental group (N=30) (cm)	Control group (N=30) (cm)
Length		
Left	91.42 ± 4.49	91.30 ± 2.68
Right	91.22 ± 4.43	91.12 ± 2.63
Greatest circumference		
Left	37.08 ± 1.65	36.33 ± 1.56
Right	37.20 ± 1.55	36.40 ± 1.53
Smallest circumference		
Left	23.30 ± 0.91	23.18 ± 1.10
Right	23.33 ± 0.94	23.22 ± 1.05

Table 4. Sum of angles of the
spinal curvatures

Group	Sum of angles $6°-26°$	Sum of angles $28°-45°$
Experimental	19	11
Control	11	19

either test. The small differences in the results between groups did not show any differences as far as the motor memory was concerned.

DISCUSSION

The asymmetrical leg kick in the breaststroke is a symptom of a functional lateralization of man. The problems of structural, dynamic, and/or functional lateralization constitute very complex phenomena. The essential causes of asymmetrical leg kicks could even involve the structure and function of the brain hemispheres. Since the causes of the functional asymmetry of the brain cannot be determined, we were compelled to limit ourselves to the observation of the effects and the investigation of the direct causes. It is common to observe asymmetry of the leg motion during breaststroke swimming. We often attempt to eliminate these faults through special gymnastic exercises because we assume that the cause is weak musculature or lack of flexibility due to shortened muscles. As a result of corrective exercises we may alter the body arrangement in water and therefore we may assume that perhaps the indirect cause of the asymmetrical motion is the body position which in turn has appreciable effects on the motions of the limbs. Frequently, in attempting to correct the leg motions, we may give advice or instructions since we assume that the cause of the inefficient motion is the inability to comprehend the motion or because of a weak or inexact memory of it.

The examinations of subjects from the Academy of Physical Education in Wroclaw did not indicate that a fundamental relationship exists between the appearance of the asymmetrical kick in the breaststroke and morphological or dynamic asymmetry of the subjects. The relationship between the execution of leg motion (inconsistent with basic principles) and the motor memory have not been verified. Therefore, it might be better to reconsider the presently accepted opinions and methods of pedagogical procedures in order to correct inaccurate breaststroke kicks. Further investigations of the kicking motion is needed. An investigation now being conducted deals with a more thorough and more exact determination of the problems presented in this article. This new study is also concerned with the relationship between functional laterality and the motion of kicking and the effects of pedagogical procedures used in the initial phase of instruction on the execution of correct and incorrect kicking techniques.

REFERENCES

Baley, S. and W. Nawrocka. 1952. Znaczenie bocznosci dle praktyki wychowania fizycznego. Kultura Fizyczna 11/12.
Boigey, M. 1939. Manuel Scientifique dEducation Physique, Paris.
Demel, M. and W. Sikora. 1956. Z badan nad asymetria funkcjolanlna. Kultura Fizyczna 2.
Iwanowski, W. 1968. Metoda sferosomatometryczna w badaniach pomiarowych postawy ciala. Wychowanie Fizyczne i Sport, 2.
Kubisz, E. 1962. Proba badania asymetrii ruchow konczyn dolnych w plywaniu stylem klasycznym. Kultura Fizyczna 6.
Talyszew, F. M. 1963. Izmienienje proprioceptiwnoj czuwstwitelnosti w procesje uczebno-trenirowocznych zaniati. Probliemy Fizjologii Sporta, Moskva.
Wolanski, N. 1957. Uwagi na temat asymetrii budowy ciala czlowieka w zwiazku z asymetria funkcji konczyn. Kultura Fizyczna 1.

Investigation of hydrodynamic determinants of competitive swimming strokes

U. Persyn, J. De Maeyer, and H. Vervaecke

As swimmers, coaches, and teachers, we feel an approach to an investigation from a hydrodynamically oriented standpoint is vitally important (but surely not a unique goal). In the authors' opinion competent teachers and coaches possess a biomechanical knowledge that is relatively refined for movements out of the water, but they encounter considerable difficulty when they attempt to quantify movements occurring in water.

It appears to the authors that the majority of real experts among the practitioners neither have the time nor feel the need to publish their work. On the other hand, scientists often make singular transpositions of theory into practice with little regard for the practical implications of their results. As a consequence the complexity of human motion in water is often over-simplified in experimental research. Exceptions occur when practitioners with a scientific insight and approach (Cureton, Counsilman, Carlile, for example) are able to identify problems which are amenable to research and solutions with the help of other scientists.

This study (1974) was based on a representative series of concepts which were identified by Counsilman (1968) in his classic text, *The Science of Swimming.* Since his work evolved primarily from results of film studies, it is essential that the concepts outlined undergo additional investigation. Certainly great advances in swimming performance have resulted from careful study of films. In this sense the Japanese, Hungarians, and Australians have been the leaders. In this study (1974) it was necessary to depend extensively on heterogeneous and fragmentary data derived from observation and experience rather than on published literature. Neither the films in circulation nor videotape recordings of the last Olympic Games and World Championships

214

are, by themselves, sufficiently useful. Both sources, however, complement each other to a great extent.

PURPOSE

The underlying objective of this study was to help bridge the gap between practice and research. For that reason behavior patterns of the strokes from concrete modalities of movement were investigated. These patterns can be experienced personally by swimmers and observed by others. The complete document (1974), parts of which are summarized here, does not provide for immediate application in practice. It will, however, form a sound basis for continued scientific research on the technical aspects of swimming.

The study also focused on the problem of synchronization, which is perhaps the most complex area of research on hydrodynamic and technical determinants of human motion in water. Other components, ranging from simple to more complex, are buoyancy, resistance, propulsion, balance, and continuity of movement. It would have been simpler to start with less complex characteristics, but the possibility of integrating the results was a more important consideration.

RESULTS

The results presented here represent a critical analysis of some of the concepts and principles proposed by Counsilman (1968).

Propulsion

According to Counsilman (1968), "the knees do not reach full extension until the legs are almost touching . . . there is little or no backwards pushing of the water with the soles of the feet once the legs are extended" (p. 116). In the author's opinion, the principle of propulsion of the foot in breaststroke at the beginning of the squeezing action can be compared to that of the propeller. (See Figure 1.) The knees reach full extension immediately after the vigorous initiation of the squeezing, with the rotating feet in a thrusting supinated position. Also according to Counsilman, in hand positioning for the pull it is fundamental that the hand be flat, not cupped (1968, p. 12). Comparison is suggested between the curved shape of the hand in lateral movements and that of a propeller blade or of an airplane wing with double flap deflection. Such a wing has a high maximal coefficient of lift. In lateral movements the best swimmers use a hand position between "flat" and "cupped." A related analogy exists between the principle of propulsion (path, orientation, shape)

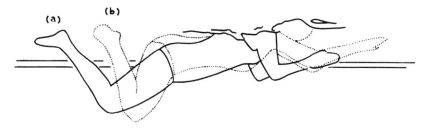

Figure 1. Behavior pattern concerning the horizontal balance and the continuity of movement in breaststroke. a, during the "normal" inhalation (first half recovery) the thighs are still about in the line of the body. The water resistance on the forearms and legs develops a "head bearing" component (allows an easy diaphragmatic respiration). b, afterwards the hips are bent and the arms are extended, so that the body drops forward into a horizontal position. This is the slowest moment. For that reason the propulsion of the kick is immediately of great importance.

of the hand in the breaststroke and that of the Voith-Schneider propeller. The blades of this propeller, oscillating around their own axes, are rotating in a horizontal plane. There is also the possibility of changing the eccentricity. (See Figure 2.)

Body roll

First a synoptic table of individual diagrams was prepared which represented the synchronization of six isochronous phases of the arm and six isochronous kicks per cycle. Figure 3 shows a synoptic behavior pattern of differences and analogies between the movements of the lower limbs during the stroke cycle of a few patterns of the crawl stroke. Three patterns (classified in six isochronous kicks per cycle) are superimposed in a circle diagram (composed of a combination of time-space-structures) (back view). Relation of movement is shown between the slow 2-beat and the 2-beat cross-over kick and between the 2-beat cross-over and the 6-beat kick. The timing concerning the 2-beat cross-over, according to Counsilman (1968, p. 32), is indicated by the *full arrows* in Figure 4. The timing in phases 6 and 1 is represented in the drawing by a *dotted line*.

Continuity of movement in the crawl and back crawl strokes

Research by Counsilman (1968) indicates that at fast speeds the kick contributes nothing to the propulsion created by the arms (p. 7) and that there is constant application of forward propulsion from the arms (p. 13). However, fluctuations in forward speed and the discontinuity of the arm propulsion have not been considered. There is a similarity in the two strokes (crawl and backcrawl) when the six arm phases, the six kicks, and the trunk position are

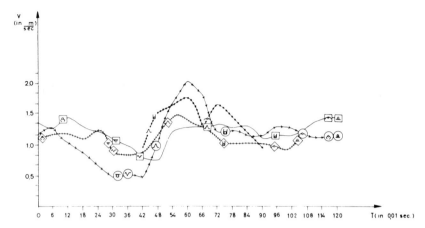

Figure 2. Superposition of individual curves of speed fluctuation during a cycle in breaststroke, synchronized to the moments delimiting the phases. The swimmers are:

		Vmin.	Vmax.	V.(m/sec)
⊦⊦⊦⊦⊦⊦	D. Schoenfield	0.85	1.47	1.09
———	G. Stepanova	0.75	1.45	1.22
→·→·→	Kisnne-Kaczander	0.45	2.05	1.13
••••••	M. Chatfield (only the most distinctive part) (Olympic Games, Munchen)			

The marks mean: ⓐ, mouth out of the water; ⊽ , mouth in the water; ⊠, feet turn outwards; ⊘ , maximal spreading of feet; ⊎, arms at shoulder breadth; ⊛, end of widest phase; ⊚ , end of bringing together. We observe: "normal" inhalation during the recovery; maximal speed during the kick; an acceleration after the maximal spreading of the feet propeller mechanics); the speed nearly maintained during the arm pull; a "normal" breathing and a deep position by Kisnne-Kaczander, but a great fluctuation of speed, late breathing by Galina Stepanova, and a "jumping" style by Dana Schoenfield but less fluctuation; a singular overlapping of propulsion by Marc Chatfield.

considered. Nevertheless, there is a considerable difference in both strokes as to the presumed duration of the high propulsive force of the arms. The most important forward thrust of the arm in the crawl amounts to 66 percent of the duration of the total cycle, in back crawl only 33 percent. (See Figure 5.)

Synchronization in the butterfly stroke

Figure 6 represents a comparison of the principle of propulsion used by an eel and one of the principles used by butterfly swimmers, as reported by Gray in 1933. There is a transfer of impulse from the lower limbs to the upper limbs, resulting in an elevation of the hips and a downward dropping of the chest. As a result, movement occurs in two planes (hips-legs; arms-head-chest). Thanks to the cambering of the chest and a stronger kick, the head is lifted by the frontal water pressure (Counsilman, 1968, pp.69,71,86,87).

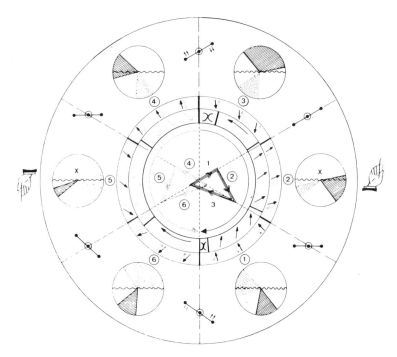

Figure 3. Synoptic behavior pattern of arm and leg movements. From inside to outside: △,path of the right foot with the 2-beat cross-over (back view);), the right foot thrusts downward in the slow 2-beat. Six kicks in the 2-beat cross-over. Six kicks in the 6-beat.⊗, synchronization of the phases of the left and the right arm (side view). The shoulder is the axis.↖, body position (roll to the right) (back view).

Practical implications

The swimming styles which have been observed in the films are dependent, of course, upon the velocity (a longer gliding position and downward press, a different beat in crawl, etc.). This does not mean that a series of generalizations are not imposed by the speed, which was of prior interest to us in this study. Limiting the analysis to one single pattern does not offer a reasonable solution because every swimmer is different in his psychomotoric and morphological capacities. It is important to attempt to find out how hydrodynamic principles can be efficiently applied to a swimmer's style. The capacities of "ordinary" swimmers require most often different applications of these principles than the capacities of the best ones. This may be temporary and dependent on the level of development. For the benefit of the methodological implications we have traced relationships of movements between the four competitive strokes and different patterns. However, we consider it necessary to make any approach relative on the basis of the four

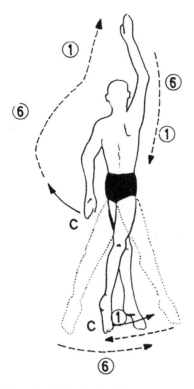

Figure 4. Timing in the 2-beat cross-over.

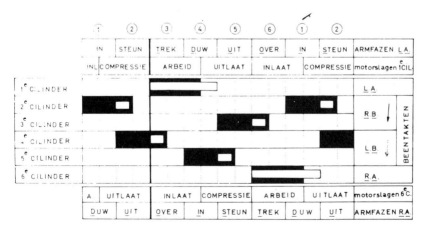

Figure 5. Remarkable similarity between the working scheme of a 6-cylinder motor (4 strokes) with a normal order of sparking (1-5-3-6-2-4) and the behavior pattern of a 6-beat crawl.■■■, order of sparking;▭, propulsion of the arms;▭, presumable propulsion of the legs; *L.A.*, left arm; *R.A.*, right arm; *L.B.*, left leg; *R.B.*, right leg.

220   Persyn *et al.*

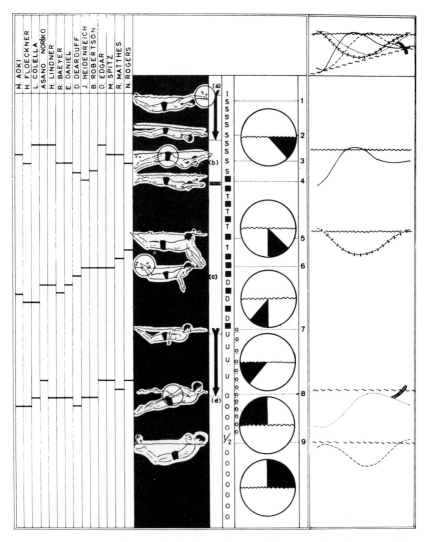

Figure 6. Comparison of propulsion pattern of competitive butterfly swimmers and the eel.

groups of strokes, when we aim at improving the knowledge of movements in aquatics.

REFERENCES

Counsilman, J. E. 1968. The Science of Swimming. Prentice Hall, Englewood Cliffs, N.J.

Counsilman, J. E. 1971. The application of Bernoulli's principle to human propulsion in water. *In:* L. Lewillie and J. P. Clarys (eds.), First International Symposium on Biomechanics in Swimming, Proceedings, pp. 59–71. Université Libre de Bruxelles, Bruxelles.

De Maeyer, J. 1973. Enkele hydrodynamische aspekten van de menselijke beweging in het water. Leuven (niet-gepubliceerde licentiaatsverhandeling, I.L.O. K.U.L.) (Promotor: U. Persyn).

Persyn, U. 1965. Zwemmen. Leuven. (niet-gepubliceerde kursus, I.L.O. K.U.L.).

Persyn, U. 1969. Hydrodynamische gegevens die aan de basis liggen van de zwemtechnieken. Sport, Tijdschrift van de lichamelijke Opleiding, de Sport en het Openluchtleven, XII n° 2(46), 119–123.

Persyn, U. 1969. Hydrodynamische toepassingen in de totaalcoördinatie van de crawlslagen. Sport, Tijdschrift van de lichamelijke Opleiding, de Sport en het Openluchtleven, XII n°4(48), 235–239.

Persyn, U. 1971–1973. Sportreferaten (Ministerie van Nederlandse Cultuur, Bestuur voor de Lichamelijke Opvoeding, de Sport en het Openluchtleven), 1–2(1971), 3–5(1972), 9–10(1973).

Persyn, U. 1974. Technisch-hydrodynamische benadering van de bewegen-de-mens-in-het-water, uitgaande van een kritische studie van de. "Science of Swimming" van Counsilman. Hermes, Vol. VIII, No. 3–4, 5–136.

Van Lammeren, W. P. A. 1944. Weerstand en voortstuwing van schepen. "De technische boekhandel." H. Stam, Amsterdam.

Films

Carlile, F. and U., New Magic of Swimming.

Carlile, F. and U., SPEEDO FILM, Swimming the American Way, prod. A. Lake.

Chateau, R. and A. Radenac, De Australische kampioenen, 1959.

Counsilman, J. E., The Science of Swimming, Indiana University, Bloomington.

Counsilman, J. E., Back Stroke.

Counsilman, J. E., Breast Stroke.

Counsilman, J. E., Butterfly.

Counsilman, J. E., Crawl Stroke.

Counsilman, J. E., Starts and Turns.

Counsilman, J. E., Swimming Technique, Indiana University, Radio and Television Service.

Counsilman, J. E., Swimming Strokes Analyses.

F.W.U., Institut fur Film und Bild, Wissenshaft und Unterricht, Grundformen der Schwimmarten, Sporthochschule Köln.

Nederlandse Sportfederatie, XIe Europese kampioenschappen Utrecht, 1966, Vrije slag, F.I.N.A., in co-operation with SPEEDO.

Nederlandse Sportfederatie, XIe Europese kampioenschappen Utrecht, 1966, Schoolslag, Rugcrawl, Dolfijn, F.I.N.A., in co-operation with Speedo.

Nilos-Ineps, Frankrijk-Australie te Parijs, 1960.

Rajki, B. Irta és rendezte (de dolfijnslag), co-operation Popper Imre, oper. Varga Vilmos.

Rajki, B., Crawl, 1955 Budapest, co-operation Popper Imre.

Rose, M., Skilled Swimming 1 and 2, Sunkist in co-operation with the American National Red Cross, prod. J. Bell, G. Nagy.

Ryan, Films, Sprint Crawl, Swimming Instruction: Serres, co-operation Yale Athletic Association and the Yale Swimming Team, prod. Dr. F. Ryan, B. Stoneback, J. M. Miller.
Speedo Film, International Swimmer-Tokio, 1964, co-operation of the international swimming coaches D. Talbot, G. Haines, T. Cathercole, J. Devitt.
Speedo Film, International Swimmer - Mexico, 1968.
Speedo Film, Carlile, F. and U., Swimming Champions of the World, 1971.
Speedo Film, International Swimmer-Munchen, 1972.

Videotapes

Olympic Games, Munchen, 1972.
World championships, Belgrado, 1973.

Swimming starts, water polo, and life saving

A biomechanical comparison of the grab and conventional sprint starts in competitive swimming

J. E. Bowers and P. R. Cavanagh

The advent of new techniques and training procedures has altered competitive swimming considerably in recent years. One such change which was widely used at the 1972 Olympic Games by many sprint swimmers was the grab start. In the grab start, the swimmer grasps the front edge of the starting block usually with both hands outside of his feet. Many coaches feel that this enables the swimmer to pull himself toward the water with his arms assisting the thrusting with his legs, thus giving more force and therefore a better start. Others believe that the posture simply allows a more forward position of the center of gravity at the time of gun flash.

Winters (1968) was among the first to demonstrate the superiority of the grip start in a group of five male college swimmers. He reported faster velocity at water entry and faster times to 10 yards. Roffer and Nelson (1972) were able to show that swimmers unfamiliar with the grab start could improve their performance on a criterion of "time to 12 feet" after a period of training in the grab start. Despite this evidence of improved performance with the grab start, the exact locus of the improvement still remains to be determined. Also, no studies have reported data on the grab start using female swimmers as subjects.

PURPOSE

It was the purpose of this investigation to determine through the use of cinematographic techniques whether differences existed between the grab and conventional (circular armswing) sprint starts as used by female competitive swimmers with respect to selected velocities, angles, and temporal components. Specifically the factors investigated included: 1) the velocity of the body center of gravity at take-off; 2) the velocity of the body center of gravity at entry; 3) the angle of projection at take-off; 4) the angle of entry with respect to the water level; 5) the position of the trunk with respect to the horizontal at the point of entry; 6) the take-off time; 7) the flight time; 8) the time to a distance of 10 yards from the starting end of the pool.

PROCEDURES

Subjects

The subjects for this study were six college age women with at least 1 year of competitive swimming experience on the varsity swimming team of either Bucknell University or The Pennsylvania State University. All of the swimmers had previous experience with both types of start and therefore no training period was required. They had a mean of 10 years of competitive swimming experience and all had participated in the 1973 Association of Intercollegiate Athletics for Women's National Swimming Championship Meet.

Instrumentation

An electrically driven 16-mm LoCam camera filming at a nominal rate of 100 frames per sec was used to record each trial. The camera was also equipped with a pulse generator which placed a timing mark on the film every 0.01 sec, which enabled the investigator to verify the frame rate of the camera. The camera was placed on a tripod 32 feet away from the mean plane of motion of the swimmer and 36 inches above the deck of the swimming pool.

Test procedures

The testing phase was conducted in a single testing session at the Pennsylvania State University Natatorium during the Spring Term of 1973. Each subject performed four starts of each style followed by a freestyle sprint at maximal speed past the 10-yard marker to simulate racing conditions. The subjects were allowed to warm-up prior to the start of the filming session, in order to familiarize themselves with the testing situation. All of the swimmers performed trial 1, then all of the swimmers performed trial 2, and they followed this pattern until all eight trials had been completed. This allowed for a sufficient amount of rest between trials. The type of start to be used in each trial was assigned randomly among the subjects, so that three began with the grab start and three began with the conventional start.

The preliminary verbal command to start each trial was "take your mark" which was followed, when the swimmer was stationary, by the firing of the gun. A panel of three judges watched each trial to determine if a false start had been committed. Any trial which was declared a false start by the judges was repeated by the swimmer. The camera was started with the preliminary verbal command to ensure that it was running at the desired speed prior to the swimmer's first movement. The camera was not stopped until the subject was beyond a point 10 yards from the starting end of the pool. An observer at the 10-yard point manually switched on a neon light when the swimmer's head reached a position directly opposite the vertical mark on the side of the pool. This provided a visible mark on the film to enable the 10-yard time to be calculated.

In order to aid the investigator in the determination of body segment end points, each subject was marked with a contrasting colored marking pen prior to the filming.

Analysis equipment

A digital data acquisition system, composed of a Vanguard motion analyzer, a digital voltmeter connected to certain interface circuitry, and a Friden Flexowriter was used to extract data from the film. This unit produced a paper tape which was later used with a Hewlett-Packard minicomputer to derive the various parameters studied. An IBM/370 computer was used to perform the analysis of variance calculations.

Method of computation

In order to compute the various velocities and angles needed in this investigation, the swimmer's center of gravity had to be determined for the segments of the trial from which these data were derived. The center of gravity of the body for each frame analyzed was determined by use of the segmental method, as described by Williams and Lissner (1962) using the relevant anthropometric data published by Dempster (1955).

Statistical analysis

A two-way analysis of variance (starting styles by subjects) was used to compare statistically the grab and conventional starting styles. Mean values from all trials of the same starting technique for one subject were used as input to the program.

A finite difference approach to differentiation was found to produce unsatisfactory velocities. An alternative technique was employed which involved the three-point moving average smoothing of the displacement data

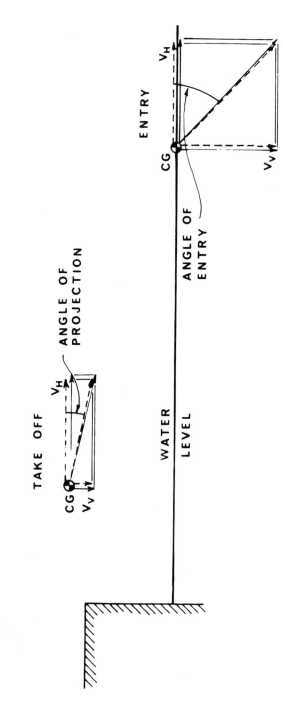

Figure 1. Components of velocity of the whole body center of gravity at take-off and entry.

followed by a second degree polynomial fit to three adjacent data points. The derivative at the central point of the three points was taken to be the velocity at that point. Further details are published elsewhere (Bowers, 1973).

RESULTS AND DISCUSSION

Velocities and angles

The horizontal and vertical components of velocity of the center of gravity at take-off were not significantly different between the two starting styles. As shown in Figure 1, these similar initial conditions resulted in angles of projection and entry and components of velocity at entry that were similar between the two styles of starting. Clearly there should also be no difference between the distance covered with the two different starts, and this was found to be the case when the center of gravity was considered. A small difference of almost $4°$ in the orientation of the body at the point of water entry was found with the flatter entry occurring in the conventional start.

This evidence would appear to suggest that any additional increment in propulsive force which is obtained by the use of the grab start is only sufficient to account for the loss in momentum due to the absence of the

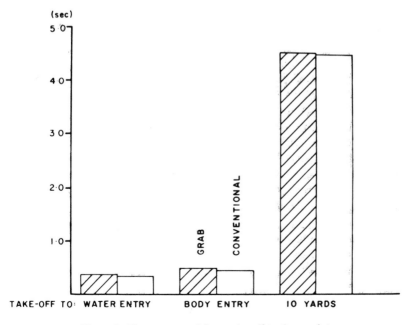

Figure 2. Times measured from take-off to three points.

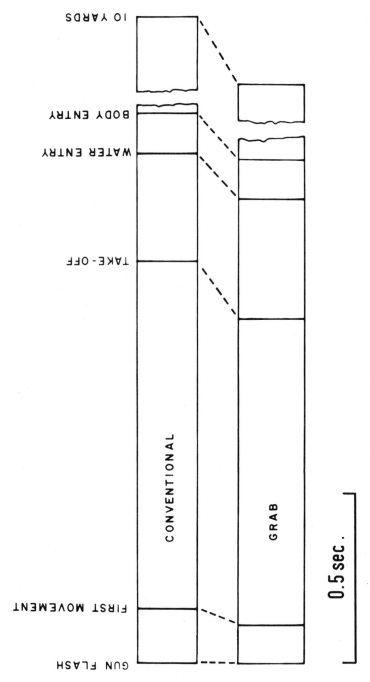

Figure 3. Times measured from gun flash to various stages of the start.

armswing. The net result, as far as conditions at take-off are concerned, is the same with either type of start.

Temporal components

In the over-all performance measure taken in this study (time from gun flash to 10 yards) the swimmers as a group were 0.184 sec faster when they used the grab start rather than the conventional start. This difference was significant at the 0.05 probability level. Figure 2 graphically illustrates the point that has already been made, that this superiority in performance did not arise from events after take-off. All the parameters were measured from the take-off as zero time and it is apparent from Figure 2 that the grab start was in fact slightly slower (though not significantly so) than the conventional start in all cases.

It is clear, then, that time spent on the block following gun flash must be the major determinant of improved performance. Figure 3 shows results which confirm this hypothesis.

The two main measures taken in this segment of the performance were gun flash to first movement and gun flash to take-off or total block time. The group showed shorter mean values when using the grab start for both these parameters, movement time being 0.15 sec faster and total block time 0.17 sec faster. Both these differences were significant at the 0.001 level of probability.

It is probable that movement time is faster in the grab start because the extensor muscles of the lower limb are able to maintain a high level of activity before gun flash, movement is prevented while in this ready position by the action of the arms. Further time is saved by the elimination of the armswing which occurs in the conventional start before the center of gravity of the body begins to move forward. The action of the arms after gun flash would appear to counteract any loss in propulsive force which occurs because of the elimination of the armswing.

CONCLUSIONS

The major reason for the superiority of the grab start over the conventional circular armswing start would appear to be that the swimmer is able to leave the blocks more quickly yet without a decrement in velocity at take-off. Further work is necessary to define the exact action of the hands in the grab start.

REFERENCES

Bowers, J. E. 1973. A biomechanical comparison of the grab and conventional sprint starts in competitive swimming. Unpublished master's thesis. Pennsylvania State University, University Park.

Dempster, W. 1955. Space requirements of the seated operator. USAF, WADC, Tech. Ref. 55–59. Wright Patterson Air Force Base, Ohio.

Roffer, B. J. and R. C. Nelson. 1972. The grab start is faster. Swimming Techn., J. Swimming, Diving, Water Polo 8: 101–102.

Williams, M. and H. Lissner. 1962. Biomechanics of Human Motion. W.B. Saunders Company, Philadelphia.

Winters, C. N. 1968. A comparison of the grip start and the conventional start in competitive swimming. Unpublished master's thesis. Southeast Missouri State College, Cape Girardeau.

A comparison of four styles of racing start in swimming

A. Ayalon, B. Van Gheluwe, and M. Kanitz

The current state of knowledge on racing starts in swimming is characterized by a diversity of opinions concerning the mechanics of the activity. Different writers advocate different methods. Some also have presented a rationale for their preferences (Smith, 1958; Counsilman, 1968; Heffner, 1960; Jorgensen, 1971; Maglischo, 1968; Groves, 1971; Torney and Clayton, 1970).

Several articles have been written advocating the grab start as the best (Hanauer, 1967, 1972; Turner, 1974). Hanauer stated that subjective observations led him to conclude that the swimmers who use the grab start leave the blocks faster, that the trajectory is lower, that the body seems to have greater velocity, and that water entry will be earlier than, but not as far from the edge of the pool as in other methods. Roffer and Nelson (1972) found that over a distance of 12 feet, the grab start was faster than conventional starts. Fitzgerald (1973) advocated a style that combines the characteristics of the bunch start in track and field and the grab start in swimming (this style was called, in the present study, bunch start).

PURPOSE

The purpose of this study was to compare four styles of swimming racing starts: 1) the conventional style (straight backswing), 2) the grab start, 3) the bunch start, and 4) the track start. The track start was similar to the bunch start except that in the track start support for the back leg was provided while the hands were on the block.

PROCEDURES

Twenty untrained male swimmers (age $\bar{X}$ = 22) were taught to perform the four styles of start. Four sessions that included 20 trials for each style were given to all the subjects. Videotape feedback was used to facilitate the learning process. The seven subjects who performed the four styles in an adequate form were chosen for participation in the investigation.

In the testing session each subject performed three trials for each style. The order of the styles was randomly chosen for each subject. The mean value for the three trials was used as the data for the final analysis. Both time and film data were gathered for each trial.

Timing device

This device measured the time between the command to start and the moment the swimmer's hips reached the distance of 5 m from the edge of the pool. It consisted of a clock (1/100 sec) and a system of switches and an electromagnet that operated the clock.

Cinematographic techniques

A Bolex, 16-mm spring-driven movie camera, operating at 51 frames per sec, was used to film the subject's performance. A bell was used to start the subjects and a light was recorded on the film at the moment the bell rang.

The film was analyzed by digitizing 17 points of the body, and these data were processed with a program for kinematic analysis using a Monroe 1860 desk computer.

RESULTS

The mean values and standard deviations for the temporal variables are presented in Figure 1. *t*-tests between the four styles for the time to leave the blocks, time in the air, total time to water entry, and time to reach 5 m are presented in Table 1.

The horizontal and vertical displacement of the center of gravity for the four styles studied is presented in Figure 2. The angular displacement of the shoulder, hip, knee, and ankle joints for each of the four styles of start are presented in Figures 3, 4, 5, and 6.

DISCUSSION

The results obtained show that with the bunch and track styles the subjects left the blocks faster than with the other styles. This can be explained by the

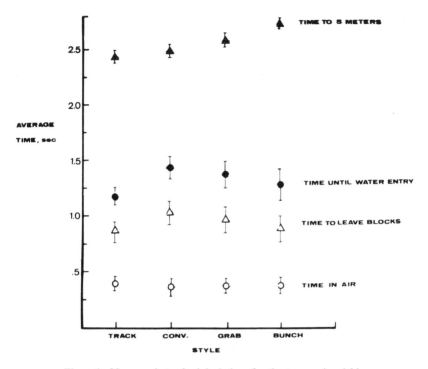

Figure 1. Means and standard deviations for the temporal variables.

low position of the body and the lack of fluctuations of the center of gravity along the y-axis in these two styles (Figure 2). In the conventional and grab styles, time is required to bring the center of gravity of the body to the line of push. Although the grab start was faster than the conventional start in leaving the blocks (see Figure 1), the difference was not statistically significant.

The time in the air was quite similar for all the styles, and no significant differences were found among these values.

The track and bunch starts were significantly faster ($p < 0.05$) than the grab start for the total time until water entry.

The bunch start proved to be the slowest start in terms of time to reach the 5-m line. This phenomenon could be explained by the fact that in this style only one leg is used for propulsion. The track style eliminated this problem by adding the action of the second leg. The back leg had a very definite effect on the acceleration of the center of gravity, as can be seen in Figure 1 (time to water entry).

No rationale was apparent for the use of the hand positions in the bunch start similar to the grab start as suggested by Fitzgerald (1973). While in the

Table 1. Results of *t*-tests among styles for
the temporal variables

	Conventional	Grab	Bunch
Time to leave block			
Grab	1.93		
Bunch	3.75*	3.39*	
Track	4.85*	2.33*	1.45
Time in air			
Grab	0.18		
Bunch	0.48	0.28	
Track	1.02	0.99	0.97
Time to water entry			
Grab	0.01		
Bunch	1.25	2.64*	
Track	2.07	3.22*	1.38
Time to 5 m			
Grab	1.10		
Bunch	2.78*	2.28	
Track	0.91	1.90	2.63*

*$p < 0.05$.

grab start elbow flexion helps to lower the center of gravity faster, this is not necessary in the bunch where the center of gravity is already low enough.

In reference to the coordination of the movement in the different styles, the summation of forces in the conventional style seems to be the most effective (see Figure 2). The propulsive action is started by the arms, then the hip, knee, and ankle extensions. In the other three styles the action of the different body parts, in the propulsive phase, was found to be quite simultaneous.

CONCLUSIONS

It can be concluded from this study that: a) the provision of support of the back leg seems to benefit a style that brings the swimmer into a low starting position; b) although in the track style the back leg pushed at about 40 cm behind the edge of the block, the faster times for leaving the blocks in this style compensated for this deficiency and allowed for better times for reaching the 5-m line; c) the bunch style was the slowest style studied; d) in spite of the fact that the grab start was faster than the conventional style for leaving the blocks, the better summation of forces of the latter could provide for a faster time to the 5-m line.

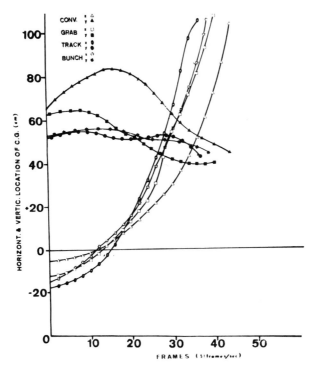

Figure 2. Horizontal and vertical displacement of the center of gravity for the different styles 0, edge of block.

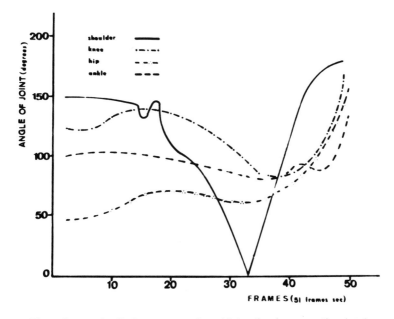

Figure 3. Angular displacement at selected joints for the conventional style.

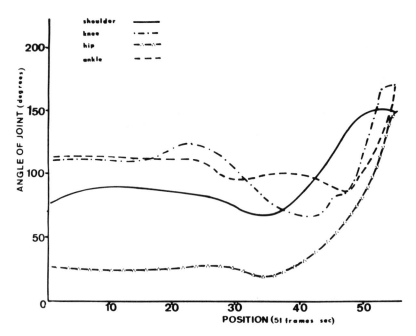

Figure 4. Angular displacement at selected joints for the grab style.

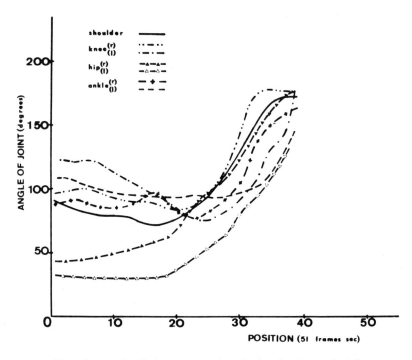

Figure 5. Angular displacement at selected joints for the bunch style.

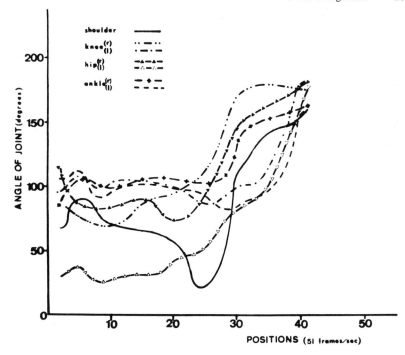

Figure 6. Angular displacement at selected joints for the track style.

A further study with larger groups of subjects and with longer training in the new styles would perhaps show more definite differences between the conventional and the other styles studied.

REFERENCES

Armbruster, D. A. 1968. Competitive Swimming and Diving. The C.V. Mosby Co., St. Louis.

Counsilman, J. E. 1968. The Science of Swimming. Prentice-Hall, Englewood Cliffs, N.J.

Fitzgerald, J. 1973. The track start in swimming. Swimming Techn. 10: 3; 89–94, October.

Gambrill, D. L. 1969. Swimming, Goodyear Publishing Co., Pacific Palisades, Calif.

Groves, R. 1971. A cinematographic analysis of four styles of racing start in swimming. Unpublished Ph.D. dissertation. University of Missouri, Columbia.

Hanauer, E. S. 1967. The grab start. Swimming World 8: 5 and 42, June.

Hanauer, E. S. 1972. Grab start faster than conventional start. Swimming World 13: 8–9 and 54–55, April.

Heffner, F. 1960. The swimming start. Athletic J. 40: 18 and 60–61, January.

Jorgensen, J. W. 1971. Cinematographic and descriptive comparison of selected racing starts. Unpublished Ph.D. dissertation. Louisiana State University, Baton Rouge.

Maglischo, E. 1968. Comparison of three racing starts in competitive swimming. Res. Quart. 39: September, 604–609.

Roffer, B. J. and R. C. Nelson. 1972. The grab start is faster. Swimming Techn. 8: April, pp. 101–102.

Smith, A. 1958. The coiled spring racing dive. Athletic J. 38: 51–52, January.

Torney, J. A. and R. D. Clayton. 1970. Aquatic Instruction, Coaching and Management. Burgess Publishing Co., St. Paul, Minn.

Turner, J. C. 1974. The mechanical advantages of the grab start speak for themselves. Swimming Techn. 10: No. 4; pp. 111–112, January.

Analysis of the egg beater and breaststroke kicks in water polo

J. P. Clarys

Fundamentally, the game of waterpolo is played above the surface of the water, therefore dictating that a player keep his head above water and have both arms available for playing the ball whenever possible. Consequently, a large demand is placed on the legs for stability and locomotion (Beatty, 1973).

Experienced poloists are able to propel themselves upward so that their entire torsos, from the waist up, are out of the water (Hines, 1967). Balance and body control are essential to correct throwing, and it is necessary that beginners learn how to. tread water to ensure this balance and control (Barr, 1964). For the most part this is accomplished by employing the egg beater kick and to a certain extent a modified breaststroke kick. The former is basically a frog kick as used in the breaststroke with the exception that the legs move alternately instead of moving symmetrically together. The latter differs from the normal kick because the legs must not come together during the propulsive phase.

The egg beater kick as shown in Figure 1 has been described in different textbooks on water polo (*e.g.,* Barr, 1964; Hines, 1967; Lambert-Gaughran, 1969) and has been biomechanically analyzed by Beatty (1973).

This study was undertaken to investigate the efficacy of the egg beater kick in comparison with the breaststroke kick using a device that employed pressure transducers.

APPARATUS

The use of pressure transducers is not very common in aquatic research. Boichev *et al.* (1969, 1971) studied the synchronization between legs and

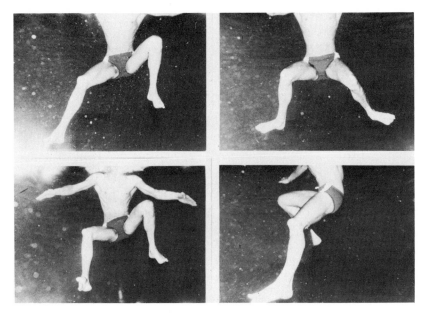

Figure 1. The vertical egg beater kick.

arms and the coordination of the swimming movement in general using an electrotensiometric transformer. Belokovsky (1971) investigated the pulling motions of the arms during the sprint crawl stroke using pressure transducers controlled by accelerometers. Recently, similar to Belokovsky, Rijken and Sitters (1974) studied different types of pressure on the palms of the hands of a group of top class Dutch front crawl swimmers. The pressure transducers used were developed at the Netherlands Ship Model Basin.

The apparatus shown and explained in Figure 2 was used for the comparison of the egg beater kick with the breaststroke leg movement. The electrical signal of the strain gauges was amplified and registered on a ultraviolet recorder. The velocity variations of the feet through the water generated different electrical signals, which corresponded to the exerted mechanical pressures. The pressure transducers were fixed on two identical wooden boards and were calibrated at different velocities prior to the collection of data.

PROCEDURES

One top class water polo player and all around swimmer was selected as a subject because of his precise egg beater movement and outstanding breaststroke performances.

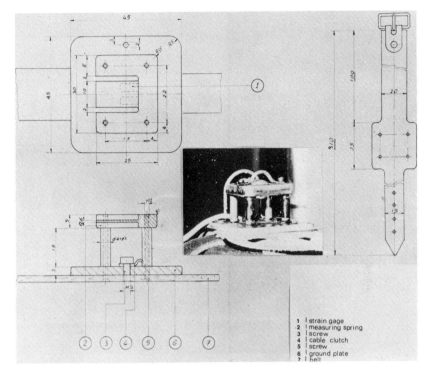

Figure 2. The pressure transducer device.

The pressure transducers were fixed on the left and right tibial malleoli of the subject. After the subject completed a preliminary warm-up, the following kicks were performed: a) egg beater kick in vertical ball handling position, hands upon the water surface; b) breaststroke kick under the same circumstances; c) egg beater kick in an horizontal position, hands together in front of the body; and d) breaststroke kick under the same circumstances.

Each kick was executed 10 times during 20 sec with a 1-min rest between the executions. The subsequent kicking sequence was started after complete recuperation of the subject.

During the horizontal tests, velocity was measured by means of a carriage that could be driven electrically at accurate, adjustable speeds. This device followed the subject, and the corresponding velocity was recorded by a photoelectric cell system.

RESULTS AND DISCUSSION

Over-all pressure patterns of the egg beater and breaststroke kick in both vertical and horizontal positions are shown in Figure 3. Only the absolute

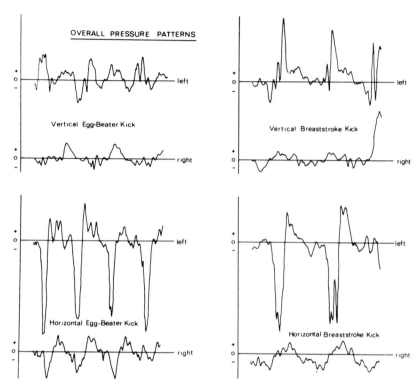

Figure 3. Over-all pressure patterns of the egg beater kick and breaststroke kick in vertical and horizontal positions.

values of the results were considered, and these must be taken as a basis for further research.

The general pattern for both leg movements and for the different executions within one kick show a high reproducibility. This may be an indication of the technical skill of the subject and the over-all correctness of the different executions.

In order to evaluate and compare the different kicks and the left and right legs, respectively, we calibrated both pressure transducers under the same circumstances at a velocity of 3.00 $m \cdot sec^{-1}$. The deviation from the baseline (zero) over a time period of 10 sec was considered as the relative 100 percent of the pressure.

The mean percentages for all kicks are listed in Table 1. These lead to the following assumptions: a) in both egg beater and breaststroke kicks there was a lack of over-all pressure symmetry between right and left leg movements in contradiction to the cinematographically stated symmetry or alternative synchronization; b) although no significant visual difference could be found in the leg motion of the two positions, no indication was found of any similarity in the pressure patterns between the horizontal and vertical posi-

Table 1. Relative pressure percentages for the egg-beater (E.B.) and breaststroke (B.S.) kick in vertical (V) and horizontal (H) positions*

	Left leg (%)	Right leg (%)	Velocity $(m \cdot sec^{-1})$
Pressure at $3 \; m \cdot sec^{-1}$	100	100	
V.E.B. +	19.5	11.3	
V.E.B. −	10.9	5.9	
V.B.S. +	37.3	14.4	
V.B.S. −	41.0	14.1	
H.E.B. +	11.8	7.1	0.88
H.E.B. −	42.7	23.4	
H.B.S. +	12.0	5.3	0.82
H.B.S. −	40.5	17.2	

*+ indicates positive or propulsive pressure; − indicates negative or contramovement pressure.

tions; c) there was no resemblance between the kicks in a vertical position, but we presumed a relative similarity of pressure pattern existed in the horizontal position; d) in both vertical kicks the propulsive action resulted in the highest pressure; e) in the horizontal position, the contramovement (negative pressure registration) of both egg beater and breaststroke kicks showed the highest pressures.

CONCLUSIONS

Although these statements have been made on one carefully selected subject, we found important differences between the left and right leg pressure patterns. We also noted marked differences between the egg beater and breaststroke kicks in the vertical position. The differences were not as pronounced in the horizontal position although the locomotion pattern was the same.

The contramovement pressure seems to be important. Both movements are frequently used in water polo, and these findings indicate that if studied in more detail using a larger sample and combined with electromyography and goniometry more valuable information on both leg movements would be provided and might eventually lead to a specific application in water polo.

REFERENCES

Barr, D. 1964. Guide to Waterpolo. Museum Press, London.
Beatty, G. W. 1973. Prospectus of a biomechanical analysis of the egg-beater

kick in waterpolo. Personal communication and unpublished master's thesis. University of Western Ontario, Canada.

Belokovsky, V. V. 1971. An analysis of pulling motions in the crawl arm stroke. *In:* L. Lewillie and J. P. Clarys (eds.), Proceedings of the First International Symposium on Biomechanics in Swimming, pp. 217–221. Université Libre de Bruxelles, Brussels.

Boichev, K. 1971. Devices recording the parameters of swimmers. Bull. d'info. Olympic Committee of Bulgaria 4: 28–31.

Boičev, K. *et al.* 1969. Electrotensiometric apparatus for studying the movements of swimmers under natural conditions. Problems Physical Culture 4: 222–231.

Hines, C. 1967. How to Play and Teach Waterpolo. Associated Press, New York.

Lambert, A. F. and R. Gaughran. 1969. The Technique of Waterpolo. The Swimming World Publication, North Hollywood, Calif.

Rijken, H. and B. Sitters. 1974. Effectiviteit van de handbeweging bij de vrije slag voor een aantal goed getrainde zwemsters en zwemmers. Zwemkroniek (The Netherlands) 51: 19, 439–442.

An evaluation of selected carrying methods used in lifesaving

J. G. Hay, D. R. McIntyre, and N. V. Wilson

National organizations responsible for the teaching of lifesaving typically recommend a number of carrying or towing methods for use in bringing a victim to safety. The American Red Cross, an organization which has been active in this area for over 60 years, claims that "only four [of these methods] have withstood successfully the test of time and extensive application." (American Red Cross, 1972, pp. 135–136). These four methods, most or all of which are also included (sometimes with slight modification) among those recommended by the corresponding organizations of other countries, are the tired swimmer, hair, cross-chest, and head carries. These carries are described as follows:

> *Tired Swimmer Carry.* . . . the swimmer moves . . . to the victim and instructs him to turn to a face-up floating position. He then swims to a position facing the tired swimmer and tells him to place his hands on his shoulders keeping the elbows straight, to separate the feet and to look him in the face. Thereupon, the rescuer swims a slow and easy breast stroke, pushing the victim ahead of him. . . The recovery of the arms in the breast stroke must, of course, be along the side of the victim (ARC, 1972, p. 136).

> *Hair Carry.* . . . the rescuer slides his fingers from the crown of the victim's head toward the forehead and seizes a handful of hair. Depressing the wrist and holding the arm straight, he turns on his side and tows the victim using the side stroke adaptation, either with the regular or the inverted scissors and shallow arm-pull (ARC, 1972, p. 139).

> *Cross-Chest Carry.* From a position behind the victim, the rescuer reaches over the shoulder and across the chest and grasps the side just below the arm pit. The rescuer tucks the victim's shoulder securely into his own armpit and clamps his arm firmly against the chest. At the same time, the rescuer turns on the side so that the hip is directly beneath the small of the victim's back. Either the regular or inverted scissors and the shallow arm-pull are then used. . . (ARC, 1972, p. 140).

Head Carry.... from a position behind the victim, the rescuer places a hand on each side of the head. The palms cover the victim's ears, the fingers are extended along the jaws and the thumbs are placed on the temples. The hold is firm and by depressing the wrists, the victim's head is tilted back until the chin points directly upward. The arms are held straight. The rescuer assumes a half-sitting position in the water and strokes vigorously with the legs using either an inverted scissors or breast stroke kick (ARC, 1972, pp. 141–142).

Considering the importance of carrying methods in the saving of human lives and the apparent absence of previous work in this area (an extensive review of the literature failed to reveal even one published paper devoted to a scientific analysis of carrying methods), an evaluation of these recommended methods seemed long overdue.

PURPOSE

The purposes of this study were to: a) compare the four carrying methods recommended by the American Red Cross in terms of speed, energy cost, and efficiency; b) compare the four methods in terms of selected kinematic characteristics of the motions involved; and c) attempt to relate observed differences between methods in speed, energy cost, and efficiency to observed differences in their kinematic characteristics.

PROCEDURE

Subjects

Eight experienced, college-aged, male lifesavers were used as subjects (rescuers). All of the rescuers were in good physical condition at the time of the experiments. One additional subject, a male high school student, was used as the victim in all of the trials conducted.

Trials

Two 4-hr testing sessions were conducted with four rescuers being tested in each session. Each rescuer performed four trials, one using each of the four carrying methods. Each trial proceeded as follows: a) The rescuer placed a noseclip in position to prevent exhalation via the nose and then adopted a standing position in the shallow end of the pool. b) On a shouted command, the rescuer swam 53 to 54 yards (48.5 to 49.4 m) to the other end of the pool where the victim was awaiting his arrival. In keeping with what would be appropriate in a real-life situation, the rescuer was instructed to swim this first length of the pool as fast as he could consistent with the need to conserve some energy for the return swim with the victim. All rescuers used a front crawl stroke in swimming this first length. c) Upon reaching the victim, the rescuer took hold of a mouthpiece suspended directly above him and inserted this in his mouth. This mouthpiece was connected to a meteorological balloon supported on a trolley which was moved along the poolside in unison with the rescuer during the return swim. d) The rescuer then took hold of the victim in the manner appropriate to the carrying method being employed and carried him back to his original starting point at the other end of the pool. Once again, in keeping with what might be required in a real-life situation, the rescuer was instructed to swim this second length as fast as he was able.

Trials were performed in a randomized order with one trial conducted during each 15 min of each 4-hr testing session. This procedure provided for a 1-hr rest period between consecutive trials by the same subject. Three timekeepers recorded the time taken by the subject to swim the middle 135 feet (41.1 m) of each length.

Gas collection

A sample of expired air was collected in a meteorological balloon during the middle 100 feet (30.5 m) of each return swim. The volume of the sample was determined with a Parkinson-Cowan ventilation meter and aliquots of the sample were analyzed for O_2 and CO_2 by the Micro-Scholander technique. Duplicate analyses run on each sample agreed within 0.03 percent. Oxygen uptake, ($\dot{V}O_2$), energy cost (estimated by the product of $\dot{V}O_2$ and time to complete the return swim), and the ratio of average speed to energy cost (an indicator of the rescuer's efficiency) were then calculated. (Means and standard deviations for temporal and energy cost parameters are to be found in Table 1).

Cinematography

The movements of the rescuer and the victim between 80 and 100 feet (24.4 and 30.5 m) from the beginning of the second length of each trial were recorded cinematographically with the aid of an inverse periscope (McIntyre and Hay, 1975). The periscope was mounted on the side of the pool opposite to that alongside which the subjects moved and at a distance of approximately 56 feet (17.1 m) from the subjects' "line of action." A Locam 16-mm motion picture camera was mounted on the platform of the periscope and filmed each performance at a rate of 20 frames per sec.

The films were analyzed with the aid of a Vanguard motion analyzer linked on-line to a digitizer and IBM keypunch. The x- and y-coordinates of a fixed origin and 21 landmarks on both the rescuer and victim, the x-coordinate of the center of the frame, and the y-coordinate of the surface of the

Table 1. Means and standard deviations for temporal and energy cost parameters

Parameter		Cross chest carry	Hair carry	Head carry	Tired swimmer carry
Time for first length	$\overline{X}$	23.7	23.9	23.9	23.7
(sec)	S.D.	1.2	1.5	1.0	1.3
Time for second length	$\overline{X}$	83.4	66.6	75.2	50.5
(sec)	S.D.	17.1	8.8	12.7	4.9
Oxygen uptake	$\overline{X}$	3.40	3.25	3.36	3.36
(liters/min)	S.D.	0.28	0.24	0.39	0.45
Energy cost	$\overline{X}$	23.63	18.14	21.07	14.13
(kcal)	S.D.	3.63	2.09	2.94	1.54
Efficiency	$\overline{X}$	0.07	0.12	0.09	0.19
(fps/kcal)	S.D.	0.02	0.03	0.03	0.03

water were recorded for each frame during one complete stroke cycle. The coordinates thus obtained were used in conjunction with a computer program which first corrected the data for refractive effects (see McIntyre and Hay, 1975) and then computed: a) the x- and y-coordinates of the centers of gravity of the rescuer and the victim in each frame, b) the range of vertical motion of the center of gravity of the rescuer and the victim during one stroke cycle, c) the mean angle of inclination of the trunk of the rescuer (represented by a line joining the midpoint of the hips to the midpoint of the shoulders) from the horizontal during one stroke cycle, d) the mean angle of inclination of the trunk of the victim from the horizontal during one stroke cycle, and e) the stroke length and stroke frequency of the rescuer. (Means and standard deviations for kinematic parameters are to be found in Table 2).

Statistical analysis

An analysis of variance for repeated measures on the same subjects was employed to determine if the parameters of interest differed significantly among carrying methods. Where significant F-ratios were obtained ($p < 0.05$), the Newman-Keuls test was used to test for significant differences between individual mean values. In addition, Pearson product-moment correlation coefficients were computed to determine the relationships existing among the parameters of interest.

RESULTS AND DISCUSSION

Speed, energy cost, and efficiency

Significant differences were found among carrying methods in the average speed attained by the rescuer during the return swim with the victim (average

Table 2. Means and standard deviations for kinematic parameters

Parameter		Cross chest carry	Hair carry	Head carry	Tired swimmer carry
Range of vertical motion	$\overline{X}$	0.27	0.34	0.24	0.34
of rescuer	S.D.	0.04	0.08	0.08	0.13
(ft)					
Range of vertical motion	$\overline{X}$	0.30	0.31	0.24	0.32
of victim	S.D.	0.05	0.08	0.05	0.14
(ft)					
Mean angle of trunk	$\overline{X}$	32.7	26.9	21.0	18.1
inclination of rescuer	S.D.	6.1	6.3	4.5	5.0
(deg)					
Mean angle of trunk	$\overline{X}$	25.9	17.0	21.5	19.7
inclination of victim	S.D.	10.0	4.8	4.2	4.5
(deg)					
Stroke length	$\overline{X}$	1.70	2.21	1.80	2.80
(ft)	S.D.	0.45	0.44	0.76	0.68
Stroke frequency	$\overline{X}$	0.86	0.84	1.02	0.89
(cycles/sec)	S.D.	0.04	0.04	0.12	0.10

speed = 135 feet (41.1 m)/time for the second length.) The tired swimmer carry was significantly faster than each of the others and the hair carry was significantly faster than the cross-chest carry.

Significant differences were found in energy cost in all the paired comparisons between one carrying method and another with the tired swimmer carry requiring the least energy followed, in order, by the hair, head, and cross-chest carries.

Significant differences between carrying methods were found with respect to efficiency; *i.e.,* the tired swimmer carry was more efficient than all of the others and the hair and head carries were more efficient than the cross-chest carry.

A consideration of the kinematic characteristics of the four carrying methods suggested some reasons for the observed significant differences in speed, energy cost, and efficiency.

Stroke length and stroke frequency

An analysis of the significant differences in stroke length and stroke frequency among the four carrying methods indicated that the tired swimmer carry was faster than the cross-chest and head carries because of a significantly greater stroke length and faster than the hair carry because of a significantly greater stroke frequency.

Significant correlations between stroke length and speed, energy cost, and efficiency further emphasized the important role played by stroke length. In contrast, none of the relationships between stroke frequency and these same three variables was statistically significant.

Trunk inclination of rescuer

Significant differences were found among carrying methods in the angle of inclination of the trunk of the rescuer (an angle roughly akin to the angle of attack). The mean angle for the tired swimmer and head carries was less than that for the hair carry which, in turn, was less than that for the cross-chest carry. In addition, significant relationships were found indicating that decreases in trunk inclination were associated with increases in stroke length, increases in speed, decreases in energy cost, and increases in efficiency.

The stroke length is determined by propulsive factors, which exert a positive influence, and resistive factors, which exert a negative influence. Thus, if decreases in trunk inclination are accompanied by increases in stroke length, the inclination of the trunk must somehow be involved, either in increasing propulsion or in decreasing resistance or both. While changes in trunk inclination would probably have some effect on both propulsion and resistance, it seems likely that of the two, there would be a greater effect on the resistance. For, as the trunk inclination increases, the frontal area presented to the oncoming flow of water also increases and, with it, the magnitude of the drag which the rescuer encounters. Under such circumstances, the inverse relationship between trunk inclination and stroke length can be readily understood.

Trunk inclination of victim

Only one significant difference was found among carrying methods in the mean angle of trunk inclination of the victim. The trunk inclination in the hair carry was significantly less than in the cross-chest carry—a similar finding to that involving the trunk inclination of the rescuer when using the same two carries. In keeping with this observed similarity in results, a significant relationship was found between the trunk inclinations of the rescuer and victim.

Range of vertical motion

Since increases in the vertical motion of a body moving through water are generally accompanied by increases in the drag which the body experiences, it might be hypothesized that the less the range of the rescuer's vertical motion the better his over-all performance. This hypothesis was not supported, however, since the tired swimmer and hair carries had significantly greater mean ranges of vertical motion than did the head carry. It would seem, therefore, that the propulsive benefits associated with the larger movements of the limbs in these two carries more than offset any accompanying increases in the resistance encountered due to their greater ranges of vertical motion.

CONCLUSIONS

The findings in this study appear to warrant the following conclusions: a) The tired swimmer carry is faster, less energy-consuming, and more efficient than the other carries studied and should, therefore, be used in preference to other carries whenever possible. b) The hair carry is probably the next best all around carry of those studied. It is less energy-consuming than the head carry and faster, less energy-consuming, and more efficient than the cross-chest carry. It should certainly be used in preference to the cross-chest carry whenever possible and in preference to the head carry when conserving the rescuer's energy is an important consideration. c) The cross-chest carry should only be used when speed, energy cost, and efficiency are not the dominant factors governing the choice of carry. d) Of the kinematic parameters examined, the stroke length and the trunk inclination of the rescuer appear to be most closely associated with the over-all performance. The greater the stroke length and the less the trunk inclination, the better the performance.

ACKNOWLEDGMENTS

The authors wish to express their gratitude to Dr. Carl V. Gisolfi (Stress Physiology Laboratory, University of Iowa) for his assistance with the physiological measurement techniques employed in the study, and to Dr. George G. Woodworth (Statistical Consulting Center, University of Iowa) for his assistance with the statistical analysis.

REFERENCES

American Red Cross. 1972. Life Saving and Water Safety. Doubleday and Co., Garden City, N.Y.
McIntyre, D. R. and J. G. Hay. 1975. Dual media cinematography. In: L. Lewillie and J. P. Clarys (eds.), Biomechanics of Swimming II, International Series on Sport Sciences, Vol. 2, pp. 51–57. University Park Press, Baltimore.

Instruction for normal and handicapped swimmers

A theory-based approach to teaching swimming

M. Smith

In earlier research many workers have examined differential effects of one or two factors and provided bases for improving instruction in important ways. This article deals with an effort to organize and then apply simultaneously a large number of current relevant concepts from biomechanics, motor learning, psychology, and studies of teaching style, to the task of teaching nonswimmers. This approach, in contrast to most earlier efforts, is concerned as much with the social-psychological dimensions of learning environments as with matters of the nature and sequence of tasks set for learners.

The major aspects of the study (Smith, 1974) on which this article is based included: a) a review of relevant literature from which a multidisciplinary theoretical rationale was developed; b) the expression of the important concepts from the rationale in a series of 16 "critical characteristics" that became guidelines for developing detailed curriculum materials; c) videotaping classes of nonswimmer children, 7 to 10 years old, taught by the investigator. The tapes were analyzed both by observation and by use of a modification of a widely used system of verbal interaction analysis, Hough's OSIA (Amidon and Hough, 1967), for evidence of the presence of the 16 critical characteristics in the experimental classes; and d) training four neophyte instructors and then analyzing videotapes of classes taught by those individuals.

The present article is limited to a discussion of the critical characteristics extracted from the theoretical rationale. The original 16 have been reduced to nine characteristics which will be stated and briefly discussed.

CRITICAL CHARACTERISTIC I

As an important factor in maintaining facilitative levels of arousal in learners, the teacher's behavior must be flexible with a warm, indirect style predomi-

nant in the early stages. Eysenck's (1963) work on the familiar Yerkes-Dodson law established that for complex or threatening tasks, high levels of arousal diminish performance. Bruner (1966) pointed out that high states of arousal are common in learning tasks and that when anxiety is high, ". . . instruction verges on a kind of therapy" (p. 53). Flanders' (Amidon and Hough, 1967) extensive field studies provide two additional points of support: a) that superior teachers regularly display flexible behavior in the sense that they are equally capable of being authoritarian or indirect (warm, accepting, non-threatening), and b) when learners feel uncertain or anxious, an indirect teaching style is most likely to be effective.

CRITICAL CHARACTERISTIC II

Willingness to attempt or risk tasks, either teacher or self-assigned is met with appropriate positive verbal or nonverbal reaction and/or corrective feedback. This implies that learners are free to make significant choices within the general framework set by the teacher. The active inquiry or search behavior that characterizes learning requires a persisting willingness to take risks in attempting to learn. Performance levels will be greatest when the learner assesses his own probability of success on a given task at about 50/50 (Atkinson, 1957). This situation is most likely to occur if the learner has *reasonable latitude* to attempt self-assigned tasks and to modify, reorder, or decline tasks set by the teacher. The central roles of positive reinforcement and corrective feedback in skill acquisition are well established (Skinner, 1968; Bilodeau, 1969).

CRITICAL CHARACTERISTIC III

Early tasks center on experiences in the water with the principles that influence movement in first the vertical and second the horizontal planes. Bruner (1966) stressed that new knowledge should be in concrete form; further, it should minimize the amount of information that must be held in mind and processed to achieve comprehension. It should also be effective in terms of integrating matters that may otherwise appear unrelated. Fitts and Posner (1967) stressed the importance of meaningful verbal instructions and spatial cues in the early or cognitive phase of skill learning. Smith (1974) has compiled a comprehensive summary of the physical principles involved in movement in the water which are applicable to this characteristic.

CRITICAL CHARACTERISTIC IV

Practice activities are predominantly in the water and involve chunks of movement that the learner identifies as whole units rather than a practice of intact parts of desired terminal skills. The dangers of relying on transfer of training are well known and are to be avoided. The literature regarding skill acquisition provides extensive support for whole methods of practice. It also indicates that practice of specific parts may at times be necessary for individuals. The "whole units" that are practiced must be both manageable and meaningful to the learner (Lawther, 1968).

CRITICAL CHARACTERISTIC V

Skilled functional movements emerge through a shaping, social learning process of successive modification within a framework established by the teacher but with allowances for learners to make significant choices. Bandura (1969), warned against applying simplistic learning principles drawn from animal studies in laboratories to real learning of complex skills by humans. He cited a wide variety of real-life skill acquisition and behavioral changes induced under experimental conditions primarily through learners viewing other persons being reinforced for desirable performances. Such modeled performances not only serve as demonstrations to be emulated, but give an accurate indication of which behaviors are rewarded and which behaviors bring negative results. This powerful social learning process of direct modeling is strengthened by verbal and symbolic instructional cues which Bandura (1969, p. 46) labeled "symbolic modeling." When direct and symbolic modeling cues are combined with Skinner's (1968) concept of the "shaping" of complex behavior through differential reinforcement, one has what appears to be an accurate description of the way individuals acquire complex skills, including learning to swim.

CRITICAL CHARACTERISTIC VI

Demonstrations and other instructional cues are seldom longer than 30 sec and focus on one or two specific aspects. Input to the learner's central nervous system is by no means restricted to perceptual cues arising from the environment of the individual. Particularly during early learning a good deal of confusing feedback arises within the learner as a result of the cognitive, proprioceptive, and affective processes that are involved. Thus the "limited single channel capacity" of the individual (Miller, 1956) may be severely overloaded even though an observer would consider the perceptual cues being attended to by the learner to be both simple and few in number.

CRITICAL CHARACTERISTIC VII

Initial propulsive attempts are made using the upper limbs in the preferred style of the learner, alternately or simultaneously. Secondary propulsive experience is focused on extending distance ability and adding a variety of limb actions. The superior dexterity of the upper limbs is obvious and has its origin in the evolutionary value of a variety of skills requiring accurate hand-eye coordination. This situation, combined with the well documented principle that the flutter kick is inefficient and may even be detrimental to propulsion (Counsilman, 1968), indicates that primary attention of beginners should be directed to propulsion with hands and arms. Further, since skilled performance is known to emerge slowly (Fitts and Posner, 1967; Skinner, 1968), and given the importance of a sense of achievement in maintaining motivation, secondary attention should be directed to extending nonstop distance ability while using a variety of combinations of limb patterns.

CRITICAL CHARACTERISTIC VIII

Feedback in the form of accurate, positive evaluation and/or response-correcting information is provided often and specifically in terms of distance, frequency, quality, and various combinations of these factors in relation to the learner's own past levels of achievement. Bilodeau (1969) considers feedback to be the key variable at all stages of learning. It is essential to response correction and in maintaining motivation (Fitts and Posner, 1967). Inappropriate external standards can heighten arousal to interfering levels and/or generally decrease expectations of success and, therefore, lower motivation. Difficult but realistic goals related to past performance levels can be identified much more reliably and have been shown to be consistently motivating (Locke and Bryan, 1966).

CRITICAL CHARACTERISTIC IX

As learning progresses, the teacher stretches the reinforcement schedule and becomes more discriminating in dispensing reinforcers and corrective feedback. The object of instruction should be a relatively self-sustaining performance by the learner, who has also been equipped to take over his own corrective function (Bruner, 1966). The essential ingredients are instruction that emphasizes why things are done as they are, a stretched reinforcement schedule known to stabilize behavior, and a diminution of instructional cues so that the learner assumes more and more responsibility for his own activity. As performance becomes refined, reinforcement and feedback are not only withheld over longer intervals but become more specifically concerned with important aspects of technique.

PRELIMINARY APPLICATION OF THE CURRICULUM

The detailed curriculum materials (Smith, 1974) were carefully developed to be consistent with the concepts expressed in the critical characteristics. The

Table 1. Results of preliminary application of curriculum

Instructor	Class Size	$\bar{X}$ Age (yrs)	$\bar{X}$ Height (inches)	Nonstop distance final test $\bar{X}$ (feet)		
				Front	Back	Combo
Author	12	7.84	50.6	8.1	11.7	14.6
Trainee 1	8	7.94	50.7	11.1	11.7	13.4
Trainee 2	8	7.82	53.0	20.4	32.7	15.1
Author	12	9.78	54.3	14.3	59.4	31.4
Trainee 3	8	9.63	53.4	19.6	10.1	11.9
Trainee 4	8	9.61	53.9	39.5	115.3	114.1

investigator instructed a class of 12 children, 6 of each sex, ages 7 to 8 years, and a similar class, 9 to 10 years of age, each for 10 lessons of 40 min. Only those children unable to swim any measurable distance were included in these instructional classes. Data concerning age, I.Q., S.E.S., height, and school grade of all children were collected. A taped interview with each child was conducted, prior to instruction, to assess experience and attitudes regarding the water. Then neophyte instructors, two of each sex, received 20 hr of training before teaching one class of 8 nonswimmers in each of the age ranges (7 to 8 and 9 to 10 years). Final, testing in all classes consisted of nonstop distance swims in front, back, and combination front and back positions (Table 1).

All but four children in the investigator's class of 7- to 8-year olds learned to swim some distance between 5 and 600 feet. These four were shorter in height, younger, and among the least experienced when compared with other children in the classes. They also reported more specific and general anxiety and threatening fantasies about the water than successful classmates.

It is hoped that data from the final tests and other information arising from this study will be useful as baselines for future work. The extensive observational analysis of the videotapes and the large body of information gathered through the Hough OSIA analysis of the verbal interaction during both phases of the study provided evidence that the critical characteristics were made operational in the classes.

Performances of the neophyte instructors and the classes taught by them indicated that the approach can be grasped without undue difficulty.

REFERENCES

Amidon, E. J. and J. B. Hough (eds.). 1967. Interaction Analysis: Theory, Research and Application. Addison-Wesley Publishing Co., Don Mills, Ontario.

Atkinson, J. W. 1957. Motivational determinants of risk-taking behavior. Psychol. Rev. 64: 359–372.

Bandura, A. 1969. Principles of Behavior Modification. Holt, Rinehart and Winston, New York.

Bilodeau, E. A. (ed.). 1969. Principles of Skill Acquisition. Academic Press, New York.

Bruner, J. S. 1966. Toward a Theory of Instruction. Belknap Press, Cambridge, Mass.

Counsilman, J. E. 1968. The Science of Swimming. Prentice-Hall, Englewood Cliffs, N.J.

Eysenck, H. J. 1963. The measurement of motivation. Sci. Amer. 208: 130–140.

Fitts, P. M. and M. I. Posner. 1967. Human Performance. Brooks/Cole Publishing Company, Belmont, Calif.

Lawther, J. D. 1968. The Learning of Physical Skills. Prentice-Hall, Englewood Cliffs, N.J.

Locke, E. A. and J. F. Bryan. 1966. Cognitive aspects of psychomotor performance: the effects of performance goals on level of performance. J. Appl. Psych. 50: 286–291.

Miller, G. A. 1956. The magical number seven, plus or minus two: some limits on our capacity for processing information. Psychol. Rev. 63: 81–97.

Skinner, B. F. 1968. The Technology of Teaching. Appleton-Century-Crofts, New York.

Smith, M. F. R. 1974. A psychologically-based approach to teaching swimming. Unpublished doctoral dissertation. University of Alberta, Alberta.

Special swimming instruction for the multiple handicapped

W. P. M. Vis

STARTING POINT

The human being can be looked upon as a moving object in space who finds himself between and in relation to the other objects and the environment. This can be called a fundamental aspect of human existence. In this context the swimming instruction must be considered a part of movement education and must be looked at in relation to the pedagogical and agogical perspective.

This implies that we regard our pupils as persons who are disturbed or retarded in their total development and who need our special help in order to grow up and achieve optimal human functioning. This assistance that is directed toward the individual pupil may be referred to as education. If this educational assistance has as its starting point the moving person, we refer to it as movement education. Through conscious influence of the movement behavior of the student, movement education provides an important contribution to total education. This form of education is fundamentally important, since human movement means contact with the environment and confrontations and actions with persons and objects.

These moving, manipulating, exploring actions give the pupil an *experience* and a notion of the qualities and properties of persons and objects: balls are round things with which you can roll, very near and far away, that's only a matter of distance one has to cover; high and low is a matter of climbing and falling; light and heavy is a matter of lifting up and carrying away; etc. Moreover, while moving, a pupil experiences and *unfolds* his own possibilities, and we hope he'll come to *enjoy* them; while doing he comes to a notion of himself as somebody who is able or unable to do particular things. This forms among others a base for the achievement of self-consciousness. All this means development, characterized by progress, unfolding, differentiation and integration, in which "moving" plays an essential part. Generally the mentally

263

retarded can only develop himself through actual moving among objects and persons; he can't argue or discuss things. He gets to know his world by dealing with it actively, by moving; movement is—certainly for mental retardates—a necessity for development. Herewith, we have given the motive for an essential aspect of the total education with regard to individuals who are characterized as developmentally disturbed pupils.

ASPECTS OF MOVEMENT EDUCATION

Starting from the above-mentioned philosophy, movement education with regard to mental retardates can be approached in three ways: movement stimulation, movement instruction, and movement recreation.

Movement stimulation

Movement stimulation is that form of movement education that is focused on: a) gaining the very *experience* of *fundamental movement situations* and the experience of very elementary movement forms like grasping, handling, throwing, creeping, walking, mounting and dismounting, balancing, climbing etc. and b) experiencing and exploring the *primary movement space,* in particular the ground space and the surrounding space of the body. This inviting approach mainly concerns severe mental retardates, in whom the capacity for or motivation to (directed) activity is often restricted or totally absent.

Movement stimulation, realized individually or in small groups led by trained persons, is applied: a) as a stimulating manipulation on behalf of those pupils who are not considered for schooling or for work; b) as a form of training therapy within the frame of the physiotherapy, mostly for severely physically handicapped pupils; c) in preparation for the below-mentioned movement instruction, mainly for younger pupils with a favorable prognosis concerning their (movement) development.

Movement instruction

The fundamental movement experience is central in movement stimulation. Movement instruction is mainly concerned with further *development* of *movement behavior:* on the enrichment and enlargement of the movement arsenal; on the elevation of the aiming movement, adjusted to the kind of movement situation; on the increase of movement engagement; on the improvement of insight into different movement situations; and on the development of movement association with others. For this approach, exclusively realized by movement pedagogues and taking place in groups, milder retarded pupils who have already shown certain movement skilfulness and who seem to be affected by means of our movement situations are considered. They ought to dispose of a so-called basic movement development, they ought to show a sense of task-directedness, to be instructable, to show willingness for contact, to have interest for actual moving, and not to behave aggressively or otherwise disturb the other pupils of the group. Movement instruction is to be found not only at schools for mild mental retardates, but also as a part of the day program of working pupils, who have not yet reached their movement optimum.

Movement recreation

Movement recreation, organized or guided by movement specialists, meets the needs of recreation of the pupils who have broadly common interests and possibilities. Movement recreation, in most cases based on movement instruction, can be an individual matter, but it mostly takes place in groups. It is mostly for "better" pupils, who are able and want to engage actively and spontaneously in a *playful, joyful, relaxing,* and more or less varied movement occupation. Movement recreation is applied in the form of sporting clubs in spare time, or for a change in the day program, mainly among working pupils.

Movement therapy and physiotherapy

Up to now we have been speaking about education in general and movement education in particular. Therapy, including movement therapy and physiotherapy, means something else. If a pupil presents such dominant disturbances or handicaps that the pedagogical help becomes very difficult, a specialist can be called in, so that favorable conditions for a more directed pedagogical activity can be created. In other words, special treatments (*e.g.,* movement therapy, physiotherapy, hydrotherapy, speech training, behavior therapy etc.) derive their aims from education; therapy is at the service of education. A therapy that does not suit any pedagogical frame should not be continued.

In *movement therapy and physiotherapy,* an intensive individual treatment by movement specialists and physiotherapists is focused on the realization of newly desired (movement) behavior of severely *emotionally* and *psychosocially disturbed* pupils to bring them into better contact with their environment and other people. Based on our experiences, this concerns two categories of pupils, described as follows.

The first includes younger pupils, functioning on an intellectual level of imbeciles, who are able to have a short but not lasting, directed movement, and contact relation with their environment. They present themselves as restless persons, who are rapidly irritated, who feel threatened moderately quickly, who express themselves in a chaotic way, who are very difficult to influence, and who are mainly orientated to objects at the expense of their human relations.

The other group is comprised of older pupils, functioning on high imbecile or mild mentally retarded level with a neurotic form of behavior. They can have a well directed movement and contact relation with their environment but are inhibited. They appear as less vital, retiring, suggestible pupils, who feel threatened moderately quickly, who express themselves with difficulty, and who show ambivalence of "we will, but we are not able to" in their appearance.

METHODS

Conditions

In order to teach swimming to the multiple handicapped, the physiotherapist (movement therapist) should decrease certain forms of spasm through a number of techniques in relation to the psychomotoric disturbances and/or instrumental disturbances according to the Bobath method (reflex-inhibition) to arrive at the point of dynamic, ongoing movement forms in water.

Modalities

Movement education and therapy are realized by carefully selected movement situations, each containing a movement problem, the solution of which requires activity, by which the pupil has more or less to move in space. These movement situations can be divided into two groups.

1. Movement tasks. Certain movement situations are directed toward reaching a concrete object; they are limited by a clear starting point and a clear end. In a movement task, the problem or question is always directed, restricted, and as such more comprehensible; the situation around a movement task is steady. In this situation, the available instruments, such as apparatus and tools, can structure a space, form an obstacle, make a demand, impose a limitation. Movement tasks, realized on the basis of a (played) rhythm, are also considered in this category.

2. Movement games. Certain movement situations are directed toward playful activity and characterized by continuity, surprise, unexpectedness, and more or less unpredictability. Here, the situation is not steady but variable. The comprehensibility is more difficult now. The continuously changing situation entails a continuously changing problem. This variability is determined not only by the kind of game and the choice of game agreements, but also by the interaction between the different playmates.

Conditions

The offered means should meet the following conditions: a
based upon the basic patterns of human movement; b)
concrete and clear, giving the intention directly; c) they sl
moving and joining; d) they should give sufficient opportuni
ing, exploring, and rejoicing.

PROCEDURE

The movement pedagogue, movement therapist, and phys.
members of a multidisciplinary team. In close consultation
gogue, psychologist, rehabilitation specialist, psychiatrist, and
residence group, they determine the necessity, the possibility,
ing of movement education or movement therapy. These inclu
tative aspect, referring to the results of the action motricity as
attendant expressions, namely those which oppose the acti
b) some qualitative aspects, referring to the way of contacting,
ness, instructability, interest, and sociability. The quantitative as
the concrete level of achievement concerning basic motricity; ti
aspects refer to the degree of susceptibility of the pupil by r
available movement situations. The quantitative and qualitative a
examined movement behavior are considered in their mutual coi
form the starting point. Indications for a certain kind of movemei
or movement therapy and physiotherapy and data gained with thi
examination provide us with the indications for a more justified (
of the groups. Movement education and movement therapy ;
therapy take place in a planned and programmed way. This me
work on fixed days and times, guided by teaching programs anc
plans in which the objective is described, as well as the way in
objective may be reached. To determine the extent to which these
are realized, every approach or treatment is periodically evaluated
of a movement re-examination and by our regularly fixed observai
evaluation is described in detail and submitted verbally and in wri
treatment team.

REFERENCES

Vis, W. P. 1971. Swimming as Therapy, Motoric Treatment of Dev
Disturbances, p. 180. Lemniscaat, Rotterdam.
Vis, W. P. 1973. Special Swimming Instruction for the Handicappec
Lemniscaat, Rotterdam.

Electromyography for the evaluation of handicapped swimmers

L. Maes, J. P. Clarys, and P. J. Brouwer

In the literature many authors recommend the use of a specific swimming technique for supporting and/or strengthening certain muscles or muscle groups. Very few of these recommendations are based on scientific experiences. Lorenzen (1970) mentioned the strengthening of the extensors of the back during the backcrawl. Vis (1971) indicated the breaststroke was the most effective way to develop the back musculature. According to Duffield (1969) the extensors are generally used in back and front crawl. The flexors are utilized in breaststroke and butterfly.

Experimental investigations on the function of muscles during swimming are limited. Ikaï et al. (1964) compared the electromyogram (EMG) of an Olympic champion with a University champion in breaststroke, front, and back crawl. Lewillie (1968, 1971, 1973) studied the triceps brachii, the biceps brachii, and the quadriceps femoris at different speeds using the four competitive strokes.

Clarys et al. (1973) investigated the biceps brachii, the brachio radialis, the flexor carpi ulnaris, and the triceps brachii in subjects executing the front crawl stroke in competition and in water polo. In this study the electrical potentials (EMG) of five preselected muscles were studied during three swimming techniques: a) breaststroke, b) back crawl, and c) front crawl. The results were related to the "normal" and the disabled swimmer.

PROCEDURES

The EMG technique used for the measurement of muscle potentials during swimming has been previously described by Lewillie (1968, 1971). The recordings are made by means of a telemetric apparatus. The electromyograms are synchronized with 16-mm film.

The 13 male subjects (mean age 21 years) in this study were all-around swimmers and water polo players. We realized that eventual style differences were due either to an individually different motor learning process or to anatomical differences. In a previous study, no significant differences were found in swimming motions between swimmers and certain water polo players (Clarys *et al.*, 1973).

The muscle selection was made according to several criteria.

1. Most of the superficial muscles, mentioned in the literature, were photographed on ten cadavers and a scale was developed. The relative subdermal surface of each muscle was measured by means of a planimeter (OTT 113). All muscles with a relative subdermal surface less than 10 cm^2 were omitted because of the possibility of faulty recordings.

2. The different muscles were classified according to their location and anatomical function.

3. Finally, a group of five flexors were selected that met the criteria of sufficient surface and location on each body part: the biceps brachii, the flexor carpi ulnaris, the rectus abdominis (under and above the umbilicus), the biceps femoris, and the tibialis anterior. The biceps brachii was used as the control muscle because of the possibilities for comparison with previous studies.

Data were recorded for each of the following items: a) the total relative myoelectrical activity developed by the muscle and its quantitative importance in relation to the activity developed during a maximal (isometric) contraction (Table 1); b) the relative maximal intensity reached and its quantitative importance in relation with the activity during a maximal isometric contraction (Table 1); c) the location of the different peaks in the EMG pattern in relation to the movement pattern.

RESULTS AND DISCUSSION

The recordings of the biceps brachii and the flexor carpi ulnaris in the front crawl were similar to the results reported by Clarys *et al.* (1973).

Biceps brachii

In the breaststroke ten subjects showed a double-peaked EMG pattern with a maximum at the beginning of the pull of the arm cycle and at the end of the push phase of the arm cycle, respectively. Ikaï *et al.* (1964) mentioned only one peak in their study.

Table 1.

Muscle	Total (relative)* electrical activity (%)			(Relative) maximal intensity reached (%)		
	Breaststroke	Front crawl	Back crawl	Breaststroke	Front crawl	Back crawl
Biceps brachii	29.3	48.7	33.7	61.5	94.5	66.6
Flexor carpi ulnaris	45.4	43.1	31.8	59.0	62.4	53.0
Biceps femoris	27.2	32.5	27.3	62.6	57.4	54.2
Tibialis anterior	33.3	22.7	16.9	80.4	38.7	24.8
Rectus abdominis (under umbilicus)	13.0	21.0	19.9	30.9	29.2	36.8
Rectus abdominis (above umbilicus)	22.5	31.4	25.1	42.4	52.1	38.4

*The relative 100 % = the individual isometric maximum for a specific muscle over a time period of 0.2 sec.

In the back crawl, all subjects showed a double-peaked pattern, but the film analysis revealed little resemblance among the different cycles. These results differ from the findings of Ikaï *et al.* (1964). (It should be noted that Ikaï and his associates did not record the activity of the arm flexors during the primary pull and push phases of the arm cycle.)

Flexor carpi ulnaris

During the breaststroke, ten subjects showed a double-peaked pattern with highest values near the time of maximal extension of the arm and in the middle of the pull and push phases. During the maximal extension of the arm Ikaï *et al.* (1964) also found one peak.

In the back crawl, eight subjects showed a double-peaked EMG, pattern but in three cases only one peak was found. The double-peaked electromyograms reached a maximum a) between the middle of the recovery phase and the glide phase and b) between the entry in the water and the middle of the pull and push phases (in this region the single peak maximum was also found). Ikaï *et al.* (1964) described one peak during the cycle at the same point in the stroke cycle as was found in this study.

Biceps femoris

The biceps femoris showed single-peaked pattern during the breaststroke in ten cases. Three subjects showed a double-peaked EMG. (See Figures 1–3.) The maxima occurred: a) in the middle of the counter movement of the leg and b) between the complete extension of the leg and the middle of the knee flexion (at approximately 1/4 of the knee flexion).

In the front crawl, eight subjects showed a triple-peaked pattern. The different peaks were not very pronounced. Because of inadequate synchronization between the rhythm of the arm and leg movements, it was not possible to locate the peaks in relation to the movement pattern. A similar situation existed in the cases of the biceps femoris in the back crawl and the tibialis anterior in both back and front crawl.

During the back crawl, nine subjects had triple-peaked EMG patterns, with marked individual differences in durations and amplitudes.

Tibialis anterior

All subjects in the breaststroke showed one very clear and pronounced peak in the EMG pattern, with a maximum at the end of the recovery movement of the legs. These findings are similar to those reported by Ikaï *et al.* (1964).

In the front crawl, six swimmers showed a minimal electrical activity compared to the other muscle patterns. The amount and the form of the

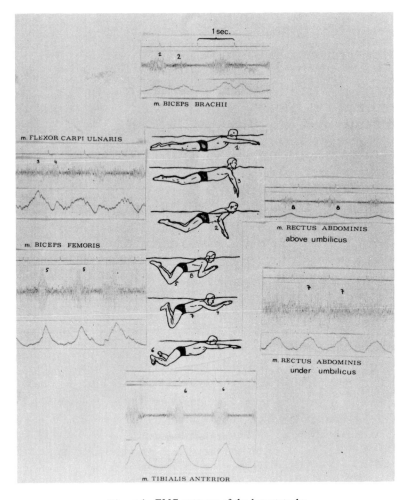

Figure 1. EMG patterns of the breaststroke.

peaks seem to indicate an important variation. Ikaï *et al.* (1964) found one peak during the leg cycle in the front crawl. A minimum of myoelectrical activity was found in this muscle during the back crawl by eight subjects. There were also important irregularities in the form and the amount of the peaks.

The EMG results derived from subjects who swam the breaststroke seem very relevant. Therefore, we suggest the use of the tibialis anterior as a control muscle in future EMG investigations of leg movements.

Rectus abdominis (under the umbilicus)

During the breaststroke, six swimmers showed a rounded single-peaked pattern, while six others had an EMG indicating minimal myoelectrical activity.

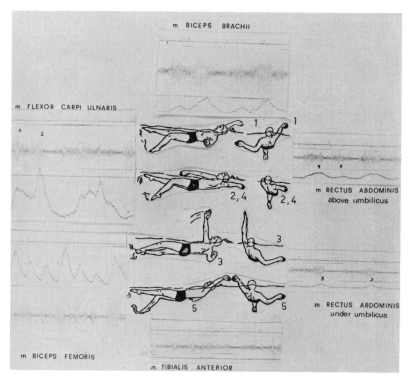

Figure 2. EMG patterns of the back crawl.

In one case, a rounded double-peaked pattern was found. The 16-mm film analysis indicated a maximum when the arm reached the middle of the recovery phase. At the same moment, the legs were almost at maximal flexion at the hip joint.

In the front crawl, six subjects showed identical patterns without pronounced peaks. One had an electrical maximum when the arms reached the middle of the pull phase. If a second peak could be seen, the maximum was found during the glide phase.

In the back crawl, six subjects showed a small pronounced single-peaked EMG pattern. No electrical activity was found in five cases. The peaks only reached the maximum during the pull and push phases of the arm.

Rectus abdominis (above the umbilicus)

In the breaststroke, a single-peaked pattern was found in seven swimmers, a double-peaked pattern in one case. Four subjects showed a constant form of myoelectrical activity without pronounced peaks. In the mono-peaked EMG, the maximum was located at the end of the push phase. In this position the legs were in maximal flexion at the hip joint.

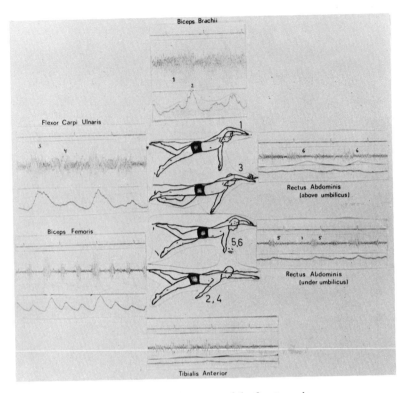

Figure 3. EMG patterns of the front crawl.

In the front crawl, a similar form of electrical activity with small peaks was found in nine patterns. Only one swimmer had a regular mono-peaked EMG. This peak was found halfway through the pull phase of the arm.

During the back crawl, very irregular patterns for most of the subjects were apparent: one little peak per cycle for three subjects, two peaks per cycle for five subjects, constant electrical activity in the case of two subjects, and no electrical activity for two subjects.

In the case of the mono-peaked patterns the maximum was found at the start of the pull phase of the arm. In the double-peaked patterns, the maxima were located at ± 1/4 and 3/4 of the same phase.

The fact that the percentages of the rectus abdominis (above the umbilicus) were always markedly higher than those of the rectus abdominis (under the umbilicus) seems to support the theory that the part of this muscle *above* the umbilicus cooperates in an active way in the total movement. During the propulsive phase of these three swimming techniques, this part will contribute to the intensity of the pull and push phase of the arms, while pulling the ribs toward the fixed pelvis. While swimming front and back crawl the two parts of the rectus abdominis would assist in augmenting the arm movement.

CONCLUSION

The assumption is made that the results of this study may be related to most handicapped cases, on the one hand. The recordings of the biceps brachii and the flexor carpi ulnaris were similar to those of Clarys *et al.* (1973). Therefore, in relation to the handicapped swimming, we presume that those two muscles can be strengthened and/or supported in all three swimming techniques. On the other hand, both measurements of the rectus abdominis showed little activity during swimming movements.

The biceps femoris and the tibialis anterior are important in the breast-stroke but none or only a small amount of activity was found during the back and front crawl, in contradiction to the findings of Lorenzen (1970) and Duffield (1969).

REFERENCES

Clarys, J. P., J. Jiskoot, and L. Lewillie. 1973. A kinematographical, electro-myographical and resistance study of waterpolo and competition front crawl. *In:* S. Cerquiglini, A. Venerando, and J. Wartenweiler (eds.), Biomechanics III, Medicine and Sport, Vol. 8, pp. 446–452. Karger, Basel.

Duffield, M. H. 1969. Exercise in Water. London.

Ikaï, M., M. Miyashita, and K. Ishii. 1964. An electromyographical study of swimming. Jap. Res. J. Phys. Educ. 7: 4.

Lewillie, L. 1968. Telemetrical analysis of the electromyogram. *In:* J. Wartenweiler, E. Jokl, and M. Hebbelinck (eds.), Biomechanics I, Medicine and Sport, Vol. 2, pp. 147–148. Karger, Basel.

Lewillie, L. 1971. Quantitative comparison of the electromyogram of the swimmer. *In:* L. Lewillie and J. P. Clarys (eds.), First International Symposium on Biomechanics on Swimming, pp. 155–159. Université Libre de Bruxelles, Brussels.

Lewillie, L. 1973. Muscular activity in swimming. *In:* S. Cerquiglini, A. Venerando, and J. Wartenweiler (eds.), Biomechanics III, Medicine and Sport, Vol. 8, pp. 440–445. Karger, Basel.

Lorenzen, H. 1970. Behinderte Schwimmen. H. Putty Verleg, Wuppertal.

Vis, W. P. M. 1971. Swemmem els therapis. Lemniscaat, Rotterdam.

Analysis of techniques used by swimmers in the Para-Olympic Games

U. Persyn, E. Surmont, L. Wouters, and J. De Maeyer

Differences in physical abilities depend upon individual handicaps and, therefore, comprise one of the main problems in competition for the physically handicapped. Competitive sport for physically handicapped individuals is meaningful only when they are divided into homogeneous groups. Based on the level of spinal cord lesion, the paralyzed are classified in five classes. Specifically, in the sport of swimming, because the lower extremities provide the primary equilibrium, the best class is divided into two categories: classes 5 and 6. This division is based upon the "muscle charting system" of the lower extremities.

PURPOSE AND PROCEDURE

We have not proposed a new system, but we do attempt to show that the present system is unsatisfactory. It can be quite frustrating to the competitors. While it is generally believed that the classification should be made on a functional basis, we propose that it also be made in an aquatic medium. This is necessary in order to compare timed performances in the water. Such a classification might even be specific for each swimming stroke.

We consider it of primary importance to identify some basic general principles rather than be involved in obtaining exact measurements. A videotape recorder has been used to evaluate the hydrodynamic principles applied by paralyzed swimmers. Our study (Surmont, 1974) of able-bodied swimmers on the world class level was the basis for our observational scheme and the grouping of results in this study. All of the swimmers of our test group were participants of the XXI Weltspiele der Gelähmten-Heidelberg, 1972. These Para-Olympic Games took place at the Institut für Sport und Sportwissenschaft Universität Heidelberg.

An individual solution for adequate movement in the water is as variable as the possible differences of handicaps; it is difficult to identify norms. Although most of the authors state clearly that any classification system should be built upon a functional basis, this has not been done. At most meetings, protests abound, and there are many athletes whose classifications are reviewed. The "Classification Manual for Doctors" (1972) points to this possibility: "One must keep in mind, that when swimming one can benefit from the remaining sensory functions and also from slight movement." In the case of partially paralyzed muscles, some can produce a slight but efficient movement. Also for able-bodied individuals in a 2-beat kick in the crawl stroke (for example the pattern of S. Gould) the need for the lower extremities is very slight. They provide stabilization but very little of the propulsive force. The "International Swimming Rules" (1973) for the paralyzed state that the legs can only be used in classes 5 and 6. Nevertheless, many swimmers were observed using one leg efficiently even in class 3: a kick when swimming (Figure 2, 10–11) and an impulsion when turning. In the existing classification system, only a subjective test of the (specific or nonspecific) muscle strength of the lower limbs is considered, independent of the swimming stroke. A main factor, joint flexibility, is ignored. This capacity, however, defines to a great extent the possible hydrodynamic solutions. We believe that, if one has an efficient movement of the upper extremities, then the flexibility and shape (streamline) of the lower extremities are more important than their strength.

In the same class, the fastest times are occasionally as much as three times faster than the slowest times (e.g., 3'25.9" and 1'24.8" for 100-m back crawl stroke: women class 5). In the same class one can identify very adequate (Figure 1, 1–2 and Figure 2, 18–21) and very poor (Figure 1, 5–6 and Figure 2, 16–17) technical swimming solutions. In different classes we find nearly the same solutions. (Figure 1, 1–2, 3–4) The present system does not provide for homogeneous classes.

STYLE EVALUATION

"Good" solutions

In the breaststroke, we found that most competitors had changed their styles so that they no longer complied with the FINA rules. The kick had become a dolphin-like kick (Figure 1, 1–2). In the crawl and back crawl if one leg still functions, it tends to roll the body along its longitudinal axis. Fundamental to total synchronization is the "crossed coordination" of the upper and lower limbs which provide a reasonable solution. During the pressing downwards of an arm, normally a downward kick of the opposite leg is given. A paralyzed individual kicks his "functioning" leg alternatively outwards-downwards and

278   Persyn *et al.*

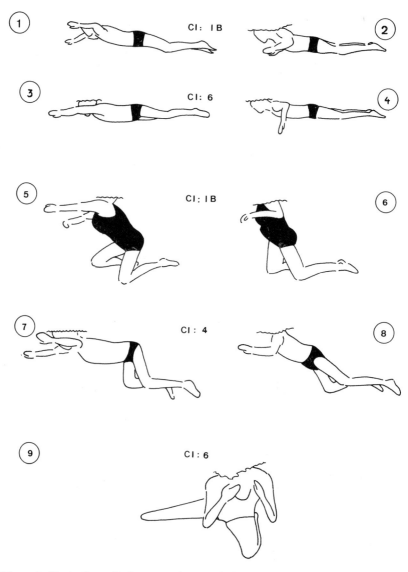

Figure 1. Illustrations of adequate and poor solutions to the problems of swimming by paraplegics.

Figure 2.

inwards (crossing-over)-downwards, which is the best solution to provide a partial screwing effect (Figure 2, 10–15). Because the lower limbs are handicapped, the synchronization of the kick in the crawl usually is reduced to a 2-beat pattern. Some, however, succeed in using a 6-beat synchronization (Figure 1, 18–21). If in the back crawl the downward-body-supporting kick is missing, a rolling results if the upper limb push is downward with a great force.

"Poor" solutions

In the back crawl a handicapped rarely uses the downward push which restores the balance. This push instead is too often replaced by a dragging downward push phase and even by a sculling movement. The pull frequently is too lateral resulting in a very large twisting movement. Often a rough circumduction is used over a too short path, a systematic fault of beginning swimmers. In the crawl the arm presses downwards too long so that the synchronization of the arms becomes similar to a glide stroke. As a result the lower limbs will sink. We even observed a trudgeon style, an extremely strong kicking style, with paraplegic patients (Figure 2, 14–15). A submerged position of the head and a deep entry of the hand and forearm is the most logical solution for the paralyzed, although not used enough. Some swimmers create a disadvantage for themselves by making exaggerated movements with the lower limbs. Since the abdominal musculature is too weak, a twisting of the trunk results, breaking the streamline features of the body (Figure 2, 16–17). In the breaststroke, the hands are pulled so that they pass the shoulder (Figure 1, 3–4). The result is a prolonged recovery of the arms and a discontinuity of movement. This is an important fault in this style because the lower limbs (dolphin kick) do not provide propulsion at the end of the recovery.

For a paralyzed person, attempting a breaststroke kick usually will be more disadvantageous than attempting a dolphin kick, even if one leg is furnishing propulsion. A similar attempt of the more severely paralyzed leg will: a) be more of a drag than a propulsing force, because of the great amplitude of the kick; b) be too slow to switch into a normal synchronization: arms and legs will overlap each other in an ineffective way (Figure 1, 9). Often the stabilizing hip flexion during the support provided when the spread of the upper limbs is too pronounced and drags too much (Figure 1, 5–8).

CONCLUSION

It appears that swimmers at this "Olympic" level often fail to receive adequate training from swimming experts. If we observe poor swimming technique among the best swimmers, then the situation is probably much worse for the remaining handicapped. People accept the fact that swimming for the physically handicapped has to be encouraged. However, we doubt the desirability of high level competition for them, since in the existing classification system the technical function related to swimming is not evaluated. Homogeneous groups cannot be obtained only on the basis of a medical examination of the level of spinal cord lesion and an inadequate muscle function test. Thus the aim for fair competition is difficult to reach.

REFERENCES

Anonymous. 1972. Classificatie handleiding ten behoeve van de geneesheren. B.L.O.S.O., Brussels.
Anonymous. 1973. Rules for the Swimming International Stoke Mandeville Games. International Swimming Trainers Association for the Paralyzed, Stoke Mandeville.
Persyn, U. 1973–1974. Technisch-hydrodynamische benadering van de bewegende-mens-in-het-water, uitgaande van een kritische studie van de "Science of Swimming" van Counsilman, Hermes, Vol. VIII, No. 3–4, pp. 5–136.
Surmont, E. 1974. Studie over de zwemsport bij fysisch gehandicapten, Leuven, Niet-gepubliceerde licentiaatsverhandeling, Departement voor Lichamelijke Opleiding - K.U.L.

Anatomical aspects of swimming

Body build and somatotype of Olympic swimmers, divers, and water polo players

M. Hebbelinck, L. Carter, and A. De Garay

Athletic ability represents an expression of psychological and biological variation of human physical activity in a quantified way within the structure of the governing rules of sport. As postulated in a previous paper presented at the Fourth International Seminar on Biomechanics (1974), body form and function are intimately related and do play an important role in achieving top class performance. For every Olympiad, samples of the best athletes from many countries are selected for competition in various sports. There is no doubt that athletes who compete in Olympic Games are endowed with aptitudes which permit them to attain an extremely high level of achievement in their special sport. Hence, a sample group of athletes participating in Olympic Games is particularly favorable for making a comparison of certain characteristics of body build and body form.

It is the purpose of this article to present a description and an analysis of anthropometric data and of the somatotypes of male and female Olympic swimmers and divers, as well as of male water polo players.

METHODS

The subjects for the aquatic sports studied in this investigation were taken from the comprehensive study of athletes of the Mexico Olympic Games, edited by De Garay, Levine, and Carter (1974). Anthropometric measures were available on 66 male swimmers, 29 female swimmers, 16 male divers, 7 female divers, and 71 male water polo players. For the somatyping, the corresponding numbers of subjects were 64, 27, 16, 7, and 70. Because the number of swimmers was not large, they were classified according to swimming style and not according to distance. All styles of swimming were represented by the male subjects, but in the female group there were no butterfly swimmers. The divers participated in either 3- or 10-m diving, or both.

The anthropometric measurements were taken following the internationally accepted techniques of Martin and Saller. These techniques as well as the instruments used are described in the volume on Olympic Athletes (De Garay *et al.*, 1974). The present study includes the report and analysis of a selected number of measures: height, weight, trunk length, biacromial width, chest depth, biiliocristal width, arm length (not including the hand), lower leg length (not including the foot), total leg length (not including the foot), thigh girth, calf girth, upper arm girth (elbow flexed), biepicondylar humerus width, biepicondylar femur width, and the sum of three skinfolds (triceps, subscapular, and suprailiac). The analyses of differences between more than two means were made using the Duncan's New Mutiple Range Test.

In order to make these somatometric data proportionally comparable, the mean values were adjusted to phantom height, and z-scores were calculated as recommended by Ross and Wilson (1973). Additionally, three anthropometric indices were calculated, *i.e.,* the weight ÷ height ponderal index of Quetelet, the biiliocristal width ÷ biacromial width index for androgyny (Bayley and Bayer, 1946), and the trunk length ÷ leg length index of Manouvrier.

All subjects were somatotyped according to the Heath-Carter Anthropometric Somatotype Method (Carter, 1972). For descriptive analyses the mean somatotype was computed for each group and subgroup, and individual somatotypes were plotted by computer on somatocharts. In addition, an indication of the dispersion of the somatoplots of each group was calculated using the somatotype dispersion index, and the dispersion standard deviation according to the formulas of Ross and Wilson (1973) and Ross, Carter, and Wilson (1974). The somatotype dispersion distances among mean somatotypes for the swimmers, divers, and water polo players and their respective subgroups were calculated to indicate the difference between the means of the various somatoplots.

RESULTS

Somatometric characteristics

The means and standard deviations for all groups of swimmers, the divers, and the water polo players are summarized in Table 1. Table 2 reveals that there were no significant differences among the groups of male swimmers in weight,

Table 1. Anthropometric values (mean and standard deviation) for Olympic swimmers, divers, and water polo players

Event*	N	Weight (kg)	Height (cm)	Trunk length (cm)	Biacromial width (cm)	Biiliocristal width (cm)	Arm length (cm)	Leg length (cm)	3 skinfolds (mm)
SWM M	66	72.1 ± 6.8	179.3 ± 6.2	54.4 ± 2.7	41.2 ± 2.0	28.1 ± 1.4	60.7 ± 3.0	82.1 ± 3.7	22.0 ± 5.1
FRS M	22	74.2 ± 7.1	181.1 ± 5.9	55.0 ± 2.4	41.7 ± 1.7	28.6 ± 1.4	62.0 ± 2.6	83.4 ± 3.9	22.9 ± 4.8
BRS M	12	69.0 ± 6.2	175.4 ± 6.3	53.2 ± 2.0	40.4 ± 2.5	26.8 ± 0.9	59.4 ± 3.5	79.8 ± 4.2	22.1 ± 4.8
BKS M	11	70.3 ± 5.8	180.3 ± 5.3	54.6 ± 3.5	41.1 ± 1.9	27.7 ± 1.1	61.7 ± 3.4	83.6 ± 3.6	21.5 ± 7.3
BUT M	10	72.2 ± 7.1	178.2 ± 5.9	54.7 ± 3.4	40.7 ± 1.9	28.5 ± 1.7	59.5 ± 2.7	81.1 ± 2.9	21.4 ± 5.2
MED M	12	73.0 ± 6.3	178.5 ± 5.8	53.9 ± 2.7	41.8 ± 1.7	28.3 ± 1.1	60.0 ± 1.5	82.1 ± 2.8	20.3 ± 3.8
SWM F	29	59.9 ± 9.1	164.4 ± 7.1	49.5 ± 2.7	37.1 ± 1.7	27.1 ± 2.0	55.1 ± 2.9	76.1 ± 4.4	34.2 ± 17.7
FRS F	7	53.4 ± 9.9	165.9 ± 8.7	49.1 ± 3.0	36.8 ± 2.4	26.1 ± 2.8	55.3 ± 3.6	77.7 ± 4.0	31.2 ± 10.6
BRS F	8	53.9 ± 7.3	160.9 ± 7.2	49.4 ± 3.6	36.8 ± 1.8	26.9 ± 1.6	55.4 ± 1.7	73.9 ± 3.6	34.9 ± 31.1
BKS F	3	57.2 ± 3.1	164.6 ± 6.4	49.7 ± 1.4	36.2 ± 1.3	27.6 ± 0.8	54.0 ± 2.6	75.1 ± 2.5	32.1 ± 11.9
MED F	10	61.8 ± 9.6	166.0 ± 6.0	49.7 ± 2.4	37.7 ± 1.0	27.8 ± 1.7	55.2 ± 3.5	77.3 ± 5.2	36.3 ± 8.4
DIV M	16	65.5 ± 5.0	172.1 ± 5.1	51.3 ± 2.2	40.2 ± 2.2	27.3 ± 1.4	58.5 ± 2.5	79.0 ± 3.6	20.0 ± 3.9
DIV F	7	52.3 ± 3.9	160.4 ± 2.9	47.9 ± 2.0	36.5 ± 1.5	26.5 ± 1.7	53.3 ± 2.6	74.4 ± 2.5	28.0 ± 6.1
WTP M	71	77.8 ± 8.5	179.9 ± 6.9	54.9 ± 2.9	42.2 ± 1.8	28.9 ± 1.7	60.4 ± 2.7	82.6 ± 4.1	29.3 ± 11.1

*SWM, swimmers; FRS, freestyle; BRS, breaststroke; BKS, backstroke; BUT, butterfly; MED, medley; DIV, divers; WTP, water polo.

Table 2. Analyses of differences among groups–swimming (men)*

Variable	*F*-ratio	Between-group differences				
Height	2.52†	Breast	Butterfly	Medley	Back	Free
Weight	1.44	Breast	Back	Butterfly	Medley	Free
Biacromial width	1.31	Breast	Butterfly	Back	Free	Medley
Biiliocristal width	4.30‡	Breast	Back	Medley	Butterfly	Free
Arm length	1.20	Back	Breast	Butterfly	Medley	Free
Leg length	2.31	Breast	Butterfly	Medley	Free	Back
Trunk length	0.90	Breast	Medley	Butterfly	Free	Back

*From De Garay *et al.* (1974).
†Significant at 0.05 level.
‡Significant at 0.01 level.

biacromial width, arm length, leg length, or trunk length. The male freestyle swimmers were taller and had wider hips than the breaststrokers.

As shown in Table 3, there were no differences among the groups of female swimmers in terms of anthropometric variables. There was a slight tendency only in terms of ranking for the female medley swimmers to be larger.

The male divers were clearly the leanest group, having a mean height of 172.1 cm and a mean weight of 65.5 kg as compared to 179.3 cm and 72.1 kg, respectively, for the total group of male swimmers. The leanness of the male divers was also demonstrated by the relatively low sum of skinfolds: mean of 20.0 mm. The small number (*N*=7) of women divers averaged 160.4 cm in height, and 52.4 kg in weight as compared to 164.4 cm and 59.9 kg for the total group of female swimmers. With a sum of skinfolds of 28.0 mm, the female divers also tended to be leaner than the total group of female swimmers, who had a mean sum of skinfolds of 34.2 mm.

The mean height of water polo players was 179.9 cm and mean weight 77.8 kg. Water polo players had larger absolute somatometric measures than male swimmers in terms of weight, skinfolds, biacromial width, biiliocristal width, and trunk length, whereas the groups did not differ significantly in height, arm length, and leg length. The average skinfolds were 29.3 mm, but the range was from a lean 14.2 mm to 70.3 mm. This large range in skinfolds was also corroborated by the 47.5-kg range for weight. It thus appears that water polo players range from fat to rather lean.

The relative body proportions and comparisons between the different groups of swimmers, divers, and water polo players are further illustrated in

Table 3. Analyses of differences among groups–swimming (women)*

Variable	F-ratio	Between-group differences			
Height	0.93	Breast	Back	Free	Medley
Weight	1.70	Free	Breast	Back	Medley
Biacromial width	0.90	Back	Breast	Free	Medley
Biiliocristal width	1.09	Free	Breast	Back	Medley
Arm length	0.17	Back	Medley	Free	Breast
Leg length	1.44	Breast	Back	Medley	Free
Trunk length	0.08	Free	Breast	Back	Medley

*From De Garay et al. (1974).

Tables 4 and 5, as well as in Figure 1, where the differences are presented in terms of z-values. In general (Table 4) the male medley swimmers were proportionally somewhat broader (biacromial and biiliocristal width, chest depth, biepicondylar widths) than the other male swimmers. Moreover, they were also the leanest (low skinfold value) and, together with the breaststroke swimmers, the most muscular (high values for upper arm girth and calf girth).

The group of male swimmers were somewhat heavy as compared to male runners and gymnasts. The water polo players appeared to be the heaviest. The proportional values of male divers were very close to the phantom values. The calf girths of most of the male swimmers and water polo players were relatively small, as well as the thigh girths except in water polo players. When compared to male runners and gymnasts (Table 4), only chest depth, skinfolds, and weight emerge as being proportionally larger somatometric characteristics for male swimmers, divers, and water polo players.

The proportional values, adjusted to phantom height, of female swimmers and divers (Table 5) were in general very close to the values of female sprinters and gymnasts, except for chest depth and skinfolds, which were somewhat larger in all styles of swimmers and in divers.

When comparing the different female swimming events according to style, it appears that medley swimmers and breaststroke swimmers are proportionally largest in biacromial width, chest depth, and upper arm girth. It should be noted that there were many similarities in the proportional anthropometric qualities between female and male swimmers and divers, except for the skinfolds and the girths.

In Figure 1 the various anthropometric values are converted into z-values, demonstrating the relative differences of the measures among the groups. For

Table 4. Anthropometric mean values, adjusted to phantom height, of male swimmers, divers, and water polo players compared to male runners (N=225) and gymnasts (N=28)*

Variable	WTP	DIV	SWM	FRS	BRST	BKST	BUT	MED	RUN	GYM	Phantom
Weight	73.6	64.8	68.4	69.5	66.9	66.0	69.0	69.7	63.3	62.5	64.6
Trunk length	51.9	50.7	51.6	51.5	51.6	51.8	52.2	51.5	50.6	51.6	51.3
Leg length	78.1	78.1	77.9	78.1	77.4	78.2	77.5	78.3	80.3	78.0	79.0
Arm length	57.1	57.9	57.6	58.1	57.6	57.9	56.9	57.2	58.0	56.7	57.1
Biacromial width	39.9	39.8	39.1	39.1	39.2	38.7	38.9	39.9	38.8	40.7	38.0
Biiliocristal width	27.3	27.0	26.7	26.8	26.0	26.2	27.2	27.0	26.5	27.2	28.8
Chest depth	20.1	19.1	19.7	19.6	19.9	19.4	20.2	19.7	18.5	19.3	17.5
Thigh girth	54.1	52.5	51.9	51.5	53.0	50.4	52.4	52.5	52.0	51.6	55.8
Calf girth	34.8	35.7	34.4	33.9	35.2	33.6	34.6	34.8	34.8	35.1	35.3
Upper arm girth	33.2	32.5	32.4	32.7	32.9	31.0	32.7	32.2	29.8	35.4	29.4
Skinfolds	27.7	19.8	20.9	21.6	21.4	20.8	20.4	19.4	17.1	16.6	
Biepicondyler humerus width	6.8	7.0	6.8	6.8	6.9	6.8	6.8	6.9	6.7	7.0	6.5
Biepicondylar femur width	9.5	9.4	9.4	9.2	9.4	9.2	9.5	9.6	9.3	9.5	9.5

*WTP, water polo; DIV, diving; SWM, all swimming strokes; FRS, freestyle; BRST, breaststroke; BKST, backstroke; BUT, butterfly; MED, medley; RUN, runners; GYM, gymnasts.

Table 5. Anthropometric mean values adjusted to phantom height, of female divers and swimmers compared to female track sprinters (N=28) and gymnasts (N=21)*

Variable	DIV	SWM	FRS	BRST	BKST	MED	SPR	GYM	Phantom
WT	55.6	58.9	54.8	57.0	59.1	63.3	58.6	54.0	64.6
TRL	50.8	51.2	50.4	52.3	51.4	51.0	50.5	51.5	51.3
LGL	78.9	78.8	79.7	78.2	77.7	79.2	80.2	78.3	79.0
ARL	56.6	57.1	56.7	58.6	55.8	56.6	57.0	56.7	57.1
BIA	38.7	38.4	37.8	38.9	37.4	38.7	37.9	38.7	38.0
BIC	28.1	28.0	26.8	28.5	28.5	28.5	27.0	27.8	28.8
CHD	18.9	19.0	18.8	19.3	18.5	19.2	17.9	17.6	17.5
THG	56.2	54.6	51.8	56.0	56.0	55.2	55.9	55.8	55.8
CAG	35.8	34.6	33.4	34.8	36.4	34.7	35.7	35.0	35.3
UAG	29.4	29.8	28.8	30.2	29.6	30.4	28.6	29.7	29.4
SKF	29.7	35.4	32.0	36.9	33.2	37.2	28.0	29.1	
BEH	6.4	6.5	6.4	6.5	6.7	6.4	6.3	6.4	6.5
BEF	9.1	9.3	9.0	9.4	9.6	9.3	9.1	9.3	9.5

*WT, weight; TRL, trunk length; LGL, leg length; ARL, arm length; BIA, biacromial width; BIC, biiliocristal width; CHD, chest depth; THG, thigh girth; CAG, calf girth; UAG, upper arm girth; SKF, sum of three skinfolds; BEH, biepicondylar humerus width; BEF, biepicondylar femur width; SPR, track sprinters. See Table 4 for explanation of other abbreviations.

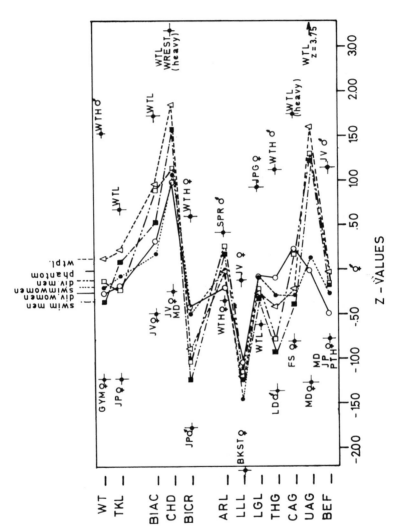

Figure 1. Comparative somatogram of female Olympic swimmers (*N*=7), and male Olympic swimmers (*N*=28), divers (*N*=16), and water polo players (*N*=71), and male Olympic swimmers (*N*=66), divers (*N*=16), and water polo players (*N*=71), extremé z-values in the Mexico Olympic sample. This and all of the following figures refer to participants in the 1968 Olympic Games in Mexico.

comparison we have also added the most extreme z-values which have been recorded in the total sample of athletes from the Mexico Olympic Games. This somatogram shows that water polo players had different body build characteristics from the swimmers and divers. In most other groups of swimmers and divers the graph follows a rather regular pattern of clustered z-values within a range of a half a z-value, except for the girths where the values are more dispersed.

Three anthropometric indices of the different swimming groups, divers, and water polo players are presented in Table 6. For comparative purposes the values of male rowers and gymnasts and female track sprinters and gymnasts are included in this table. As expected, the ponderal index (weight/ height was highest in water polo players and was comparable to that of the rowers. The female freestyle swimmers had the lowest ponderal index, similar to that of female gymnasts and also to female divers who were rather lean, having a ponderal index of 3.3. When considering the BC/BA values from 74 to 76 as intermediate values for the androgyny rating (Bayley and Bayer, 1946), it appears that all the aquatic sports athletes, males and females, of the present study were situated in the range of masculine (between 73 and 69)

Table 6. Anthropometric indices of swimmers, divers, and water polo players*

Events	WT/HT	BC/BA	TRL/LGL
SWM M	4.0	68.2	66.3
FRS M	4.1	68.6	65.9
BRST M	3.9	66.3	66.7
BKST M	3.9	67.6	66.3
BUT M	4.0	70.0	67.4
MED M	4.1	67.7	65.8
ROW M	4.4	70.8	64.3
GYM M	3.7	66.8	66.1
SWM F	3.5	73.0	65.0
FRS F	3.2	70.9	63.2
BRST F	3.4	73.1	66.8
BKST F	3.5	76.2	66.2
MED F	3.7	73.5	64.4
SPR F	3.4	71.2	63.0
GYM F	3.2	71.7	65.8
DIV M	3.8	67.9	64.9
DIV F	3.3	72.6	64.4
WTP M	4.3	68.5	66.5
Phantom	3.8	75.8	64.9

*WT/HT, weight/height; BC/BA, biiliocristal
width/biacromial width; TRL/LGL, trunk length/
leg length; ROW, rowers; other abbreviations as in
Tables 4 and 5.

and hypermasculine (68 and minus) rating values, with the only exception being the female backstroke swimmers who were at the limit of femininity with an average index of 76.2. Among the males, the butterfly swimmers had the highest BC/BA index (70.0), comparable to that of rowers (70.8), whereas male breaststroke swimmers had the lowest index (66.3), comparable to that of male gymnasts (66.8). In the female group of aquatic sports athletes, the lowest BC/BA values were obtained by the freestyle swimmers (70.9).

Finally, the trunk length/leg length index (TRL/LGL) shows a rather uniform picture with values lying close to the phantom mean value of 64.9. The male swimmers and water polo players, as well as the female breaststroke swimmers and backstroke swimmers, reached average values of 1 to 2 units above the phantom value, indicating a longer trunk in proportion to their legs. Female freestyle swimmers with a trunk to leg length index of 63.2 appeared to be the only group to be proportionally long-legged. They were comparable to female sprinters (TRL/LGL index = 63.0) in this regard.

Somatotype

The somatoplot distributions of the sport groups and event groups are presented in Figures 2 through 15. The mean and dispersion index are given on each somatoplot, and these descriptive statistics are summarized in Table 7. The mean somatoplot for each of the swimming event groups is plotted on Figure 16 and the means for the swimmers, divers, and water polo players are plotted on Figure 17.

Male swimmers The average somatotype of the male swimmer was a 2-5-3, an ectomesomorph. The most consistent aspect of the somatotype ratings of the swimmers by event was the approximate rating of 2 in endomorphy. Both mesomorphy and ectomorphy showed variations of more than ½ unit among events. The backstrokers were the lowest in mesomorphy and the highest in ectomorphy, while the breaststroke, butterfly, and medley swimmers were the highest in mesomorphy and lowest in ectomorphy. The freestylers were between the backstrokers and the other three groups. The somatotype dispersion distances among the means for the event groups are presented in Table 8 and diagram on *XY* coordinates in Figure 18. A somatotype dispersion of 2.0 is the equivalent of the change by one component rating of 1 unit. This value of 2.0 was used as an empirical critical value for estimating the significance of the differences between the mean somatoplots of event and sport groups. For the male swimmers the backstrokers were clearly different from the breaststroke, butterfly, and medley swimmers. The freestyle swimmers did not differ from any of the other four groups. For the total group of male swimmers and for each of the event groups, the majority of the swimmers were either ectomesomorphs or balanced meso-

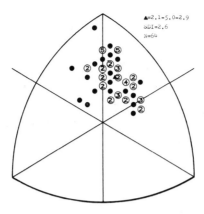

Figure 2. Somatotype distribution of male swimmers.

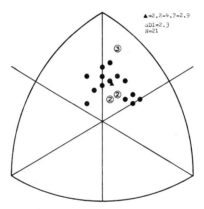

Figure 3. Somatotype distribution of male freestyle swimmers.

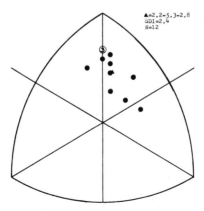

Figure 4. Somatotype distribution of male breaststroke swimmers.

295

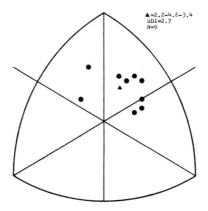

Figure 5. Somatotype distribution of male backstroke swimmers.

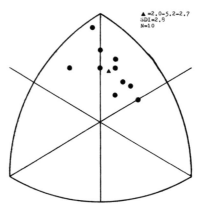

Figure 6. Somatotype distribution of male butterfly swimmers.

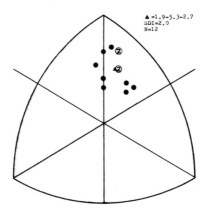

Figure 7. Somatotype distribution of male medley swimmers.

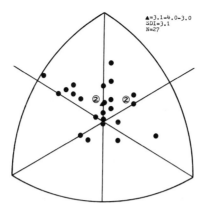

Figure 8. Somatotype distribution of female swimmers.

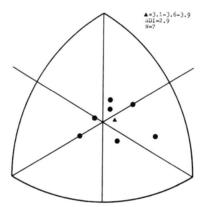

Figure 9. Somatotype distribution of female freestyle swimmers.

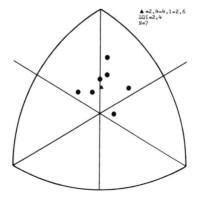

Figure 10. Somatotype distribution of female breaststroke swimmers.

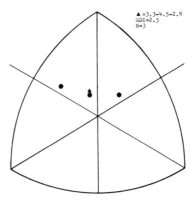

Figure 11. Somatotype distribution of female backstroke swimmers.

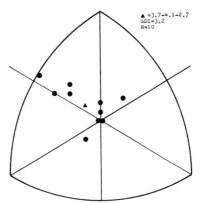

Figure 12. Somatotype distribution of female medley swimmers.

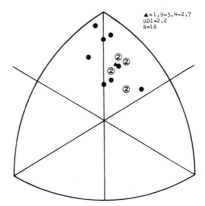

Figure 13. Somatotype distribution of male divers.

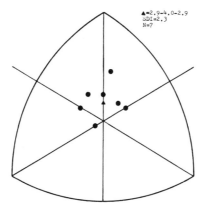

Figure 14. Somatotype distribution female divers.

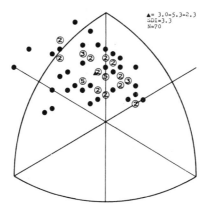

Figure 15. Somatotype distribution of water polo players.

morphs, with much smaller percentages being ectomorph-mesomorphs, or endomesomorphs.

The average dispersion of each somatoplot from its mean somatoplot (the somatotype dispersion index or SDI) is 2.6 for the total group. The backstroke and butterfly swimmers had the largest SDI (2.7 and 2.8, respectively), while the medley swimmers had the smallest SDI (2.0).

Female swimmers The average female swimmer was a 3-4-3, or a central balanced mesomorph. The small number of backstroke swimmers (*N*=3) precluded meaningful analysis; therefore, the remaining comments refer primarily to the freestyle, breaststroke, and medley swimmers. The freestyle swimmers were the least mesomorphic and most ectomorphic of these three groups. The medley swimmers were the most endomorphic and the breast-

Table 7. Mean somatotype and somatotype dispersion statistics for Olympic swimmers, divers, and water polo players (Mexico, 1968)

Group	N	Mean somatotype	Somatotype dispersion index	Dispersion standard deviation
Swimming				
Men				
Freestyle	21	2.2–4.7–2.9	2.3	1.0
Breaststroke	12	2.2–5.3–2.8	2.4	1.3
Backstroke	9	2.2–4.6–3.4	2.7	1.3
Butterfly	10	2.0–5.2–2.7	2.8	1.6
Medley	12	1.9–5.3–2.7	2.0	0.8
Total group	64	2.1–5.0–2.9	2.6	1.2
Women				
Freestyle	7	3.1–3.6–3.9	2.9	1.3
Breaststroke	7	2.4–4.1–2.6	2.4	1.1
Backstroke	3	3.3–4.5–2.8	2.5	1.8
Medley	10	3.7–4.1–2.7	3.2	1.3
Total group	27	3.1–4.0–3.0	3.1	1.8
Diving				
Men, 3 and 10 m	16	1.9–5.4–2.7	2.2	1.3
Women, 3 and 10 m	7	2.9–4.0–2.9	2.3	0.9
Water polo	70	3.0–5.3–2.3	3.3	1.8

stroke swimmers the least endomorphic. These two groups did not differ from each other on mesomorphy and ectomorphy. The analysis of the somatotype dispersion distances among the events shows that the freestyle swimmers differed from all of the groups, and the medley and breaststroke swimmers differed from each other (Figure 18).

Considering the smaller number of female swimmers than male swimmers, the larger SDI (3.1 compared to 2.6) was surprising. Observation of the somatocharts indicate that the variety of somatotypes in each of the strokes is not too different from the males for freestyle, breaststroke, and backstroke, but the SDIs for medley (3.2) and for the total group of swimmers (3.1) are higher than those of the male groups.

The greatest frequency of somatotypes in the total group were in the balanced endomorph-mesomorph area, balanced mesomorphy, and the central area of the somatochart. The freestyle swimmers were almost all to the right of the mesomorphy axis and towards ectomorphy, while the medley swimmers were balanced endomorph-mesomorphs or central somatotypes, on the left-hand side of the mesomorphic axis. The large SDI of the event groups around the center of the somatochart makes it difficult to summarize the component dominance of the female swimmers by events.

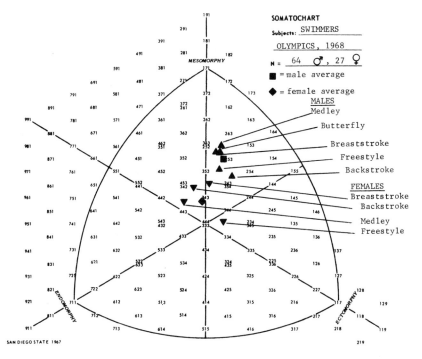

Figure 16. Somatoplots of mean somatotypes of male and female swimmers according to style.

Diving

Male divers The typical male diver had a somatotype of 2-5.5-2.5, and most were either balanced mesomorphs or ectomesomorphs.

Female divers The female diver had a somatotype of 3-4-3, a balanced central mesomorphic physique; however, the somatoplots were scattered around the central category, and only one physique actually fell within this category. The SDI of 2.3 is fairly large for the small number of subjects.

Water polo players

The average somatotype of the water polo player was 3-5.5-2.5, an endo-morphic-mesomorph. Almost all of the somatotypes were in the meso-morphic sector of the somatochart, but the greatest frequencies occurred in endomesomorphy and balanced mesomorphy. In contrast to male swimmers, the somatotypes were on the endomorphic side of the mesomorphic axis, whereas the swimmers were largely on the ectomorphic side of the axis. There were several extreme endomesomorphs (those outside the arc connecting the

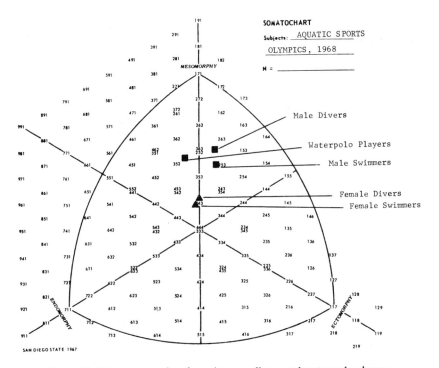

Figure 17. Mean somatoplots for swimmers, divers, and water polo players.

5-5-1 and the 1-7-1 somatotype) among water polo players. The wide range of physiques in water polo is fairly apparent, and the SDI of 3.3 reflects this wide dispersion.

Comparisons among sports

We have seen already that the somatotype distributions of the various sport groups differed somewhat from one another, and an indication of the magnitude of these differences can be obtained by calculating the somatotype dispersion distances between pairs of means. The relevant differences are shown in Table 8. The differences between the means of the male swimmers and water polo players and of the water polo players and the divers exceeded the critical value of 2.0. On the other hand, the difference between the mean somatoplots of the female divers and swimmers was extremely small. The somatotype dispersion distance between the means for the male and female swimmers was 3.46, and between the divers, 4.23. Because the female divers and swimmers had approximately the same mean somatoplot, the difference was accounted for in the greater mesomorphy of the male divers relative to the male swimmers.

Table 8. Somatotype dispersion distances among sports and events for Olympic swimmers, divers, and water polo players (Mexico, 1968)

| | Male swimmers | | | |
	Backstroke	Breaststroke	Butterfly	Medley
Freestyle	0.98	1.31	1.40	1.71
Backstroke		2.18	2.21	2.46
Breaststroke			0.20	0.35
Butterfly				0.34

| | Female swimmers | | |
	Backstroke	Breaststroke	Medley
Freestyle	3.51	3.18	3.50
Backstroke		1.25	1.40
Breaststroke			2.51

| | Swimmers, divers, water polo players | | | |
	Swimming ♀	Diving ♂	Diving ♀	Water Polo ♂
Swimming ♂	3.46	1.20		2.62
Swimming ♀			0.34	
Diving ♂			4.23	2.75

DISCUSSION

Water polo players were found to be larger than swimmers and divers and relatively larger with respect to weight and girth. They also had the largest skinfolds among the male athletes, which may account in part for the greater girths. Male divers were similar in skinfolds to the male swimmers, but the female divers had lower skinfolds than the swimmers. The relative thigh girth of the female athletes in this study exceeded that of the male athletes, while the relative calf girth values were similar for both sexes and the upper arm girth values were lower for females than males. This indicates that there was greater tissue mass in the lower limb than in the upper limb for females as compared to males. Again, the greater skinfolds in the females may account for part of these differences. Compared to other sportspersons, water polo players and male and female swimmers appear to have relatively greater trunk length (and probably area) than leg length. In terms of biomechanics the greater "planing" surface of the trunk and the higher skinfolds (associated with lower specific gravity) should be an advantage in these sports. Divers showed similar body structure patterns to gymnasts both absolutely and

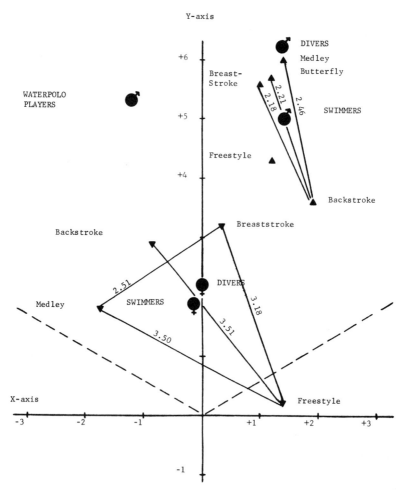

Figure 18. Mean somatoplots for sports and events plotted on *XY* coordinates. Significant somatotype dispersion distances are indicated by *solid lines* between events.

relatively. However, the female divers and swimmers were more like each other than were the male divers and swimmers.

The average somatotype for Cureton's U.S. Olympic swimmers was 2.9 − 5.4 − 2.7, and for San Diego State University swimmers, 2.4 − 5.4 − 2.6 (Carter, 1970). The sample of athletes in the Mexico Olympic Games was more ectomesomorphic than these two samples. Belgian water polo players studied by Clarys and Borms (1971) had a mean somatotype of 3.4 − 5.3 − 1.8, which is more endomesomorphic than the Mexico Olympians. The Olympic athletes were less endomorphic and more ectomorphic than the Belgians, but were equal in mesomorphy. The reduced endomorphic ratings for the Mexican Olympic swimmers and water polo players compared to the other samples suggest differences in training intensities which may affect the accumulation of relative fatness.

CONCLUSION

On the basis of the descriptive and statistical analyses presented, the following generalizations appear to be justified. The body dimensions and somatotypes of Olympic swimmers, divers, and water polo players show characteristic tendencies related to their sport and, in some cases, to their event. The variation within some events and sports is considerable, but in general they can be differentiated from athletes in some other sports.

REFERENCES

Bayley, N. and L. M. Bayer. 1946. The assessment of somatic androgyny. Amer. J. Phys. Anthrop. N.S. 4: 433.

Carter, J. E. L. 1972. The Heath-Carter somatotype method. San Diego College, San Diego (offset printed manual).

Carter, J. E. L. 1970. The somatotypes of athletes—a review. Human Biol. 42: 535.

Clarys, J. and J. Borms. 1971. Typologische studie van waterpolospielers en gymnasten. Geneeskunde en Sport 4: 2.

De Garay, A. L., L. Levine, and J. E. L. Carter (eds.). 1974. Genetic and Anthropological Studies of Olympic Athletes. Academic Press, New York.

Heath, B. H. and J. E. L. Carter. 1963. Need for modification of somatotyping methodology. Amer. J. Phys. Anthrop. 21: 227.

Hebbelinck, M. and W. D. Ross. 1974. Kinanthropometry and biomechanics. In: R. C. Nelson and C. A. Morehouse (eds.), Biomechanics IV, International Series on Sport Sciences, Vol. 1, pp. 537–552. University Park Press, Baltimore.

Ross, W. D., J. E. L. Carter, and B. D. Wilson. 1974. Tactics and formulae for somatotype analysis. In Press.

Ross, W. D. and B. D. Wilson. 1973. A somatotype dispersion index. Res. Quart. 44: 372.

Ross, W. D. and N. C. Wilson. 1974. A strategem for proportional growth assessment. Acta Paediat. Belg. 28: 169.

Lung volumes
and swimming

J. L. Ghesquiere

Four years ago the author noted that few people of African origin excel in water sports, swimming in particular. Although the primary reason for this is probably in social differences and attitudes, hence, motivation; the problem of buoyancy may also affect the Africans' performance in swimming, especially over long distances. This factor may also play a critical role in learning to swim, and in water safety. In a theoretical discussion, the author pointed out that, as a rule, the buoyancy of the African was less than that of people of European or Asian origin—not taking into account the interindividual differences within the group. Buoyancy will be affected by three principal factors: a) the ratio of fat to fat-free body-mass; b) the ratio of volume to weight or density; and c) the relative volume of the lungs (residual volume as well as total lung volume). The two first factors have been discussed in detail in a paper presented at the First Symposium of Biomechanics in Swimming (1971). The author is not aware of any study comparing the relative density of Negro to white, as could be measured by underwater weighing techniques. (Fat percentage, assessed by anthropometric methods; skinfold thickness, for example, rarely exceeds 10 to 11 percent of total body weight, among the people in Zaire). However, the reader's attention should be directed to the relative size of lung volumes and their influence upon swimming performance. Differences in Negro-white lung volumes are by no means a new discovery. Shortly after the invention of a practical spirometer by Hutchinson in 1846, these differences were reported by Gould in 1869, who found smaller vital capacity among Negroes as compared to whites by as much as 11 percent (height taken into account) in his famous study on Civil War soldiers.

Damon (1966) presented a survey of earlier literature related to Negro-white differences in lung volumes and concluded that there is a real difference in lung functions between healthy whites and Negroes. These findings have, in more recent years, been corroborated by studies on the African Continent (Table 1), notably in South Africa and in Zaire. To the author's knowledge,

Table 1. Forced vital capacity (FVC), 1-sec forced expiratory capacity (FEC$_1$), and percent of FEC on FVC for some African samples compared to American and European samples*

	N	Observed	Predicted	Difference (%)
FVC				
Sweden, Göteborg	152	4.890	3.810	22
U.S. Army				
White	392	4.747	3.771	21
Negro	61	4.116	3.790	8
Zaire				
Students	50	4.350	3.540	18
Kivu, rural	45	3.703	3.316	10
Kivu, pygmies	21	3.183	2.914	8
South African Negro	120	3.427	3.427	
FEC$_1$				
Sweden, Göteborg	152	3.760	3.660	
U.S. Army				
White	392	3.781	3.101	18
Negro	61	3.297	3.098	6
Zaire				
Students	50	3.646	2.908	19
Kivu, rural	45	2.944	2.734	7
Kivu, pygmies	21	2.558	2.435	5
South African Negro	120	2.661	2.661	
FEC$_1$/FVC				
Sweden, Göteborg	152	79	76	
U.S. Army				
White	392	82	80	
Negro	61	82	80	
Zaire				
Students	50	83	81	
Kivu, rural	45	82	80	
Kivu, pygmies	21	81	80	
South African Negro	120	78	78	

*Observed values and predicted values according to Johanssen and Erasmus (1968) (based on a population sample of Pretoria, S.A.).

very little attention has been given to this fact among people interested in sports medicine and exercise physiology. If we look at performances and sports records established by Africans, we can only conclude that, at least for "surface" sports, these differences in lung volumes do not affect the capacity for athletic performance, be it in short or long distance efforts.

We know that for a healthy person under normal circumstances (excluding high altitude or other partial pressure problems) lung ventilation is not the limiting factor affecting physical performances. Indeed, the critical factor is not the volume of air ventilated by the lungs, but the amount of oxygen made available to the muscle tissue per unit of time. In surface sports, the airways are in permanent contact with the ambient air, and gas exchange (O_2 and CO_2) between alveolae and ambient air is maintained at an adequate level. The limiting factors are: a) transfer factor between alveolae and lung capillary bed; b) means of transport, mainly the quantity of blood and the amount of hemoglobin available; c) speed of circulation, itself affected by the cardiovascular system and viscosity of the blood; d) diffusion between blood and tissue; and e) the capacity of the tissue to utilize oxygen.

During swimming, two new factors appear. a) The body has to be kept on or near the surface of the water. (A skilled swimmer will keep his body as much as possible under the water level, where turbulence is lower than at the surface. Except for the breaststroke, arms will be moved to a forward position out of the water, and inhalation, of course, has to be done above the water level, while underwater swimming has been ruled out.) b) The airways are in contact with open air only a fraction of the total time during which the muscular exertion is performed, which may result in a diminished alveolar P_{O_2} and augmented P_{CO_2}, since expiration, done under the surface, is performed against the resistance of water.

Will smaller lung volumes affect these factors? Buoyancy, although probably playing a minor role in competitive swimming, will be affected by the size of lung volumes. A short analysis of the respiratory cycle during swimming shows that a swimmer a) inhales in a short, open-mouthed inhalation, then blocks his respiration; b) performs a slower expiration, under water; and c) then proceeds immediately to the following inhalation. At the start and during turning, respiration may remain blocked for several seconds in inspiration. The size of lung volumes, forming a bellows inside the chest, should obviously affect buoyancy: 1.5 to 2 liters more of air will make the trunk float that much easier.

Swimmers are known to have large lung volumes, but even an average size Negro at 1.70 m tall with a total lung volume of 5,500 cc, functional residual capacity of 2,200 cc and residual volume of 1,000 cc, will be at a disadvantage compared to a 1.70-m tall European with a total lung volume of 7,000 cc, a functional residual capacity of 3,000 cc, and a residual volume of 1,500 cc. In reference to ventilation in a nonswimming sport, so far we can only theorize that the Negro athlete may try to make up for his smaller lung volumes by breathing more frequently. However, this is a disadvantage, since his alveolar ventilation will be diminished even when his lung ventilation remains at the same level as that of his white counterpart:

$$\dot{V}_A = (\dot{V}_T - \text{deadspace}) \times f$$
$$\dot{V}_E = \dot{V}_T \times f$$

where $\dot{V}_A$ = alveolar ventilation; $\dot{V}_T$ = tidal volume; f = breathing frequency per minute; and $\dot{V}_E$ = ventilation or minute respiratory volume.

In swimming the pace of breathing is determined by the arm movements. Respiratory variation in blood-gas tension will be more pronounced, and the limit of tolerance at which CO_2 can accumulate in the lungs will be reached faster, or at a slower swimming speed, unless there is a marked difference in dead space and/or an easier and faster air flow through his air passages.

The author is not aware of any studies where the alveolar air sample of swimmers has been measured and to what extent their alveolar air composition may relate to their actual swimming performance. Modern techniques, notably the water treadmill available to European and American investigators, should make such measurements possible.

REFERENCES

Damon, A. 1966. Negro-white differences in pulmonary function. Hum. Biol. 38: 380–393.

Ghesquire, J. L. and M. J. Kavonen. 1971. Anthropometric factors affecting buoyancy in the African. *In:* L. Lewillie and J. P. Clarys (eds.), First International Symposium on Biomechanics in Swimming, pp. 175–182. Université Libre de Bruxelles, Brussels.

Johanssen, Z. M. and L. D. Erasmus. 1968. Clinical spirometry in normal Bantu. Amer. Rev. Resp. Dis. 97: 585–597.

Residual reflex patterns as a basis for diagnosing stroke faults

D. Swartz and M. Allen

Why is the backstroker turning his head from side to side? Why isn't the freestyler crossing the midline of his body in the pull-through? Why does the breaststroker have difficulty with the position of his head? Why do some butterflyers have more flexion in one elbow while the other forearm is extended?

Some of these common stroke faults may have a residual reflex base. These residual reflexes can interfere with stroke mechanics. Once observed and diagnosed, these reflexes can be integrated so that the fault in the stroke is removed. Activities designed to integrate the reflexes can be part of the swim program itself. An understanding of reflex development is important to the success of such a program.

Cortically directed motion usually has as a basis the reflexes (Ayres, 1972, p. 46). There is a hierarchy of reflex development. Each reflex sequence sets the level for the next reflex stage. As more mature reflex patterns appear, earlier reflex patterns gradually diminish or are inhibited. The normal developmental sequence is from primitive postural reflexes, the tonic neck reflex (TNR), and the tonic labyrinthine reflex (TLR) to more mature righting and equilibrium reactions. The latter continue to develop for a number of years.

The earlier primitive postural reflex, called the tonic labyrinthine reflex, is a progravity response. This reflex pulls the body and its limbs toward the earth. The stimulus which evokes the TLR is the earth's gravitational force. It acts on the neuromuscular system in such a way that when the head is prone, flexor muscles are facilitated and when the head is supine, extensor muscles are facilitated. In the prone position in the water the TLR would appear similar to the jellyfish float with legs tucked up toward the chest. In the supine position the head is back and extension of the limbs makes the TLR appear similar to the back float. Within the first few weeks of postnatal life, the tonic labyrinthine reflex is noticeable. It is a protective response. Perhaps in water it is even a survival mechanism of early infancy.

The tonic neck reflex is another primitive postural reflex. The asymmetrical TNR can be elicited in infancy by stimulation of receptors in the joints between the cervical vertebrae in the neck region. If the head is turned to the right, so that the chin approximates the shoulder, extensor tone is increased in the right arm, and flexor tone is increased in the left arm (Ayres, 1972, p. 80). When the head is turned the opposite way, the opposite arrangement of muscle tone is evident in the arms. Thus, the head and arms approximate the position a track and field shot putter holds while standing in readiness in the circle before casting the shot. This TNR is a protective, survival mechanism. When the head is turned to the side, the arm on that side extends pushing anything away from the face and the opposite arm flexes protecting the back of the head. As a survival reflex, it is sometimes difficult to inhibit.

The tonic neck reflex will often elicit a leg pattern as well, although it varies somewhat from child to child. The most frequent pattern is increased extensor tone in the leg ipsilateral to the arm with increased extensor tone. One sees increased flexor tone in the other leg. Sometimes a child will elicit a crossed diagonal pattern.

A symmetrical tonic neck reflex is apparent in some children. Flexion of the head facilitates flexor tone in all four extremities and raising the head facilitates extensor tone. This reflex can affect head position in the breast-stroke of a young swimmer.

These reflexes become integrated into the central nervous system largely through inhibition. They do not totally disappear but are integrated, and the degree to which an individual supresses them reflects the degree of maturation and integration of postural mechanisms. Too much residual TNR and TLR is considered abnormal (Ayres, 1972, p. 82). It is estimated that perhaps 30 percent of school-aged children in the United States lack the integration of these reflexes. Many of these children are in age group swim programs, for frequently doctors recommend swimming programs for them. In some individuals, these reflexes are elicited under stress in the prone or supine position, the positions required in swimming.

What problems do these residual reflexes cause? If these reflexes are not properly inhibited, the individual may have inadequate muscle tone, lack of independent movement of the head and extremities, problems in crossing the midline of the body, or difficulty learning strokes automatically. These early primitive reflexes interfere with proper stroke mechanics. Perhaps an analogy can serve as an example. If a polliwog retained its tail when it grew into a frog, the tail would interfere with the frog kick. A swimmer with strong residual primitive postural reflexes has interference from the reflexes when executing proper stroke mechanics.

Why do these neck reflexes, either asymmetrical or symmetrical, still react strongly for some individuals? We know that the brain stem normally controls the primitive reflexes, but in some individuals higher cortical levels must control them instead because there is some brain stem dysfunction. Moore (1969) has noted that the neck cavity areas are of very high neuro-muscular spindle density and perhaps the last areas of the total body muscula-ture to develop to their highest functional degree. She postulated: "That the greater the spindle population, the longer it takes for this musculature to mature. It would appear that the higher the spindle density (and thus the greater the number of alpha-gamma linkages) the longer it takes to learn to control these muscles and eventually use them to their maximum (Moore, 1969, p. 87). This is relevant to the mechanics of swimming strokes as it is often the head position that is most difficult for the swimmer to control.

Our purpose is to identify the TLR, TNR, midline, or unilateral disregard (a disregard of one side of the body subcortically) when it is the basic cause of faulty stroke mechanics or of the swimmer's inability to learn the stroke. We use videotape for diagnostic purposes. In addition, we have used some simple motor tests to confirm our observations:

1. Arm extension test—to test TNR and independent head movement
2. Kraus-Weber test—to determine upper girdle strength
3. Arm circles—subcortical test of crossing the midline
4. Pivot prone position held to a count—to test TLR
5. Cocontraction test of arm muscles
6. Test tonic muscle tone
7. Test of unilateral disregard
8. Tactile test—to test tactile defensiveness and discrimination

The test for unilateral disregard is only used if the swimmer seems to exhibit a problem in strokes related to one side of the body. For example, a backstroker who consistently misses the back flip turn only when the left arm is extended at the wall is screened for unilateral disregard. Since this is a subcortical function, it will not be manifest when the swimmer is attending to it, as in practice. But during a race, when the swimmer is focusing on the cognitive tasks, this subcortical disregard may consistently appear.

The tactile test can provide information about the swimmer that is helpful to the age group coaching staff. If the swimmer shows tactile defen-siveness, he often exhibits aggressive behavior (his primitive tactile system is not integrated). Asking him to wear a swim cap will reduce some of the dual tactile input he is receiving. Towel rubbing can be applied along with touch pressure to help integrate his tactile system. Results will be seen almost immediately.

Activities to assist integration of the neck reflexes are done on the deck and in the pool as part of the swim practice. The activities involve vestibular, proprioceptive, and tactile stimulation, in part. The vestibular system has a strong influence on muscle tone both generally and more specifically through certain neuromuscular reflexes. This influence is mediated:

... through the lateral and medial vestibular nuclei on efferent transmission down the spinal cord. It has a highly facilitatory effect on the gamma efferent neuron to the muscle spindle. By activating the gamma efferent neuron of the spindle, the afferent impulse flow from the spindle is maintained and regulated for assistance with motor function (Ayres, 1970, p. 57).

Vestibular stimulation seems to enhance kinesthesia as well. The tactile system is related to motor reflexes and the ability for motor planning. Both of these systems are used for input in the activities.

Structuring the aquatic activities and requiring an adaptive response from the swimmers is necessary for such a program to be successful. Some of the activities have been adapted for the pool from activities designed for the classroom by Ayres (1972). The TNR tunnel is made by swimmers leaning against the pool wall. One swimmer swims through the tunnel. The position against the wall is one to help inhibit the TNR.

Pulsing is used in the swim program. The hyperactive swimmer tends to have no kinesthetic sense of his heart beat and pulsing helps establish this. Co-contraction activities can be towel pulls between two swimmers seated on the deck. Diagonal arm movements and water polo activities can be structured to work on a midline problem.

Within 6 weeks the results of such a program should be revealed in improved times, greater efficiency in the water, increased kinesthetic sensation, and inhibition of the primitive reflexes and thus a correction in the stroke mechanics.

This basic diagnosis and correction can be incorporated in a swim program. The swimmers find the activities novel and challenging. Many swimmers can benefit from this program at the same time.

Descriptions of the tests and the corrective activities are available by contacting the authors.

REFERENCES

Ayres, A. J. 1972. Sensory Integration and Learning Disorders. Western Psychological Services, Los Angeles.
Moore, J. C. 1969. Neuroanatomy Simplified, Some Basic Concepts for Understanding Rehabilitation Techniques. Kendall Hunt Publishing Company, Dubuque.

The shape of the pectoralis major muscle in swimmers

G. D. Maas

In the course of anthropometric research on top sportsmen in different sports (Maas, 1974), it struck me that in nearly all crawl, butterfly, and dolphin swimmers the major pectoral muscle has a typical shape, which is characterized by the relatively great distance between the clavicle and the caudal-costal origin. The muscles show an orientation which is more longitudinal than in "normal" cases. As far as I am able to ascertain, the caudal origin is on the fifth rib and its cartilage and occasionally on the sixth rib (see Figure 1).

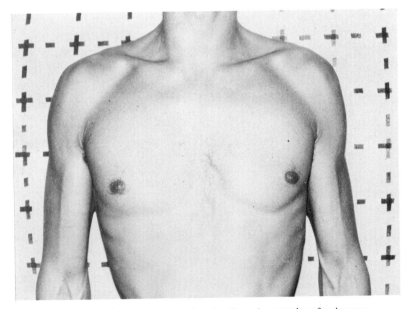

Figure 1. Typical appearance of pectoralis major muscles of swimmers.

314

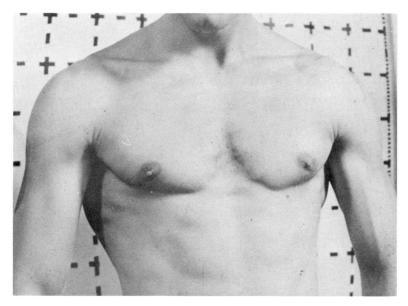

Figure 2. Typical appearance of pectoralis major muscles of gymnasts.

The greater distance between the clavicle and the caudal origin of the muscle can mean either a greater distance between the upper margins of the successive ribs, including a longer sternum, or a different position of the ribs in the thorax of these swimmers. I have no evidence to support either of these two possibilities.

In well developed and typical cases, the caudal part of the muscle is thicker than the cranial, sternoclavicular, part. This observation goes very well with the action of the muscle during a stroke: the caudal or sternocostal part is in the best position to assist in the propulsion.

The observed shape of the muscle is also found in primates: Ashton and Oxnard (1963) described it as typical in the quadruped monkeys, whereas the brachiators have pectoral muscles which are more laterally oriented and shorter in the cranio-caudal direction. Pectoral muscles fitting this description can be found among gymnasts (see Figure 2).

This observation illustrates the author's belief that in biomechanics and in anthropometry we may have to examine details which have hitherto been given little attention.

REFERENCES

Ashton, E. H. and C. E. Oxnard. 1963. The musculature of the primate shoulder. Trans. Zool. Soc. London. 29: 553.
Maas, G. D. 1974. The Physique of Athletes. Leiden University Press, Leiden, Netherlands.

Spherosomatometric method for analysis of anteroposterior spine curvatures in swimmers

W. Iwanowski

A spherosomatometric study was made of the anteroposterior curvatures of the spine among competitive swimmers who had trained a minimum of 3 years. They were grouped according to the stroke in which they specialized. The study was carried out in the years 1969, 1970, and 1974. The number of individuals under study totaled 102 male and 85 female swimmers. The age of the boys ranged from 13 to 16 years, with a mean of 15.1 years. The girls' ages ranged from 11.5 to 14.5 years, with a mean of 13.8 years. Table 1 presents a summary of the number of male and female swimmers who swam each stroke.

METHOD

A measuring device called the spherosomatometric recorder, designed by the investigator (Iwanowski, 1968), was used in this study. The recorder was used for the determination of selected anthropometric measurements, especially those involving the curvature of the spine. The principle of the technique involves division of the spatial curve, which corresponds to the shape of the spine, into two curves in the frontal and sagittal planes (Iwanowski, 1972). A permanent record is obtained on a paper tape which is used for purposes of analysis (Figure 1). On the diagram the extreme *points* are marked and connected by a *straight line*. Next a *vertical reference line* is drawn to obtain the following angles: α, for the upper kyphosis; β, for the lower kyphosis; and γ, for the lumbar lordosis.

Table 1. Number of competitors under study

Stroke	♀	♂	Total ($N = 187$)
		Number	
Butterfly	14	19	33
Breaststroke	23	28	51
Crawl	27	31	58
Backstroke	21	24	45

Instructions for use of the sperosomatometric recorder are as follows (Figure 2).

1. Before beginning the measurement, marks should be made on the skin of the standing subject at points corresponding to the apexes of the spinous processes, from C_7 to L_5.

2. After placing the subject on the platform of the apparatus in a relaxed posture, the investigator should wait 10 to 15 sec before fixing the subject at the level of the anterior superior iliac spines and at the external occipital protuberance.

3. The measurement is taken while the subject holds his breath following an inspiration.

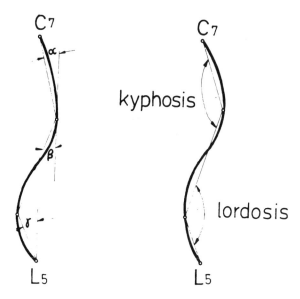

Figure 1. Diagram analysis. Determination of angles.

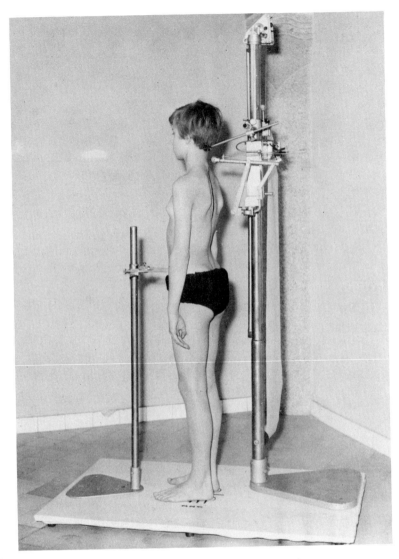

Figure 2. Use of spherosomatometric recorder.

The statistical results of previous studies (Zbajnowska, 1965; Biliński, 1969) on anteroposterior spine curvatures involving the spherosomatometric method indicated that nine subsequent measurements are necessary to obtain information at the 1 percent confidence level in individual studies. Five measurements, taken similarly, render information at the 5 percent confidence level. In mass studies of uniform sex and age groups of more than 50 subjects, three measurements of each subject are sufficient to produce information at the 1 percent confidence level (Iwanowski, 1974; Fecica, 1974).

FINDINGS

Figure 3 presents the shape of the anteroposterior spine curvatures, based on the values of the α, β, and γ angles for males and females for each swimming style. As can be seen in Figure 3, the greatest differences were found in the α and β angles, between butterfly stroke swimmers and backstroke swimmers. The values of the γ angles differ slightly, and no statistically significant differences were found in any of the cases under study.

Results for the female subjects indicate values for the α angle which differ significantly ($p \leqslant 0.05$) between backstroke swimmers and butterfly and breaststroke swimmers. In angle β, significant differences at $p \leqslant 0.05$ between backstroke swimmers and the other swimming styles were observed. For the γ angle no significant differences were found.

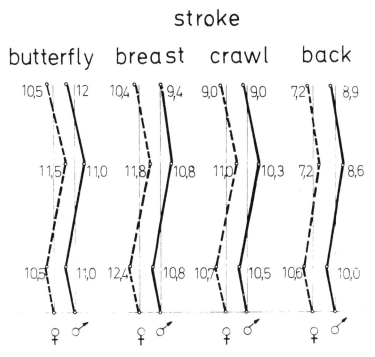

Figure 3. Spine curvatures of competitors aged 13.5 to 15.5 years, training in swimming for 3 years.

The values for the α angle for the male swimmer show statistically significant differences ($p \leq 0.05$) only between backstroke and butterfly stroke swimmers. For the β angle similar differences ($p \leq 0.05$) were found between backstroke and butterfly stroke swimmers. For the γ angle no significant differences were observed.

The results presented point toward another differentiating factor in body build of sportsmen within the same sport but training in different swimming styles. It is difficult to conclude at present whether the observed phenomenon is a result of selection of the candidates or, perhaps, the result of specific training. Future studies will be directed toward this problem.

The observed differences in the shape of spinal curvatures point toward the possibility of applying swimming exercises for purposes of correction of postural defects in children. In cases of round back, "dorsum rotundum," backstroke swimming seems to be advisable, whereas in cases of flat back, "dorsum planum," the butterfly stroke would seem to be of some value.

REFERENCES

Biliński, J. 1969. Wplyw dlugotrwalego treningu plywackiego na ksztalt-owanie krzywizn przednio-tylnych kręgoslupa. Kultura Fizyczna 23: No. 5.

Fecica, D. 1974. Zachowanie się krzywizn kręgoslupa studentów WSWF w okresie trzyletnich obserwacji. Zeszyty Naukowe AWF-Wroclaw, No. 5.

Iwanowski, W. 1968. Metoda sferosomatometryczna w badaniach pomiaro-wych postawy cizla. Wychowanie Fizyczne i Sport 12: No. 2.

Iwanowski, W. 1972. Aparat do rejestrowania pomiarów antropometrycz-nych., Patent discription -65708, Urząd Patentowy PRL, 15, XI.

Iwanowski, W. 1974. Próba oceny zmian kifo-lordozy u uczniów technikum Rolniczego w latach (1969–73). Zeszyty Naukowe AWF-Wroclaw, No. 16.

Zbajnowska, F. 1965. Porównanie fizjologicznych krzywizn przednio-tylnych kręgoslupa u dziewcząt wroclawskich w wieku 11–15 lat uprawiających i nieuprawiających sportu plywackiego. Manuscript, Library of the Academy of Physical Education in Wroclaw.

Symposium
activities

International
Coaches Clinic

In organizing this Second International Symposium on the Biomechanics of Swimming, a concerted effort was made to include scientific studies that would be of interest and value to the practitioner as well as the researcher. One of the major attempts to realize this goal was the International Coaches Clinic held on Wednesday evening.

This meeting was jointly organized by Jan P. Clarys of the Instituut voor Morfologie of Vrije Universiteit Brussel and Jean Pierre Coenraets from the Institut Superieur d'Education Physique of the Université Libre de Bruxelles, in collaboration with the major Belgian swimming organizations and the

Figure 1. The panel and audience listen to a response from G. Hoecke of the DDR (*L*. to *R*.) Verbauwen (Belgium), Pierson (Belgium), Heutinick (Belgium), Bleasdale (FINA), Cureton (USA), Sitters (The Netherlands), Hoecke (DDR), Jiskoot (The Netherlands), Bouws (DBR), Racham (Great Britain), Barr (Great Britain), and Francis (USA). Moderator Clarys and Secretary Coenraetes are seated at the left.

Figure 2. A large group of interested coaches taking notes on the experts' responses to questions.

ministeries of Dutch and French Cultures (A.D.E.P.S. and B.L.O.S.O.). The sport organizations included The Royal Belgian Swimming and Life Saving Federation (K.B.Z.R.B — F.B.B.N.S.), Vrienden Kring der Zwemtrainers von Belgie, Amicale des Entraineurs de Natation de Belgique and the Federation Belge d'Education Physique — Belgische Bond voor Lichamelijke Opvoeding (F.B.E.F. — B.B.L.O.).

More than 250 sport club coaches and competitors in swimming, diving, and water polo came from all parts of Belgium to engage in a dialogue with a panel of 12 experts in several areas of research. The panel of researchers included representatives from Belgium, German Democratic Republic (DDR), German Federal Republic (DBR), Great Britain, The Netherlands, and the United States of America.

The group engaged in a lively discussion of several broad topics that had been distributed prior to the symposium to both the Belgian swimming coaches and the panel. The following are examples of some of the topics that were discussed.

1. Research indicates that training schemes are based upon the same fundamental principles, yet each coach seems to add a personal touch to his training program.

  a. What procedures are currently being employed in the respective countries?

b. Which factors in the over-all training regimens seem to make the greatest contributions to the success of these programs?

2. In some countries there are different views concerning the training of competitive swimmers and water polo players. Several investigations have indicated that water polo training is more strenuous than training for competitive swimming events. On the other hand, in swimming, the training is more specific than for water polo.

a. Is it justifiable to simultaneously include training for both activities?
b. Does the playing and training for water polo during the season have a positive or negative effect on the performances of young swimmers?
c. Is it feasible to include water polo as a part of a conditioning program for swimmers?

3. Swimming is one of the sports in which younger athletes frequently give the best performances. Nevertheless, many promising swimmers drop out of competition for several reasons. Among these are a) the time required for training, b) the lack of competition, c) the lack of personal drive to improve, and d) family circumstances.

a. What are some of the techniques employed in keeping individual swimmers highly motivated?
b. What are the criteria and at what age should young swimmers be encouraged to follow a specific training regimen?

4. The methods used in the teaching of swimming vary considerably in different countries. In spite of recent pedagogical and research findings, many clubs and educational institutions utilize a standardized program of instruction.

a. Should one adhere to the accepted structured progressions during the initial phases of learning or is it better for the educator to adapt the exercises to the individual or to the group?
b. What is your personal opinion and the prevailing practice in the respective countries concerning this problem?

5. During the First International Symposium on Biomechanics of Swimming, trainers and coaches criticized on several occasions the high scientific level of some of the research. The presentations could not always be comprehended by everyone and therefore direct applications of the results were limited.

a. Is scientific research related to swimming necessary and justifiable?
b. Is direct collaboration or cooperation between researchers and swimming coaches (trainers) desirable or necessary? If so, how should such cooperation be realized?
c. Is it possible for science to precede technical evolution by providing a theoretical basis for change or must practical problems be solved in the swimming pool by means of applied research investigations?

Jan Clarys, assisted by Jean Coenraets, moderated the 3-hr discussions. The group was exceedingly large and there was insufficient equipment for simultaneous translations. Unfortunately, there was not enough time for each panel member to speak to each of the topics and there were so many questions from the audience that it was impossible to answer them all. In spite of these shortcomings, the session was very informative and quite worthwhile.

Special activities

The symposium program included a variety of special activities which complemented the formal scientific program. These included the opportunity for informal discussions, an extensive book exhibit, wives program, cocktail reception at the famous Castle of Ham, and an enjoyable banquet which was a fitting climax to a very successful symposium. As an adjunct activity one of the cosponsoring organizations, the International Society of Biomechanics, held the first annual meeting of its Executive Council on Wednesday evening during the week of the symposium.

INFORMAL DISCUSSIONS

Many opportunities for informal discussion and personal interaction were provided. Coffee breaks were held in the lobby adjacent to the lecture hall. Participants met as a group for lunch at the University dining facility nearby. The Tuesday evening visit to the Castle of Ham and Thursday night banquet made it possible for participants to become acquainted and discuss their mutual professional interests.

BOOK EXHIBIT

A very popular feature of the symposium was the Book Exhibit conveniently located in the lobby of the Conference Center. A variety of literature in biomechanics, medicine, anatomy, physical therapy, and swimming was included.

WIVES PROGRAM

A special tour of the historic Grand-Place in the heart of the city of Brussels was conducted on Thursday afternoon. This historic baroque theater dates back to the 12th century and has gracefully withstood the passing of time. The wives of the participants enjoyed seeing this historically significant

Figure 1. Symposium Headquarters and Conference Center.

Figure 2. Participants during the Opening Session.

Figure 3. The coffee breaks held in Book Exhibit Area were popular.

Figure 4. Castle of Ham at Steenockkerzeel, site of Symposium Reception.

Figure 5. Castle grounds provided a picturesque setting for participants.

structure as well as the area in the heart of the old city. This and other activities provided ample time for the wives to become acquainted and develop new friendships.

SYMPOSIUM COCKTAIL AT THE CASTLE OF HAM

At the close of the scientific program on Tuesday afternoon, all symposium participants were transported by bus to the famous Castle of Ham which is located in the small village of Steenokkerzeel just outside Brussels.

This castle has a long history dating back to the 8th century when Pepin of Herstal organized a prayer meeting at the tomb of Saint Trudo. At the time of his death in 714, he presented the properties of "Ham" and "Ochinsala" to the Abbey of Saint Trudo. Several noblemen have resided at the castle. One of its most renowned residents was Karel de Lannoy, Great General and diplomat of Emperor Charles, the Viceroy of Naples, who as the victor in the Battle of Pavia was successful in capturing Francis I, King of France.

The castle and the grounds have been rebuilt several times over the several centuries of its existence, yet two small towers near the rear of the inner court are evidence of the existence of the original fortification. The castle is

Figure 6. Distinguished guests included (*L.* to *R.*), Dr. Ernst Jokl (ICSPE), H.H. Prince de Merode (International Olympic Committee), Dr. Leon Lewillie, Symposium President, and Dr. Jurg Wartenweiler (ISB).

Figure 7. Prof. P.J. Brouwer, member of Scientific Committee, reviews highlights of the symposium during the banquet.

now used for the entertainment of visitors and is a very popular tourist attraction.

The group thoroughly enjoyed the informal conversations and the excellent refreshments that were served in the beautiful outdoor setting of the garden of the Castle of Ham.

Figure 8. Jan P. Clarys, Secretary General, addresses participants at the banquet.

THE SYMPOSIUM BANQUET

The site chosen for the symposium banquet on Thursday evening was the old house of "Moeder Lambic" a well known establishment of the "Bois de la Cambre." This Belgian inn, today named the "Orangerie de la Cambre," has existed since 1672, when it was merely a farm located along a muddy path.

This famous inn, which has played an important part in the history of suburban Brussels, has survived the changes that have occurred in the outlying districts of Brussels over the more than 300 years of its existence.

The symposium participants were served a typical Belgian cuisine in this historic setting. The banquet was followed by a short program that included remarks by the symposium organizers. This evening was a fitting climax to a highly successful symposium and will be remembered for a long time by those in attendance.

ISB EXECUTIVE COUNCIL MEETING

The symposium afforded the Executive Council of the International Society on Biomechanics the opportunity to hold its first annual meeting following the founding of the Society in August, 1973. The meeting was held Wednesday evening at the home of the Symposium President, Leon Lewillie. Society President Jurg Wartenweiler (Switzerland) chaired the session which was attended by: Vice President Richard C. Nelson (USA), General Secretary Jaap Vredenbregt (Netherlands) and Council Members, Wolfgang Gutewort (DDR), Marcel Hebbelinck (Belgium), Ernst Jokl (USA), and Gunther Rau, (BRD). In addition to discussion of a number of topics pertinent to the Society activities, the council received a progress report from Paavo Komi, organizer of the Fifth International Congress on Biomechanics to be held in Jyväskylä, Finland, June 29 to July 3, 1975. Appreciation is extended by the Executive Council to the Symposium Organizers for making possible this historic first Executive Council meeting.

Acknowledgments

The Symposium President and Secretary General wish to acknowledge the help and cooperation of the many organizations and individuals who contributed so much to the successful conduct of the Symposium. Special thanks are given to the members of the organizing committee, Jean Claude de Potter, Mrs. M. Plasch, Miss B. Pion, and Jean Pierre Coenraets. Valuable service was also rendered by the many assistants from the Instituut voor Morfologie: Marc Bourgeois, Arnold De Baeremaker, Tiny Franssen, Luk Maes, Guido Piette, Rene Stien, Hugo Van Bastelaer, Fernand Van Bont, Gerardus Van Der Tempel, Vera Van Velthoven, and Luk Vertommen; and from the Laboratoire de L'Effort: Micheline De Potter, Anne-Marie Lewillie, Andre Mairesse, and Rene Robeaux.

Appreciation is extended to the following professional organizations who helped support and promote the total Symposium program: The International Society of Biomechanics; The Research Committee of the International Council of Sport and Physical Education (UNESCO); The Ministers of National Education; The Ministers of Public Health and Family; The Ministers of Culture; The Royal Belgian Swimming and Life Saving Federation.

The organizers were very fortunate to have a number of sponsoring organizations who provided valuable assistance. These were: Laboratoire de l'effort. Université Libre de Bruxelles (U.L.B.); Instituut voor Morfologie, Vrije Universiteit Brussel (V.U.B.); Administration de l'Education Physique, des Sports et de la vie en Plein Air (A.D.E.P.S.); Bestuur voor Lichamelijke Opvoeding, Sport en Openiuchtieven (B.L.O.S.O.); Faculty of Medicine of the Vrije Universiteit Brussel.

In addition to these groups the following commercial firms served as co-sponsors and assisted through their financial contributions and participation in the exhibits: Simes International; Upjohn; Siemens; Sabena; Stella Artois; Jacquemotte; Coca Cola; Bic; Bayer; Marnix and Story Scientia, Scientific/Booksellers.

Finally, the contribution of the members of the Board of Honor is gratefully acknowledged. These included: 1st International Seminar on Biomechanics, Zürich 1967, J. Wartenweiler, Switzerland; 2nd International Seminar on Biomechanics, Eindhoven 1969, J. F. Schouten, The Netherlands, and J. Vredenbregt, The Netherlands; 3rd International Seminar on Biomechanics, Rome 1971, S. Cerquiglini, Italy, and A. Dal Monte, Italy; 1st International Symposium on Problems of Motion-Biology (Biomechanics) in Track and Field, Budapest 1971, K. Lissak, Hungary, and J. Antal, Hungary; 4th International Seminar on Biomechanics, Penn. State University, R. C. Nelson, U.S.A., and C. A. Morehouse, U.S.A.; The Research Committee of the International Council of Sport and Physical Education, E. Jokl, U.S.A., and M. Hebbelinck, Belgium.

Certainly the symposium would not have been possible without the cooperation and assistance of these groups. We shall be ever thankful for their generous contributions.

Léon Lewillie, *President*
Jan Clarys, *Secretary General*